SHAKING YOUR FAMILY TREE

A Basic Guide To Tracing Your Family's Genealogy

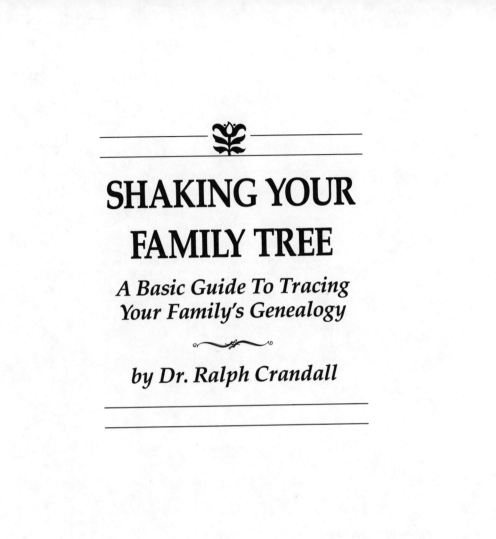

SHAKING YOUR FAMILY TREE

A Basic Guide To Tracing Your Family's Genealogy

by Dr. Ralph Crandall

Designed by Alison Scott

Yankee Publishing Incorporated
Dublin, New Hampshire 03444

Fifth Printing, 1988
Copyright 1986 by Ralph Crandall

Library of Congress Catalogue Card Number: 85-40718

ISBN 0-89909-088-5

In loving memory of
Reginald A. Morse

PREFACE

Genealogy is a fascinating activity that has captured the interest of the American people. We have always been intrigued by the possibility of descent from kings, noblemen, or *Mayflower* families. But thanks to Alex Haley's *Roots* and the American bicentennial, our focus has broadened, and what attracts us to genealogy today is at once more complex and more fundamental. Like Haley, many Americans — even those whose ancestors immigrated to this country only three or four generations ago — are realizing that we live in a virtual historical vacuum. We simply have no idea about our family experience in America or overseas. We do not know when our families came to this country or what happened to them after they arrived. Most of us live in nuclear households — little cocoons — and we have not been asked or expected to keep track, historically speaking, of grandparents or great-grandparents. Most of us would fail the test miserably if asked to name all eight of our great-grandparents. Such ignorance is part of the nation's indifference to fundamental historical matters.

But this attitude is changing as people recognize the importance and value of remembering families. It is exciting to reconstruct our families and to discover how much we are an expression of a unique family heritage. To see our families in a historical context increases our understanding and appreciation of their struggles and successes, and it promotes a measure of objectivity that can help in facing life. If we can kindle an interest in family history in our young people, we will find that their appreciation of American history, and of their families, will be deepened by the experience.

Who are your great-grandparents? *Shaking Your Family Tree* has been written to help you answer this and many other questions as you attempt to trace your family history. It offers a basic, up-to-date guide to libraries, archives, and other depositories, both public and private, that house genealogical data. It also introduces you to the methods employed by the best genealogists in compiling family histories. With *Shaking Your Family Tree*, you are set to embark on a fascinating, perhaps lifelong, historical adventure.

Whatever is good about *Shaking Your Family Tree* is owed to my friends and colleagues at the New England Historic Genealogical Society and to many other friends who have so generously participated in the creation of this book. I am especially grateful to my colleagues David Curtis Dearborn and Gary Boyd Roberts for their invaluable contributions. David has shared his enormous expertise as a genealogist and his lifelong scholarship on the Dearborn family, so that Dearborn examples enliven and inform every chapter of the book. Gary has patiently and skillfully edited every draft of the manuscript, and his unparalleled knowledge of genealogical libraries and published sources is reflected throughout.

I would also like to thank Robert Charles Anderson, Dr. David L. Greene, Cj Stevens, Ambassador Francis H. Russell, Edward W. Hanson, and Colonel Leonard H. Smith for their helpful comments and suggestions on several drafts of the book. I have also benefitted greatly from studying *The Source* and *Guide to Genealogical Research in the National Archives*. I am indebted to *Yankee* editors Sandra Taylor and Mark Corsey, whose persistent prodding brought the volume to full term. Without Linda Naylor's assistance, there would be no *Shaking Your Family Tree*. Besides skillfully handling the day-to-day matters of the director's office, she also found time to enter *Shaking Your Family Tree* on the computer and make all the corrections and additions. Special thanks are due my constant friend and mentor, John A. Schutz, not only for his invaluable advice on this book, but also for what he has taught me about life and history.

Finally, I wish to thank my wife, Linda Morse, and our children, Elizabeth, Meredith, and Catherine, for the unconditional love and endless support that only a family can give.

Ralph J. Crandall

CONTENTS

CHAPTER ONE

INTRODUCTION

Sources and Resources

An excerpt from the Bollinger family record, the first genealogy published in America. It was produced as a broadside in Pennsylvania in 1763. NEHGS

A turn-of-the-century Danish family portrait. Ben Watson

Many people today are tracing their family histories. Some are young people who have been asked by their teachers to research and describe their families over three or four generations. Some are members of immigrant families who wish to know more about their Old World ancestry and American family experience. Some have had their imaginations sparked by the discovery of a cache of family documents — old deeds and wills, early photographs, or a family Bible record — stored in an attic. There may even be a half-completed family chart that some relative began many years ago. Whatever the motivation, someone's curiosity is aroused, and that person decides it is time to begin finding the missing pieces in his or her unique ancestral puzzle. If you are reading these words, chances are that someone is you!

Now that you are interested, I must warn you that you may spend much of your leisure time during the next few years chasing ancestors. No need for alarm — it's great fun! The hunt could take you to some of the greatest libraries in the world. But you will do much of the work at home, as you write letters to relatives and contact courthouses, cemeteries, and historical societies. In the process, you will gain a better understanding of many subjects, including history and law. You will have the chance to meet unknown members of your family, both close and distant cousins, whose ancestors at some time in the past lost touch with your branch of the family.

Prepare yourself for many pleasant surprises and a few startling discoveries. Who knows what will hang on your family tree? You will find individuals from all walks of life — perhaps a senator, a king or two, a bank president, or even a bandit. But finding out is half the fun!

Begin the search with what is familiar and close at hand. Interview older family members, and go through the attic, old trunks, and closets looking for family documents. Next, visit a nearby library that has a good genealogical collection. Some of your family might be mentioned in an old biographical dictionary, a county history, or an obituary column. Beyond the library, the search becomes even more interesting. You will find yourself writing or visiting nearby archives that contain "primary" records such as wills or deeds, which may establish a family connection. In the end you will have amassed an astonishing amount of material on many ancestors. But your job will be only half-finished. Next, you will have to organize your newfound information into a well-substantiated family history.

Now you have the challenge. To help you do the job right, let's take some time to review the basic methods of gathering and organizing genealogical information.

Documenting Family Findings

What do you know about your family? That is not a frivolous question because the genealogist must work from the known to the unknown. Is what you know accurate? Most people would accept your testimony about your parents

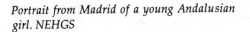

Portrait from Madrid of a young Andalusian girl. NEHGS

and brothers and sisters because you were an eyewitness to much of what has happened in their lives. But it is not so clear that your recollections would be enough to document the vital events in your grandparents' lives. This brings us to an obvious but important rule in genealogy: although all statements must be documented, the greater the separation in time and place between a researcher and an ancestor, the more necessary it is to corroborate personal testimony with information from other sources.

To illustrate this rule, let's assume that your mother claims her maternal great-grandfather and great-grandmother were Josiah Dearborn and Sarah Ann Wells, who were married in Wood County, Texas. You have heard many times the colorful tale behind this marriage. Your great-great-grandfather, the son of a Yankee farmer living in Effingham, New Hampshire, ran off as a young man to the California gold fields in 1849. Later, he moved to Texas, where he practiced law. There he met a beautiful southern belle, Sarah Ann Wells, a young widow. The tale continues that he and Sarah Ann were married in Wood County, Texas. At the outbreak of the Civil War, he was forced to join the Confederate cavalry, but later he deserted to the Union forces. After the war, he returned to Texas to find that his wife had died, leaving their little daughter behind. Met with an inhospitable reception in Texas, he moved with his daughter to Shawnee County, Kansas, where he lived thereafter.

As a family historian, you could have at least two reactions to this story, which has been repeated by four generations. A naive response would be to accept the tale as fact without further checking. The problems with this approach are obvious. Too much time has passed, and too many people have repeated the tale. The chance for error is enormous. The task of the family genealogist is to try to corroborate or disprove the story by research in primary records.

You could check a number of statements presented in the story: first, Josiah's involvement in the California gold rush; second, the marriage of Josiah to Sarah Ann in Wood County, Texas; third, Josiah's purported service in both the Confederate and Union armies; and finally, Josiah's later residence in Shawnee County, Kansas.

Published passenger lists, which are available at most genealogical libraries and include the names of ship passengers, do not reveal Josiah's participation in the California gold rush (although many forty-niners do appear on such lists). However, a search of the 1850 United States Census for California does reveal the presence of a J.H. Dearborn of the correct age and birthplace. A search of the 1860 federal census for Wood County,

"Pine Cottage," winter quarters for soldiers during the Civil War. Military records sometimes provide important genealogical data.

Texas, definitely shows Josiah living there as a lawyer. Correspondence with the Wood County courthouse brings a reply that the marriage to Sarah Ann took place there on January 16, 1861.

Similar correspondence with the National Archives in Washington, D.C., not only confirms the story of Josiah's serving on both sides in the war, but also brings to light the existence of a very informative Civil War pension application. The military records consulted at the National Archives confirm Josiah's service as a private in the Tenth Texas Cavalry and also his later service as a lieutenant in the United States Seventh Regiment of Colored Troops. (This discovery might also have provided the researcher with an added history lesson if he had not known previously that all-black units of soldiers served in the Union army and that most officers for these units were, like Dearborn, white.) Even more interestingly, his application for a pension, a copy of which was also received from the National Archives, details his service in his own words. The 1870 and 1880 federal censuses indeed show him and his family living in Shawnee County, Kansas. While we cannot find any hard evidence that Josiah returned to Texas following the Civil War, the 1870 census shows him reunited with his daughter. In the case of this family story, available documentary evidence seems to support a long-cherished tradition. And so you would, after all, want to include it as part of the family history.

Sources of Genealogical Information

Now let's look at what we did and did not use in authenticating Josiah and Sarah Ann's story. Our sources included oral tradition and public documents but no "literary records" such as correspondence, diaries, or journals. Don't be surprised by this. Josiah and Sarah Ann, like many of our ancestors, were too pressed by life to save such material, and they probably had no idea it would ever be needed. But we do know, at least, that Josiah was literate. His application for a Civil War pension seems to be written in his own hand, and he was, for a time at least, a lawyer.

Our failure to uncover literary records for Josiah and Sarah Ann reminds us that in genealogical research, we can trace few American families entirely through private documents. Either our ancestors were barely able to read and write, or like the Dearborns, their letters and memorabilia were lost as they moved, fought wars, or suffered accidents. Thus, we relied on public or institutional sources (the courthouse, military, and census records) to document Josiah's and Sarah Ann's odyssey. So far so good. These records have given us the essential facts — and even more.

Some families, of course, have preserved correspondence and other literary materials, often deposited in historical societies. A few notable American families, such as the Adamses, Washingtons, and Hamiltons, left large quantities of private material, much of which is now published. In searching our own ancestral lines, we will be pleased to discover a letter or two, and elated if we find a Bible record, but we will continue to hope that further digging may eventually produce a cache of letters, a diary, or a long and informative obituary of Josiah or Sarah Ann.

Another point worth raising is the importance of separating primary and secondary sources. Recall for a moment the written records we found to document Josiah and Sarah Ann's marriage. They are primary records. Why? Because they were created at the time of the marriage or shortly thereafter. In other words, primary records are contemporary documents. Wills, deeds, ship passenger lists, obituaries, and letters are all primary records. Such records are largely unpublished.

In contrast, secondary sources are often written many years after the person lived or an event occurred, and we must depend on the author or "compiler" — if it is a genealogy — to report the events accurately. These are not contemporary documents. Most books in genealogical libraries are secondary sources.

Is a primary source better than a secondary source? In some cases, yes, but you can't be fussy. Any kind of record that tells something about your family will be important because often information is scarce and extensive research is required to uncover any new facts. If there is a published genealogy, you should start with it. A description in a county history can also be very helpful. But remember, accuracy is important. Your goal is to produce a *factual* family history. Sometimes the search need not extend beyond secondary sources, or you might not have the time or money to conduct a nationwide search for lost ancestors. In addition, many published histories have been prepared by exceedingly careful scholars. Using their work, you can save months of effort, trace many ancestors more easily, and find numerous clues for many more. Still, with secondary sources there is always the nagging concern that the compiler might have been wrong. Perhaps he or she misinterpreted a document and put the wrong person in your ancestry. The best policy is to be conservative. When in doubt — and remember, just because it's in print doesn't mean it's true! — go back to primary records and piece the story together yourself.

What about oral history, the personal interviews you will conduct with family members? By all means, oral interviews should be part of your overall research plan. What elderly grandparents, great-uncles and aunts, and cousins — especially younger first cousins of each of your great-grandparents — know from memory might take you years to reconstruct from records. But remember that memory plays tricks; dates, places, and relationships are often confused. Treat oral history as the "opening statement" on your family rather than the final word.

Late 19th-century grammar school portrait. Such items, commonly found in private manuscripts and local archives, often provide valuable details for family histories. NEHGS

Library Resources

Now let's look more closely at the library. Once you have combed family sources and interviewed living relatives, visiting a genealogical library should be your next step. What might you expect to find there?

Look first for a published genealogy on each family in your ancestry. Such works often exist, especially for old New England families like the Dearborns from our earlier example. A genealogy can be a veritable gold mine, frequently tracing most Americans with a given surname to their immigrant ancestors. Look next for county histories or "mugbooks," which frequently contain biographical accounts and photographs. Further evidence on the Dearborn family might be found in a Shawnee County history, for example. Families often wrote their own biographies for these histories, and in return they were expected to buy the book.

After published genealogies and county histories, look for published vital records or city directories. These may give you dates and residences. Who knows what else you might find in a genealogical collection: town histories, selectmen's records, ship passenger lists, Civil War muster rolls, newspaper obituaries, cemetery epitaphs. Much is available, and many happy hours of ancestor hunting await you in the genealogy room of your local library.

Organizing Data

Soon you will have a mountain of names, dates, and places that cry out for organization. Keeping a system of files labeled by family groups is a good way to start. You should have a file for each head of household you are researching, into which you will place any information you obtain about his or her spouse and children. Begin with yourself if you are married, or with your parents if you are single. As the data grows, record your information on family group charts, large, preprinted forms that organize the essential facts about each family unit — husband, wife, and children. (Examples of these forms are included in appendix E.) Record birth, marriage, and death dates for each person, noting where and when each event occurred and where you obtained the information. In addition, for the head of household and his or her spouse, add biographical details such as education, occupation, religious affiliation, military experience, and any other data that will add color and interest to your family history.

A computer can help, too. Genealogy and the computer were made for each other. Several software packages are designed specifically for the genealogist. With appropriate software, the computer offers obvious benefits. It eliminates the need to maintain manually an ever-growing system of files, and it allows you to make additions and corrections easily. Just be sure to print a hard copy of your research periodically in case you should push the wrong button and erase everything — forever!

Another important organizing concern is which period of your family history you tackle first — the present or the past. You can present your family history on an ancestor table or on a table of descendants. With ancestor tables, also known as pedigree charts, you begin with yourself and ascend generation by generation until you finally arrive at each of your American immigrant ancestors, or you can cross the ocean and include even earlier generations when these are known. You can continue until the evidence finally disappears entirely.

By contrast, a table of descendants usually begins with the immigrant to America and descends to every living member of your family including yourself, tracing as far as possible all men and women in each generation. For several reasons you are much wiser to begin your genealogical research by preparing a table of ancestors. By identifying your ancestors in ascending order you will be able to determine all known immigrant ancestors in your numerous paternal and maternal lines. If you begin with descendant tables, however, you might make the mistake

of beginning your family history with someone bearing your surname who is not actually your ancestor.

Prepare your ancestor table on a standard pedigree chart, which has a special numbering system well worth memorizing. List yourself as number 1, your father as 2, your mother as 3, your paternal grandfather as 4, your paternal grandmother as 5, your maternal grandfather as 6, your maternal grandmother as 7, your patrilineal great-grandfather as 8, and so on, in consecutive fashion. (This numbering system can be used on the four-generation chart found in appendix E.)

You will soon note some patterns. First, each new generation has double the number of ancestors of the previous generation. Thus, you have four grandparents, eight great-grandparents, sixteen great-great-grandparents, and so on. By the tenth generation (assuming your parents as the first generation), you will have completed research on more than two thousand ancestors. Second, every father on the chart will have an even number that is twice that of his child, and every woman will have an odd number that is her husband's plus one. Thus, as your number is 1, your father's number will be 2, his father's number will be 4, and your patrilineal great-grandfather will be 8. Similarly your mother's number will be 3, her mother 7, and your matrilineal great-grandmother 15.

Assigning the correct numbers will allow you to identify immediately your kinship to a distant ancestor. Remember always to keep a person's name and his or her assigned number together, regardless of where they may appear. For instance, if you start a new chart with ancestor number 12 (your mother's paternal grandfather), do *not* renumber him as 1, but continue your numbering as started so that his father will have number 24, his mother 25, and his grandparents 48, 49, 50, and 51.

Another efficient way of organizing your pedigree is to put it in the form of an *Ahnentafel* (German for "ancestor table"). This method takes the numbering system described above and uses it to create a continuous list of ancestors instead of a chart. An Ahnentafel is particularly useful when you are corresponding with another family genealogist because it will allow him to see immediately where your genealogical research ends and also where your family and his might have common ancestry.

Your Ahnentafel

1. your name
2. your father
3. your mother
4. your father's father
5. your father's mother
6. your mother's father
7. your mother's mother
8. your father's father's father
9. your father's father's mother
10. your father's mother's father
11. your father's mother's mother
12. your mother's father's father
13. your mother's father's mother
14. your mother's mother's father
15. your mother's mother's mother

In This Book

We have covered briefly many of the points that will be treated more fully in subsequent chapters. The advice you will find encompasses the spectrum of genealogical research. It is supplemented with examples of the types of discoveries that result from successful research efforts. (Many of the examples feature our old friends, the Dearborn family.) In addition, a summary of "Pointers and Pitfalls" is provided at the end of each chapter to remind you of the techniques you will — and will not — want to take with you into your personal genealogical adventure. The appendixes contain information on the availability of the many genealogical resources mentioned throughout the book, as well as some that are not mentioned.

The most important fact to remember, of course, is that tracing a family history is an immensely rewarding and emotionally satisfying experience. You will meet many new people, correspond with many more, learn much about our nation's past, and ultimately produce a work that your family will cherish for generations.

Remember, too, that you are engaged in a factual study, so accuracy is of the utmost importance. Appendix E contains examples of several forms you will find most helpful in organizing your findings neatly and efficiently. And don't be surprised to find yourself calling on resources not directly related to your genealogical research as you seek the more general historical knowledge that will enable you to put your family history into broader historical perspective. This, too, is a part of the joy of genealogy.

To identify many of the ancestors who make up that unique pool of genes shared only by you and your siblings is a challenge — and a pleasure.

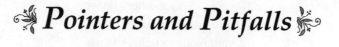

Pointers and Pitfalls

Sources and Resources

1. Genealogy is fun!
2. Begin your research with resources close at hand — your family — and proceed from the known to the unknown. Regard oral history as a starting point, not the last word, on a subject.
3. The greater the separation in time and place between you and your ancestor, the more important it is to corroborate personal testimony with information from other sources.
4. Primary sources are contemporary sources. Secondary sources are not.
5. Private documents such as letters and diaries are rare, and most people cannot rely on them to trace a major portion of their family history.
6. After you have exhausted family resources, turn to genealogical library collections.
7. After gathering data, you will have to organize it. The sample forms in appendix E can help you. A computer is also a helpful tool for genealogists.
8. Use the special numbering system of the standard pedigree chart to organize data.

CHAPTER TWO

JOYS IN THE ATTIC

Discovering Clues Within the Family

Initiating one of the new arrivals at the planting camp. National Archives

"Field study." Interviewing older family members whose memories may extend back several generations is an important part of your research. *Yankee*

racing your ancestry is like putting together a large jigsaw puzzle. To start the adventure, you must sift through a pile of shapes and locate those straight-edged pieces that form the border.

Your research should begin with pieces that fit easily, what we call genealogical clues within the family. These consist of bits of information gleaned from interviewing relatives and friends and from sifting through photographs, letters, and memorabilia gathered over many years of family life. Searching for such information will bring its surprises, and you will probably meet distant relatives of whom you had no previous knowledge. Overall success in tracing ancestral history is often directly proportional to skills developed during the initial research within the family. Combing sources at home and interviewing relatives will not only teach you much about evidence, but it will also stimulate your desire to continue searching in public archives and libraries.

The Genealogical Interview

How much can you expect to learn about your family from interviewing relatives or friends? No answer is applicable to all cases, but most families have collective memories that extend three to five generations. Thus, you can obtain basic information on your own generation and those of your parents and grandparents from interviewing relatives and searching family records.

The acid test, and perhaps the key to your entire genealogical success, will lie in how much the family can tell you about your eight great-grandparents and sixteen great-great-grandparents, who probably lived in the early and middle decades of the nineteenth century. The century from the American Revolution or slightly earlier to 1875 or so is unquestionably the most difficult in American genealogy. Families often disappeared entirely from written records during this period of expansion and large-scale migration. A New England family from Connecticut might have lived in four or five places, ranging from southern Vermont, to western New York, to Ohio or Illinois, then to Missouri or Kansas, and finally to Oregon or California. Similarly, a Virginia family might have followed paths through the Shenandoah Valley to Kentucky, then moved into the border states of Tennessee and Missouri, and settled finally in Arkansas, Louisiana, or Texas. In these "pioneer states," official records such as land, probate, and court records were usually poorly kept if they were kept at all. If you can identify most of your ancestors who lived between the American Revolution and the Civil War, the remainder of your research should be easier.

Your hunt for these elusive nineteenth-century forebears should begin with living relatives, for you may find that their memory extends considerably beyond three generations. Listen to their stories and gossip, note their comments and biases, and do not be afraid to contact relatives who don't know you but may remember your parents or grandparents.

One or more of your grandparents may still be living; if not, several of their younger first cousins may be. Each of these first cousins will share ancestors with you, and their knowledge may extend to your great- and great-great-grandparents. A few first cousins of one or more of your great-grandparents may survive as well. The births of your oldest and youngest great-grandparents may be separated by twenty-five or thirty years, so a first cousin of one of your grandparents might be older than a first cousin of a great-grandparent. Interview all such elderly cousins as early as possible in your research.

Conducting the Interview

One important objective is to uncover information that may lead to other persons or sources of information. Before arranging your first interview with an unknown relative, you might want to familiarize yourself with the methods oral historians use. A good basic textbook is Edward D. Ives's *The Tape-Recorded Interview: A Manual for Field Workers in Folklore and Oral History.*

The interview process can be divided into three stages: the initial contact, the interview itself, and the pursuit of all new clues. How you approach your relative is critical. Although many people, in particular older relatives, welcome the chance to reminisce and share the memories of parents and childhood, you should proceed tactfully. Some people are sensitive about being questioned, especially about their families.

Unless you are interviewing a close and known relative, such as an aunt, uncle, or grandparent, with whom you can usually arrange the interview by telephone, your initial contact should be by letter. It will allow you to introduce yourself and explain what inspired you to begin your genealogical project. It will also give you the opportunity to tell how you found the relative's name and address and what information you seek. In addition, you can inform him of any kind of special equipment, such as a tape recorder, that you would like to bring to the interview.

Give your relative some time to receive your letter and think about your request, then telephone him to set a specific date for the interview. At this time you should find out whether he objects to the use of a tape recorder, many of which are now quite unobtrusive. You might point out the value of recording the full conversation, which you could not do using pen and paper, but do not insist. You want to instill trust and confidence, and not inhibit the person in any way.

Your questions should be simple, direct, and focused on the type of biographical and vital information you need. Typical questions might be "Do you remember the names of your grandmother's brothers and sisters?", "When did your grandmother marry?", and "When did your father's mother immigrate to the United States?" Some may not recall specific dates and ages, but you can sometimes compensate for this by associating questions with a particular period in your relative's life or with a major episode in American or world history. Such questions might be "Were your grandparents still alive when you were in high school?" or "Was your grandmother alive during the First World War?"

Some people have a tendency to respond to specific questions with a "life and times" answer. In such cases, be careful not to interrupt, or you may lose much valuable information that such "free association" evokes. Try instead to redirect the answer through questions that will focus your relative's thoughts more narrowly. If your relative has launched into a long discourse on, say, his father's career as a ship captain, you might return to the subject by asking him, "How many of his children were married when he retired from the sea?"

If your relative expresses an interest in what you are doing, offer to share your information. People are often more generous if they know they aren't doing all the giving. In addition, you will probably gain a valuable correspondent, a source of further information, and a friend.

Following the interview, listen to the tape carefully, perhaps several times, extracting all information pertinent to your research. Very likely the interview will suggest new questions and further avenues of research and thus lead to further meetings with this relative.

If an oral interview is not possible because of distance, expense, or sickness, you might prepare a questionnaire. Outline what you already know about each individual or family, and leave space for your relative to complete the missing information. Such a form might read as follows:

Your father, Richard Davis, was born on _____ (date), in _____ (place). He married Martha _____ (maiden surname) on _____ (date), in _____ (place), and they had _____ (number) children. He died on _____, in _____, California. His wife died on _____ in _____ (California?). The names of their children are (in chronological order): _____

In addition to the questionnaire, enclose a family group chart (see appendix E) in case the person can supply even more information.

If your relative is comfortable expressing himself in writing, you might ask him to flesh out the information he provides on the questionnaire with details or anecdotes. Not everyone will be willing or able to do this, of course, but the most important thing is to obtain whatever vital data your relative can provide.

How good is evidence generated through interviews or question-naires? There is no infallible source of genealogical information. The possibility of error is obvious when memory is involved, but it is present in so-called "primary sources" as well. A minister or town clerk might mistakenly record a day, month, or year when completing a baptismal or birth certificate. A printer's error might result in an unwanted change of name or location. Or an ancestor may have deliberately reported false information, perhaps to enlist in the military or hide the facts of an illegitimate birth. Try to corroborate all vital information with as many sources as possible. If evidence conflicts (for example, a date supplied by a relative differs from that recorded in vital records), follow the source closest to the time of the actual event.

Here's an example. According to his descendants, Lauren Dearborn, a farm boy from Corinna, Maine, spent his winters as a young man working as a carpenter in the silver mines of Virginia City, Nevada. Because this story was repeated by Lauren's two children, who died less than twenty years ago, it would seem likely to be true. Indeed, a search through forgotten memorabilia in a family attic uncovered Lauren's membership card in the Storey County (Nevada) carpenter's union. In addition, his name was located in Storey County in the 1880 federal census, and his obituary notice in the local Andover, Massachusetts, newspaper repeated the story of his adventurous youth in Nevada.

Searching through the Attic

As you build a network of contacts with relatives, ask them for copies of any genealogical notes or manuscripts they may possess. Many families have at least one family member who, during the past three or four generations, has undertaken some research or composed some kind of family memoir. Such data can exist in almost any form: a file of genealogical charts and random notes; a short filial biography never intended for publication; or a massive compilation filling several boxes and representing years of effort.

Make every effort to locate these genealogical manuscripts. Perhaps they are tucked away in some corner of a relative's closet or attic. Another good place to look is the local historical society or public library, or one of the country's major genealogical repositories such as the New England Historic Genealogical Society in Boston or the library of the Church of Jesus Christ of Latter-day Saints in Salt Lake City.

Portrait of a great-grandfather, discovered in a grandmother's attic. Sometimes identifying the subjects of such treasures means painstaking investigation. Sharon Smith

Family associations also may be helpful in finding genealogical manuscripts. (Family associations bring together people descended from a common ancestor. There are several hundred such associations in the United States.) Through various publications — a newsletter, an annual report, or even a compiled genealogy — they often serve as major clearing-houses for information on almost any American surname. To determine which family associations might be pertinent to your research, contact the reference department of a library with major genealogical collections or consult the newsletters of local societies.

Finally, you might advertise your search for family manuscripts in the query columns of several genealogical magazines. General periodicals where you might place a query include *Yankee* magazine, *NEHGS Nexus*, *The Connecticut Nutmegger*, the *National Genealogical Society Newsletter*, and *The Genealogical Helper*. The query might be worded as follows: "Wanted: information on the Albert C. Jones family of Ipswich, Massachusetts, 1800-1850. Especially interested in genealogical manuscripts compiled by members of this family." You may also place ads in local periodicals, such as county historical society newsletters.

While looking for genealogical manuscripts, do not ignore other sources of family history. In addition to inherited furniture, silver, and portraits, many American families possess Bibles, heirlooms, letters, diaries, wills, deeds, photographs, and military papers. How much of this material your relatives own depends on many circumstances: when your family's American experience began, how wealthy it became, how frequently it moved, and how much it valued a sense of history.

If your family was here by 1800 — and probably one hundred

million living Americans are descended from the twenty-five thousand New Englanders of 1620 to 1650 alone — it may have made and lost several fortunes, moved far from its ancestral home, and become widely scattered in the past two centuries. For such "pioneer" families, many recent photographs are likely to have survived, but little or nothing may exist from the period before the Civil War. You may belong to one of those rare American families who have lived in the same New England town or Virginia parish for a dozen generations. Or you may be the fourth or fifth generation of a nineteenth-century immigrant family, your great-great-grandparents among the millions of Europeans who came here after the Civil War in search of freedom and work in the New World. Through different ancestors you could, in fact, belong to all three kinds of families — the pioneer, the "sedentary," and the ethnic. Whether your family has just a small box of grandmother's letters or an attic bulging with memorabilia from several generations, you should examine all this material with the careful eye of a Sherlock Holmes.

If you find photographs, inspect the back of each picture carefully for names, dates, and ages. Look, too, for the name and address of the photographer or studio. This might be a valuable clue to an ancestor's place of residence. When interviewing older relations, bring pictures along and ask your kinsmen to identify both the subjects and occasions for the photographs. Also likely to be saved are more recent wedding books, frequently signed by spouses, parents, and witnesses; baby books, sometimes including genealogical charts; passports with name, age, and residence information; and military papers, which note age, residence, health, occupation, and physical description.

Items your family might have saved from the early and middle decades of the nineteenth century could include several old daguerreotypes dating from the 1840s and 1850s showing your great-great-grandparents and possibly a portrait or silhouette of a great-great-great-grandparent. Check the backs and frames of these objects to see whether they were signed by either the subject or the photographer or artist. An artist's signature, or a silversmith's on family silver, will give you a name that might be listed in a city directory.

Examine jewelry carefully. Wedding rings, anniversary rings, and lockets might be engraved with marriage and anniversary dates, or even birth and death data. Sometimes people have saved samplers and mourning memorials from the first half of the nineteenth century. Occasionally the theme of such an early nineteenth-century sampler is a family tree.

A Mormon wagon caravan, circa 1879. The large westward migration of the 1800s often makes it difficult to find family records from this period. National Archives

Although it is more likely that such attic treasures will exist if you descend from a "settled" family, pioneer families often held onto family memorabilia as a physical link with their former homes. One such family now living in Arizona owns the family Bible kept by their ancestor, a steamboat captain on the Mississippi and Ohio rivers who died near New Madrid, Missouri, in a cholera epidemic in 1834. Almost twenty years later the man's widow and children migrated from their home in southern Indiana to Roseburg, Oregon, via the Isthmus of Panama, taking the Bible with them. The family record in the Bible shows the man's date of birth (February 28, 1792), along with the names of his parents and siblings. With this information, his descendants easily discovered a record of his birth in Candia, New Hampshire. Interestingly, the man's New Hampshire relatives were aware of his midwestern nautical career, but had lost track of his descendants.

Another especially valuable genealogical resource consists of what are called family archives. These are diaries, journals, letters, wills, deeds, Bible records, and genealogical manuscripts. Until well into the nine-

A page from the family Bible record of Johannes Ast, a 19th-century German immigrant. NEHGS teenth century, many states were casual about maintaining their public records. Consequently, family archives may prove essential to your research; they are often the only proof of affiliation to a Colonial family traceable before 1750 but very difficult to follow thereafter. Land divisions within families were often unrecorded until an issue over title arose. Deeds themselves were held by families; those found today at county courthouses are only copies.

You should conduct a special search for family Bible records. Thousands of Americans have used the spaces provided in most Bibles to record the births, marriages, and deaths of individual family members. Such documents are genealogically invaluable and if available may well supersede all other sources as the cornerstone of your family history. But a note of caution is in order. Frequently a later member of the family, perhaps your mother, father, or grandparents, will purchase a new Bible and endeavor to record several generations from memory. Clearly such a record is subject to more error than if vital events were entered as they occurred. You can quickly determine which method was used by noting the Bible's publication date and studying the handwriting used to enter the family data. If the Bible's publication date does not precede all recorded vital events, or if the data covering several generations is in one handwriting, then almost certainly it is based, at least in part, on a relative's memory. But if the date of the first record is later than the publication date and the handwriting, pen, and ink vary from generation to generation or entry to entry, then the vital data was probably entered close to the time of the actual events and is therefore much more reliable. When copying family information from Bibles, do so word for word, misspellings and all. Errors often creep in when you first attempt to interpret difficult handwriting.

The search within your family for clues to its history will be an exciting, at times frustrating, but ultimately rewarding experience. You will meet many relatives for the first time and make new friends, but as you persist in unraveling the family's well-kept secrets, you may also make one or two enemies. Be tactful and expect to encounter a few disappointments. Sometimes family members who have lost touch with one another have done so by design, not by accident, and reopening an old wound — even inadvertently — can damage or hinder your research effort. But pursue every clue possible, because information gleaned from the family forms the border of your genealogical puzzle. And finding all the straight-edged pieces will greatly facilitate the next step, research in the library.

❧ *Pointers and Pitfalls* ❧

Discovering Clues Within the Family

1. Family research provides the border for your genealogical jigsaw puzzle.

2. Don't be afraid to contact relatives who don't know you but who might remember your parents or grandparents.

3. For interviews: Proceed tactfully; contact distant or unknown relatives by mail first; use special devices such as tape recorders only if the subject approves; ask simple, direct questions; keep the discussion focused, but do not interrupt free association that might provide valuable information; offer to share your data with any interested relative; follow up your initial interview as necessary.

4. Use a questionnaire when a face-to-face interview is not practical.

5. Use as many sources as possible to verify findings. When there is a discrepancy between two sources, use the one closest to the time of the actual event.

6. Ask other family members to share their genealogical findings with you.

7. Seek published genealogies of your ancestors from local genealogical and historical societies and from major genealogical libraries. And don't overlook genealogical periodicals.

8. Seek out family archives that are especially helpful in answering questions about the period before states started keeping careful public records (the period before the mid-1800s).

9. Family Bible records are especially informative, but beware of Bible records re-created from memory many years after the events recorded in them.

10. Expect to encounter a few disappointments and to make a few enemies in your search, but persevere!

CHAPTER THREE

TREASURED AISLES

Using Library Resources

ELIZABETH ROSS,

By Copley.—1751–1831.

Elizabeth Ross, at the age of sixteen, by Copley, from Portland (Maine) in the Past, *published in 1886.*

Local library. After you have exhausted all family resources, this will be your next stop. Yankee

nce you have completed the initial search for information within your family, your next resource is the library. Your local library is the first place to look, even though it may have only a small selection of books concerning genealogy and local history. Next, try to visit several of the major genealogical collections in public libraries and historical societies throughout the country.

To begin your library search, select the family line that most interests you or for which you already have the most information. Work on it at the library until your sources of information are exhausted. Then look for material on all your other lines. Often families you might least expect to be well covered are the easiest to pursue.

Your success in using libraries will vary greatly — depending on the size of the genealogical collection, the knowledge of the librarian assigned to it, and the library's overall commitment to genealogy. If you have the opportunity to use a very large collection, such as that of the Church of Jesus Christ of Latter-day Saints or the New England Historic Genealogical Society, begin by asking for an orientation to the library. The Church of Jesus Christ of Latter-day Saints, for example, provides a slide presentation, which describes its holdings and catalog system, and a walk-through orientation conducted by a volunteer. Similarly, the New England Historic Genealogical Society provides regularly scheduled orientation tours. Even large libraries whose collections are devoted only partially to genealogy often provide published guides to their genealogical holdings. You can save much time and effort by first asking for these guides, for they often list not only major published holdings but also any special collections unique to that particular library.

After learning all you can about the library through orientations and written guides, the next step is to familiarize yourself with the card catalog and how the genealogical collection is organized. Begin by asking the librarian whether the catalog reflects any special features or problems. Some major libraries are gradually shifting to the modern Library of Congress classification system. Part of their holdings are still catalogued under the old system and may actually be placed separately on the shelves. Manuscripts are often catalogued separately, and you should not expect to find them integrated with book catalogs. Look, too, for genealogical "analytical" indexes. In a few libraries, such as the Los Angeles Public Library genealogical room, librarians over the years have entered brief analytical descriptions of many periodical articles under family surnames in the catalog.

In addition to consulting the librarian about the catalog, you should also ask for guidance with regard to the specific genealogical problems you are researching. In many instances, genealogical reference librarians are themselves first-rate genealogists and may even share an interest in the particular family lines you are researching. It is immensely helpful and timesaving when the librarian can immediately direct you to the books or manuscript collections pertinent to your research.

Finally, be aware of any special conditions or time limitations that might affect access to the library you are visiting. Many genealogical libraries have special hours and are not open on a standard Monday to Saturday basis. Others, especially historical societies, might not allow users or nonmembers access to the stacks area where books are shelved. Not being able to read the shelves for all available books on a particular name will slow your research enormously.

Your work in libraries should be governed by where you live now and where your ancestors once resided. In the best of worlds, you might still dwell in the area where your family has lived since before the American Revolution — perhaps even in the same house. But several generations of migrations might have scattered your family across the

United States, so one set of great-grandparents may have lived in Belfast, Maine, another in Buffalo, New York, another in Fort Hays, Kansas, and so on. Your task as a researcher is to seek out the unique information sources that may exist in the localities where your ancestors lived, and at the same time to consult the best genealogical libraries available in your own area.

Fortunately, more than fifteen hundred organizations in the United States have special genealogical collections of published and unpublished sources. Thirteen of the largest are listed later in this chapter. Many others appear in the *American Library Directory*, the *Directory of Historical Societies and Agencies in the United States and Canada*, published by the American Association of State and Local History, and Mary K. Meyer's *Directory of Genealogical Societies in the U.S.A. and Canada*.

Unless you plan a research trip as part of your vacation, it might be difficult to visit the library in the town where your ancestor lived. If so, the next best procedure is to write to that library. Indeed, as you get further into your research, you will discover that much of it can be conducted by mail.

When asking a reference librarian for information about an ancestor, always be brief and specific. Most reference librarians are too busy to respond to vague requests such as "Can you help me discover if I am related to the Hinman family of your town?" Also do not expect the librarian to examine post-haste a pedigree chart or file of notes that you enclose. As a matter of course, it is best not to include such material with your initial request. Focus instead on a single family, preferably one individual, and include as much information about that family or individual as possible. Your letter might read as follows:

Dear Sir/Madam,

I am seeking information on my great-grandfather, Stephen S. Rand, who, according to family tradition, worked as a lumberman in Bangor, Maine, soon after the Civil War. His wife was Margaret (Stevens) Wheeler, and they were married in Portsmouth, New Hampshire, in 1855. I am especially interested in knowing of any children born in Bangor and whether any member of this family died there.

I will be deeply grateful for any assistance you can give me and shall be happy to pay any standard research fee or photocopy costs. Please find enclosed a self-addressed stamped envelope.

Sincerely yours,

Genealogical collections in American libraries can be divided into three basic groups: those in small-town public libraries or historical societies that consist of a few items pertaining primarily to the locality; those at medium-size or major metropolitan libraries that have a large budget and often a separate reading area devoted exclusively to genealogy and local history; libraries such as the New England Historic Genealogical Society in Boston or the Latter-day Saints Genealogical Society Library in Salt Lake City that have massive collections of books and manuscripts and promote genealogical research and scholarship.

Small-Town Libraries and Societies

Public libraries or genealogical or historical societies in the area where each of your ancestors lived are usually the most likely depositories for books and manuscripts about the locality and its people. Frequently such works are written or compiled by local residents and cannot be found elsewhere.

In some communities you might find an immensely knowledgeable and dedicated person known as the "town historian" or "town genealogist." Such a person sometimes devotes a lifetime to transcribing various local records, which are then deposited in the town library. If a town has an active genealogical or historical society, its informal headquarters, regular meeting place, and the major beneficiary of its prodigious transcribing is often the local library.

Types of sources you can expect to find at a local public library or historical society include the following:

County Histories.

County histories, especially those published in the late nineteenth century, often in three or four volumes, usually consist of two sections. The first is a history of the county, arranged by town and/or topic; the second is a biographical account containing profiles of prominent individuals and families living in the county when the book was published. The individuals so profiled were often children and grandchildren of the original founders of the county, who are sometimes covered as well. These works are frequently called "mugbooks" because they often include photographs of persons mentioned.

These antiquarian histories, as well as their twentieth-century counterparts, are invaluable to genealogists because the information contained in them was usually obtained directly from local families. Interviewed or sent questionnaires, they supplied information that was often published with little or no revision. As such, these profiles amount to published "oral histories." Although such data should be used with caution and verified through other sources, these biographies may provide an invaluable clue for identifying the origin of an early nineteenth-century ancestor. Some may even outline the entire patrilineal descent.

In *History of Strafford County, New Hampshire, and Representative Citizens*, compiled by John Scales and published in Chicago (as were many such books) in 1914, the entry for Col. Thomas Haines Dearborn begins as follows:

⁓⁀

Col. Thomas Haines Dearborn was born August 21, 1860, at Northfield, N.H. He is eighth in descent from the immigrant ancestor, Godfrey Dearborn, who was born in Exeter, England about 1605 and came to New England about 1636. He was one of the company that started the settlement at Exeter, N.H. under the leadership of Rev. John Wheelright. His name appears among the signers of the Combination for Good Government in 1639, in that town. Settled in Hampton before 1648 and became a large property owner there and was one of the prominent citizens.

His son Thomas was born in Exeter, England, in 1634 and came over with his parents. His son Jonathan was born in Hampton in 1686; he is known in history as "Cornet" Jonathan Dearborn, as during the Indian wars he held that office in a company of militia that served in the wars. His son Shubael was born in Hampton in 1719, May 17th.

Note that the use of the somewhat ambiguous phrase "his son" can cause confusion for the researcher. A hasty reading, without careful attention to birthdates, might lead you to conclude that Thomas, Jonathan, and Shubael are all sons of Godfrey. In fact, only Thomas is Godfrey's son. Jonathan was Thomas's son, and Shubael, in turn, was Jonathan's. In addition, you might need to check the title cornet to learn what office Jonathan held in the militia.

The entry continues with Shubael as its subject.

He married Sarah Fogg of Hampton. He removed from Hampton to Northfield in 1770 and was one of the first settlers in that town; in fact it was not set off from Canterbury and made a township until after that date. He was a soldier in the last colonial war with the French and Indians, under King George, against whom he afterwards rebelled. He also was a soldier in the siege of Louisburg, under command of Sir William Pepperell. At the capture he secured for himself and brought home a good French musket. At Northfield he was a prosperous farmer. His son Shubael was born at Hampton, July 12, 1753, and came to Northfield with his parents. In 1779 he married Ruth Leavitt of Hampton and they commenced housekeeping in a log house in Northfield, but before long he built a new frame house, all the materials for which, except the chimney and wood-work, he hauled from Portsmouth with an ox-team; it was a nice, good-stepping team of young oxen that could walk as fast as a man could walk. But before marriage he served in the Revolutionary army. Mr. Dearborn was 22 years old when the war began. His father, too old to go, took down from the hooks over the fire-place his French musket, which he had kept bright and shining ever since he "gobbled it up" at Louisburg, and putting it into his son's hands told him to join the New Hampshire troops and use it for the defense of his country against the attack of King George's Hessians. The son obeyed. He enlisted in Captain Jeremiah Clough's company of Canterbury and Northfield men, which company became a part of Col. Enoch Poor's regiment, which marched from Exeter to Cambridge, June 27, 1775; the next ten days after the battle of Bunker Hill his company took part in the siege of Boston, which continued until March 1776. He continued service in Colonel Poor's regiment in later campaigns. He brought that gun home and it was used again in the War of 1812-15 by another member of the Dearborn family. It is now in the possession of Shubael Dearborn of Concord.

The information in this portion of the entry is detailed and fascinating, revealing not only vital data but also clues to the character and attitudes of the subjects. Such findings are not common, but even one such discovery about an ancestor will be a delight and triumph. Remember, however, that any information found in one source must be documented thoroughly with other sources — ideally primary sources — whenever possible.

⁓♋⁓

This second Shubael had a son he named Shubael; he was born in 1783, on the old farm on Dearborn Hill, Northfield. He was twice married; his second wife was Sally Glines.

Their son John S. Dearborn was born Sept. 8, 1824. He married Hannah Haines in 1850. He inherited the farm of his grandfather and was a prosperous farmer on Dearborn Hill. His health failing, he removed to Dover, where he died in 1896. His wife survived him several years, living to be 87 years of age. She died at Exeter, being at the time with her son-in-law, Hon. W.H.C. Follansby. Their son, Colonel Thomas H. Dearborn, is the subject of this sketch . . . .

In this case, nearly all the information on the ancestors of the subject is correct. But there is no guarantee of such accuracy. The error committed is that Godfrey, the immigrant, is said to have come from Exeter, England, to New Hampshire. But an article by V.C. Sanborn in volume 68 of *The New England Historical and Genealogical Register* shows that Godfrey Dearborn was actually a native of Lincolnshire. (This article is illustrative of the numerous "corrections and additions" to family histories that appear in leading genealogical journals.)

Always check each fact if possible. Often the amount of specific detail about each ancestor is the best clue to the accuracy of the sketch as a whole. Few specific details about any ancestor indicate the possibility of a weak connection.

Sometimes the self-serving nature of these sketches somewhat enlarges the subject's local prominence or omits anything unattractive or scandalous. One member of the Dearborn family was featured in an early twentieth-century biographical history of Montana. After only a decade's residence in a central Montana city, this man had become a major participant in local real estate development and oil exploration and had been elected mayor. According to county court records, however, only a few years after publication of the "mugbook" he defaulted on

Samuel L.T. Wright, author of History of the West Part of Southampton (Massachusetts) *called Foamer, a 19th-century town history. NEHGS*

several mortgages, the bank foreclosed on his properties and investments, and Mr. Dearborn quickly and rather ignominiously left town, never to be heard from in Montana again.

Town Histories.

Besides county histories, a local public library is likely to have all published town histories covering nearby communities. Treasure troves of genealogical information, many town histories were produced for either the American centennial (1876) or bicentennial (1976) celebrations.

The period beginning with the centennial celebrations and extending into the first two or three decades of the twentieth century is rightfully called the "golden age" of American antiquarian history, for during this half-century or so were published many of the best or most often used town, county, state, and single-family histories that now compose the bulk of our national genealogical literature. You can distinguish the good antiquarian town history from its more recent academic counterpart in that the former is as concerned with chronicling the lives of the individuals and families who lived in the town as with those large historical forces that shaped its destiny. Thus, a nineteenth-century town history may begin with the "founding fathers" of the community, then proceed to give numerous profiles of local political leaders, doctors, lawyers, ministers, and educators. Often it will list in several appendixes all those men who served in important political offices, fought in the Revolution or Civil War, or were college graduates. Finally, many of these early works conclude with a large section, sometimes an entire volume, that is a "genealogical register" of all families residing in the town to that date. These registers often absorbed the town's readily available vital data and sometimes private, church, probate, cemetery, and land records as well.

As compared to county compendia of this era, town histories, including genealogical sections, were carefully prepared and are usually more reliable. A few are authoritative. You should spot-check even the best town histories, however, and when in doubt, or when using one that seems mediocre, always check each name, date, and kinship carefully in both town and county records.

The second great outpouring of town histories, prompted by the recent bicentennial, included far fewer works of enduring genealogical interest. Many older towns with good earlier histories sponsored a bicentennial sequel that begins where the previous volume ends and chronicles the town's development during the past century only. In many cases, these works were supervised by a historical commission created expressly for the purpose of updating the older work or preparing a history where none existed previously. But regardless of purpose, these newer works, with several notable exceptions, are much more concerned with chronicling the events in a community than identifying the people who lived in it. While this may be good news for the historian, it is often disappointing for genealogists searching for an elusive ancestor. Still, these new town histories might contain a few hidden facts and should not be overlooked. Even the narrative history of a community in which many of your ancestors once lived might suggest new possibilities for research.

A muster list from History of Carroll County *(New Hampshire), published in 1889.*

NEW HAMPSHIRE VOLUNTEER CAVALRY.			
Pierce L. Wiggin, C, Captain,	Ossipee	John Williams, G,	Wakefield
Stephen R. Tibbitts, C, wounded June 3, 1864,	,,	John C. Caryl, I, commissioned Serg't, promoted 1st Lieut,	Brookfield
Thomas Barnes, D,	,,	Charles H. Norton, I,	Wakefield
George Brown, D,	,,	Nathaniel H. Munsey, M, died of disease,	
Charles Burke, D,	,,	Nov. 17, 1864.	Albany
John Knight, D,	,,	Thomas Richie, M,	Eaton
James McGuire, D,	Wakefield	John Clark,	Wakefield
William Chauncey, G,	,,	Charles Whitehouse,	Albany
Hiram Peck, G,	,,		

VETERAN RESERVE CORPS.			
Sewell R. Aldrich, mustered Aug. 22, 1863,	Conway	John McLachlin, Sept. 24, 1863,	Conway
Samuel Adams, Jan. 8, 1864,	Effingham	Horace S. Parrott, Jan. 1, 1864,	Sandwich
John T. Adams, April 30, 1864,	Wakefield	Daniel F. Parrott, Jan. 1, 1864.	,,
Oliver L. Allen, May 13, 1864,	,,	Enoch J. Quimby, Oct. 1, 1863,	Conway
John Delaney, Oct. 5, 1863,	Conway	George W. Ramsdell, Aug. 21, 1863,	,,
Martin V. Drew, Dec. 23, 1863,	Tamworth	Michael Sullivan, Aug. 20, 1863,	,,
Hezekiah Davis, Jan. 5, 1864,	Sandwich	Thomas B. Seaver, Aug. 25, 1863,	,,
Samuel Floyd, Jan. 2, 1864,	,,	Patrick Sherry, Dec. 23, 1863,	Tamworth
John C. Frost, Aug. 27, 1864,	Madison	Michael Scanlan, Jan. 1, 1864,	Moultonborough

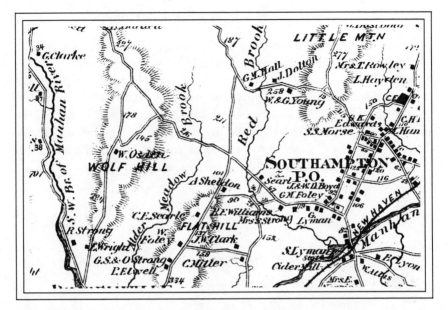

Section of a town map from Wright's History of the West Part of Southampton. *Such early maps sometimes show landowners' names as well as property boundaries.* NEHGS

County Atlases, Old Platbooks, and Local Maps.

Various commercial firms of the late nineteenth century published elaborate county atlases, with individual maps of each town or township and special maps of villages and urban areas. Frequently each farm or house is identified by the name of an owner or occupant. Such atlases are a major boon to the genealogist seeking an ancestor's homestead. Some also show the location of cemeteries. Small public libraries usually have copies of the atlases covering their counties.

County platbooks are common in the Midwest. Regularly issued by specialty publishers or title companies, they contain detailed maps indicating ownership of every piece of land. (A "plat" is a map or chart of a piece of land. Those referred to here showed original land grants to individuals from the state or federal government. A "title company" determined and guaranteed ownership of a piece of land.) You can usually find back copies in local libraries and county courthouses. Useful for determining where an ancestor lived, these volumes also show who currently owns the land.

Historical/Genealogical Society Publications.

Many towns and cities have active historical societies that publish journals or newsletters, source material (vital or marriage data, will abstracts, deeds, or court records), or both. In many instances, such efforts date from the nineteenth century. For example, *Historical Collections of the Topsfield Historical Society* began annual publication in 1895. Like older town histories, these works usually share a biographical focus. Thus, the table of contents for a typical volume (12) in the *Historical Collections of the Topsfield Historical Society* reads as follows:

Funeral Sermon on the Death of Rev. Joseph Green of Salem Village . . .

Elegy on the Death of Rev. Joseph Green . . .

Topsfield Streets and ways . . .

Biographical Sketch of Jacob Kimball . . .

John Redington of Topsfield, and Some of his Descendants . . .

Letter to Lieut. John Gould regarding his Military Company . . .

Memorandum concerning the Congregational Meeting House in 1817 . . .

Certificate Concerning Philip McKenzie . . .

Newspaper Items Relating to Topsfield, 1816-1829 . . .

Topsfield Vital Statistics, 1906 . . .

Buildings Constructed, 1906 . . .

While historical societies in many American communities are more than fifty years old and are sometimes well endowed, most local genealogical societies are fledgling organizations founded in the past decade. Although they can seldom undertake extensive publication programs, these groups are often more concerned than the local historical society with preserving the area's primary sources. Much of their time is spent transcribing unpublished local records and photocopying them for nearby public libraries. Because of such efforts, these libraries may have transcribed and indexed copies of a large percentage of the primary sources of their town, county, or region.

Institutional Histories.

Histories of local institutions — churches, banks, charitable societies, patriotic organizations, etc. — are also often written to commemorate an anniversary such as a centennial or bicentennial. Like older antiquarian town histories, these works — even the modern ones — are interested in profiling individual members (founders and officers especially) and an organization's history. The institutional history most often used by active genealogists is unquestionably Oliver Ayer Roberts's *History of the Military Company of the Massachusetts Now Called The Ancient and Honorable Artillery Company of Massachusetts*. Published in four volumes between 1895 and 1901, this work commemorates the 250th anniversary of the oldest military organization in America. Nearly the entire four volumes are devoted to short biographies of the company's members, a virtual "who's who" of Colonial, Revolutionary, and nineteenth-century civic leaders of Boston.

A "sewing circle," circa 1908. The researcher called on a ninety-year-old nursing home resident to identify herself and the others in the photograph. Sharon Smith

City Directories, Annual Town Reports, and Telephone Directories.

Many public libraries own complete sets of local city directories, annual reports, and local telephone books. City directories span the entire nineteenth century. Boston's first volume dates from 1789; by 1850 most major American cities and many rural areas had directories as well.

These volumes, alphabetically arranged, list all adult residents by name, occupation, and home and work address. At times, city directories include information that is even more genealogically useful, such as Cincinnati's 1840 directory listing of birthplaces by state or country.

The following entries from the 1888 directory for Biddeford, Saco, and Old Orchard, Maine, are typical:

Kimball N. & Son (Nathaniel and Nathaniel E. Kimball) brick mnfrs. Alfred road (see p. 463)

King Charles, laborer (Saco), boards 4 Kossuth

King Henry M., shoemaker, 11 South, house Main, 3d beyond Eastern division depot, B & M R.R.

Kinison Benjamin A., stone cutter, house 81 Alfred

Kinney Fred Weston, clerk, 170 Main, boards 4 Pearl

Note that two of the above (Charles King and F.W. Kinney) were boarders who may have moved frequently, lived in various New England towns, or eventually left the region altogether. City directories are among the few published sources useful for tracing these "urban migrants," an unstable and often overlooked but surprisingly large portion of the nineteenth-century population.

By carefully analyzing the city directory entries for any ancestor from year to year, you can learn much about his economic and social position. Over a period of time he may have moved from a poorer to a wealthier section of town, acquired his own home, or progressed from laborer to machinist or manager. You may, alas, find a pattern of downward social mobility as well.

In general, far fewer city directories are published today than in the nineteenth century or early 1900s. Some major urban areas such as Boston, however, still have city directories comparable to the best of their predecessors. Locating yourself or near relatives in these volumes is often a startling experience.

Besides city directories, most libraries have a complete run of annual town reports. While these publications are generally not as useful as city directories, they do contain valuable information. If your ancestor worked for the town, was involved in town politics, or served jury duty, he will probably be listed in the town report. But town reports are most valuable because they usually include the births, marriages, and deaths that occurred during the year.

Telephone books can fill much of the gap caused by the discontinuance of city directories. A telephone directory is not nearly as comprehensive as a city directory because many residents do not own telephones or prefer unlisted numbers. Still, a substantial proportion (if not a majority) of the adult population of every American community is listed in the telephone directory by name and address. Such information can be invaluable in locating living relatives or friends of your parents or grandparents. When visiting any town where an ancestor with a rare surname may have left descendants, it is advisable to begin your research by contacting whoever with that surname is listed in the local directory.

Vital and Town Records.

Vital and town records exist for many communities where your ancestors lived. If published, this data may be secured by your town library. Vital records, the cornerstone for all genealogical research, are discussed in some detail in chapter 4. Many printed VRs, as they are often called, include not only births, marriages, and deaths recorded by the town clerk, but also local church and cemetery records and even family information from private sources such as journals and diaries.

Town selectmen's records, a largely New England resource, are less well known, but contain invaluable information. They have been published for some older communities, usually by a local historical society or an interested individual. These selectmen's records often include lists of town founders, officers (usually elected annually), taxpayers, land grantees (whenever the town is grantor), residents who owe the town money or have been paid for certain services, new inhabitants, and persons "warned out" of town.

Miscellaneous Books and Manuscripts.

In addition to the standard types of genealogical sources mentioned above, local libraries are often repositories of gifts of genealogies and historical manuscripts that may not be found anywhere else. There is usually no rhyme or reason to these collections. Perhaps the last surviving widow of a family that had lived in the area for several generations willed more than a century's correspondence to the library; or perhaps her executor gave it, largely because he was reluctant to discard the material, but didn't quite know what to do with it. Distant relations frequently have no interest in the family and prefer to inherit clothing or furniture or to keep a watch or piece of linen as a memento.

Among this collection of miscellaneous books and manuscripts may be several privately printed, typescript, or even photocopied family histories prepared by individuals living nearby. Frequently such works were intended primarily for family members and are not widely distributed. Indeed, the only copy of such a work, besides some owned by family members and perhaps now lost, may be in the local library. Its existence there may be generally unknown.

Special Indexes.

Among the transcriptions prepared by local genealogical societies or by local librarians and/or volunteers may be various indexes of obituaries and marriages in local newspapers or of local cemetery inscriptions. Such an index may be "in progress" or cover only a certain time period. Whenever you visit a small library, always ask whether any such resources are available.

The Local Library as a Clearing-House of Genealogical Information.

In addition to holding books and manuscripts of immense value for tracing local ancestors, town libraries are usually the best sources of information on other nearby persons or groups who may also be able to help you. The reference librarian should have the names and addresses of any town historian or genealogist and of all local historical and genealogical societies. The librarian can usually direct you to local repositories of primary records, especially county courthouses and town halls. Indeed, the librarian himself may be familiar with holdings at most local repositories and have some literature that describes them. In short, the local library and librarian may be your best introduction to genealogical research in many areas throughout the country.

Libraries with Medium-Size Genealogical Collections

In the United States today, more than fifteen hundred public libraries, historical societies, and genealogical societies have well-organized
genealogy book collections. In addition to materials you would ordinari-

*John Singleton Copley's portrait of Frances Deering Wentworth, after whom Frances-
town (New Hampshire) is named. Good selections of both town and family histories
exist in many larger libraries. New York Public Library*

ly find in local libraries, these libraries often include many basic genealogical reference works, a good selection of town and family histories, various major genealogical periodicals, and important collections on microfilm or microfiche. The number of volumes at libraries with middle-size genealogical collections may range from a few hundred to several thousand. Usually, however, their holdings include many of the following titles, research aids, and types of sources.

Genealogical Bibliographies.

During the past two decades several excellent bibliographies have inventoried most printed genealogical literature. For reference works and finding aids, the major guide is P. William Filby's *American and British Genealogy and Heraldry: A Selected List of Books,* 3rd ed. The more than nine thousand entries in this work, often annotated with a brief description of contents, include many major articles and works in English concerning many foreign countries. Family genealogies are amply covered in Marion J. Kaminkow's *Genealogies in the Library of Congress: A Bibliography,* 2 vols., 1972, *Supplement, 1972-76,* 1977, and *A Complement to Genealogies in the Library of Congress,*1981. The first of these works is a list of all entries from the sixty-drawer "Family Name Index" catalog of the Local History and Genealogy section of the Library of Congress. The third lists all other genealogies in many libraries, including the Allen County (Fort Wayne, Indiana), Los Angeles, and New York Public Libraries, the Historical Society of Pennsylvania, and the Minnesota Historical Society. Also immensely useful are *Family Histories and Genealogies (National Society, Daughters of the American Revolution Library Catalog,* vol. 1) and two immense dictionary catalogs produced by the New York Public Library, one covering the library's Local History and Genealogy Division (18 vols.) and the other covering all their research libraries (800 vols.).

Local history is covered by Kaminkow's *United States Local Histories in the Library of Congress,* 5 vols., by P.W. Filby's *A Bibliography of American County Histories,* 1985., and by the ongoing bibliographies of the six New England states prepared by the Committee for a New England Bibliography. Single-state bibliographies also exist for some other states.

Many of these bibliographies list several works or items pertinent to almost every researcher. Collectively these volumes list most genealogical books — but not manuscripts — in American libraries today.

Indexes.

Not only has most genealogical literature been listed and inventoried; much (far less but still a huge quantity) has been collectively, or analytically, indexed. An analytical index usually contains references for anywhere between five hundred and five thousand books. Most analytical indexes — of surnames or surnames and given names — were compiled by librarians as each genealogy book arrived. Since some of the books so surveyed are among the ten percent or so of all published genealogies that are themselves unindexed, these analytical compendia sometimes represent the only indexes of certain individual volumes.

The first of these major compendia, the *Index to American Genealogies* issued by Joel Munsell Publishers in 1900 (with several earlier editions beginning in 1868), is a surname index to genealogies and local histories published in the nineteenth century. Each of its sixty thousand entries covering most New England and many mid-Atlantic and southern surnames, includes author, title, and page numbers. Although many genealogies and local histories were surveyed, only principal surnames (often one per genealogy) were indexed. Despite these limitations, this work remains extremely useful; it is usually called simply Munsell's.

Its chronological sequel is *The Genealogy Index of the Newberry Library*, a surname index to books acquired by the Newberry Library in Chicago between 1896 and 1918. This four-volume set includes more than five hundred thousand entries. A third work, *The Greenlaw Index of the New England Historic Genealogical Society,* is a subject index to one thousand or so major volumes acquired by the New England Historic Genealogical Society between 1895 and 1940. In addition to listing the source, author, publication date, and page number of each of its thirty-three thousand entries, this index includes the full name of the immigrant ancestor or later central figure of each sketch, the towns or counties in which the family *in that line* resided, the time period covered (often more than a century), and the length of the entry. The fourth general analytical index is the ongoing *American Genealogical-Biographical Index,* currently indexing names starting with P and more than 135 volumes in length. This massive work covers all genealogical materials at the Godfrey Memorial Library in Middletown, Connecticut.

Other indexes are more specialized. *The Biography and Genealogy Dictionaries Master Index* (13 vols.) lists more than 725,000 persons who appear in sixty past and current editions of *Who's Who* and other works of collective biography. *Passenger and Immigration Lists Index* (3 vols.) plus four supplements to date, compiled by P. William Filby and Mary K. Meyer, identifies more than one million immigrants (gleaned from all known published passenger lists) to the United States and Canada before 1820.

Special mention should be made of the *International Genealogical Index (IGI)*. By far the largest analytical index yet created, the *IGI* is an ongoing project of the Church of Jesus Christ of Latter-day Saints Genealogical Society Library in Salt Lake City. Incorporating births or christenings, marriages, and other vital sources from more than ninety countries, the current edition, produced in 1983-1984, contains more than eighty-six million entries. Although computerized, the *IGI* is published on microfiche and is currently available at branch libraries of the Genealogical Society Library of the Mormon Church (more on this library appears later in this chapter), the New England Historic Genealogical Society in Boston, the Society of Genealogists in London, and elsewhere. Data for each entry includes the name of the person identified in the source; the name(s) of either his or her parents or spouse; the sex of the individual; the type of event (such as birth or marriage); the date; and the place of the event. Listing deceased persons only, the *IGI* contains, among other enormous consolidations, all Massachusetts births (and many marriages) from the printed vital records, more than twenty percent of all baptisms and marriages recorded in English parish registers since the 1530s, and millions of Scandinavian (especially Finnish) extracts. Guides for using the *IGI* appear in two periodicals: the *Register*, vol. 137 (1983): pp. 193-217 and vol. 138 (1984): p. 39, and *Genealogists' Magazine*, vol. 21 (1983): pp. 60-63, 83-87.

Genealogical Periodicals.

Numerous periodicals are available in most genealogical collections. While the content of genealogical journals varies, you are likely to find Register-Form genealogies (more on these in chapter 12), ancestor tables, extracts from various source records, "how-to" articles, and pedagogical case studies. Foremost among these periodicals is *The New England Historical and Genealogical Register*. Begun in 1847, it is the oldest genealogical journal in the world and the leading published source for New England families generally. The country's second major genealogical quarterly is *The New York Genealogical and Biographical Record*, begun in 1870, which offers coverage for New York and many New Jersey families. Other important genealogical journals begun in the twentieth century that are national in scope and contain articles helpful to almost any genealogist include *The American Genealogist, The National Genealogical Society Quarterly, The Genealogist* (New York), *The Detroit Society for Genealogical Research Magazine, Genealogical Journal,* and *The Genealogical Helper.* (More detailed information on all of these can be found in appendix A.)

Many nineteenth- and early twentieth-century historical journals also published much genealogical material, a practice that unfortunately ceased in the 1930s and after. The Genealogical Publishing Company has consolidated a great deal of this material. A review of the company's program, with some comments on these historical journals, appears in the *Register,* vol. 138 (1984): pp. 46-51. A few decades after genealogy was dropped from many historical journals, local genealogists founded a new generation of regional periodicals. *The Kentucky Genealogist* was begun in 1950 by Martha P. Miller, and *The Virginia Genealogist* in 1957 by her nephew, John Frederick Dorman. *The Maryland and Delaware Genealogist* was started in 1959 by Raymond B. Clark Jr., and the *Rhode Island Genealogical Register* in 1978 by Alden G. Beaman. This movement extended to states without major legacies of periodical literature, such as North Carolina and Georgia. Many county, city, and local groups began periodicals as well.

Genealogical journals have also been extensively indexed, largely by Donald Lines Jacobus in *Index to Genealogical Periodicals together with "My Own Index,"* 1973 (originally published in three volumes, 1932, 1948, and 1952, and recently consolidated by Carl Boyer III as *Donald Lines Jacobus' Index to Genealogical Periodicals, rev. ed.,* 1983). "Multiancestor" volumes covering all known forebears of an individual or couple often contain the best recent material on Colonial families. In "My Own Index," an appendix to volume 3 of the *Index to Genealogical Periodicals,* Jacobus included sixty of the best of these volumes. Seventy other good multiancestor works are listed in *Genealogical Research in New England,* pp. 110-112, 114.

The successor to Jacobus's index is the *Genealogical Periodical Annual Index,* which now runs to seventeen volumes and covers the years 1962-1969 and 1974-1982. A guide to these indexes, which are not comprehensive, is Kip Sperry's *A Survey of American Genealogical Periodicals and Periodical Indexes*. Among indexes to individual periodicals, note specifically Jean D. Worden's *The New York Genealogical and Biographical Record 113 Years Master Index*. (See appendix A for other listings.) Also notable are the indexes (per volume) to the various sets of periodical extracts produced by Genealogical Publishing Company of Baltimore in the past five years. These indexes often cover the entire body of genealogical material in the extracted periodical — to date the major journals of Rhode Island, Pennsylvania, Maryland, Virginia, Kentucky, and the island of Barbados.

Genealogical Compendia.

In addition to bibliographies and analytical indexes, medium-size genealogical collections usually own most major compendia. Genealogical compendia are large compilations of family pedigrees often organized by geographical area or topic. Such works are voluminous and constantly used. Some of the best are listed in appendix B.

Major Genealogical Libraries

Among the thousands of public libraries and historical and genealogical societies in the United States, thirteen have collections that rank them far above the rest. These thirteen, listed here, are among the greatest libraries in the world.

New England Historic Genealogical Society, 101 Newbury Street, Boston, MA 02116

New York Public Library, 5th Avenue and 42nd Street, New York, NY 10016

New York Genealogical and Biographical Society, 122-6 East 58th Street, New York, NY 10022

Library of Congress, Washington, DC 20540

Library, National Society, Daughters of the American Revolution, 1776 "D" Street NW, Washington, DC 20006 (Use in conjunction with the Library of Congress and the National Genealogical Society Library, 4527 17th Street N, Arlington, VA 22207.)

Western Reserve Historical Society, 10825 East Blvd., Cleveland, OH 44106

Burton Collection, Detroit Public Library, 5201 Woodward Avenue, Detroit, MI 48202

Public Library of Fort Wayne & Allen County, 301 West Wayne Street, Ft. Wayne, IN 46802

Newberry Library, 60 West Walton Street, Chicago, IL 60610

State Historical Society of Wisconsin, 816 State Street, Madison, WI 53703

Dallas Public Library, 1515 Young Street, Dallas, TX 75201

The Genealogical Society Library, 50 East North Temple Street, Salt Lake City, UT 84150

Los Angeles Public Library, 630 West 5th Street, Los Angeles, CA 90071

Two of these organizations, the New England Historic Genealogical Society and the Genealogical Society Library in Salt Lake City, deserve special mention because of the size of their collections and the genealogical services they provide.

New England Historic Genealogical Society (NEHGS).

Founded in 1845, the NEHGS is the oldest and largest genealogical organization in the world, with a current membership of more than nine thousand. The society's open-stack research library contains nearly four hundred thousand volumes, and its manuscript holdings total more than a million items. Major collections at the society include the John Hutchinson Cook Library of Continental and British Genealogy (eleven thousand volumes on royal, noble, and gentry families of Spain, Italy, France, Germany, the Netherlands, England, and other European countries); the papers of many nineteenth- and twentieth-century genealogical scholars; the Corbin Collection of genealogical data relating to central and western Massachusetts; the Sprague, Welch, and Weeden Collections on families of Braintree and Scituate, Massachusetts, and Berwick, Maine; C.A. Torrey's listing of New England marriages prior to 1700; the Crowell and Eaton Collections on Nova Scotia families; and the Maine and Massachusetts Direct Tax Census of 1798. (The Corbin, Torrey, Sprague, and Crowell collections and the 1798 Direct Tax Census have also been published on microfilm by the society in recent years.)

One of the more valuable services provided by the NEHGS is its lending library of more than thirty thousand volumes, duplicate copies of the most frequently used books in the society's main library. Members may borrow through the mail up to three books at a time for three weeks' use. A multivolume catalog gives members an up-to-date bibliography of this collection.

NEHGS also provides a professional research service for members. Answers to simple research queries are provided at no cost; more complex queries are undertaken for an hourly fee. Educational programs at the NEHGS include frequent lectures in Boston, seminars and programs cosponsored with groups across the country, and video-taped presentations for use by members and organizations.

Genealogical Society Library (GSL) in Salt Lake City.

Founded in 1894 by the Genealogical Society of Utah and funded and administered by the Church of Jesus Christ of Latter-day Saints (commonly called the Mormons), this great library has collected a vast quantity of genealogical materials used by church members for religious purposes, but it is open to the general public as well. The library now contains more than 150,000 published volumes and 1.25 million reels of microfilm gathered from throughout the world. These records identify more than a billion people, cover more than one hundred countries, and span several continents. For the British Isles and continental Europe, the library has 573,000 reels, representing nearly half of its total microfilm collection. For the United States and Canada, there are 390,000 reels, or approximately a third of the total. The collection for Latin America includes 172,000 reels, and for Asia and the Pacific "rim" 30,100. The microfilm collection at the GSL increases at a rate of about forty thousand one hundred-foot reels of microfilm yearly. In addition to books and microfilms of primary sources, the GSL has also collected oral histories from native families of the South Pacific and elsewhere.

The basic collection development policy of the GSL is to acquire those records "that uniquely identify individuals and their family relationships." It attempts to secure the "one source for each country and time period that identifies the greatest proportion of their historical population." Thus, for the nineteenth-century Western world, it has focused on civil records, censuses, immigration registers, passenger lists, naturalization records, and passports. But for the period from 1600 to 1800 in Europe, it has found the best source to be ecclesiastical (i.e., parish) registers containing entries for birth or baptism, marriage, and death or burial.

You have access to this vast collection of microfilm material, as well as to the extensive holdings of books, through the microfiche GSL catalog. The catalog is divided into four sections: author/title, locality, surname, and subject. In addition to the main library in Salt Lake City, there are four hundred branch libraries distributed throughout the United States, Canada, Mexico and elsewhere. Each of these has a copy of the main GSL catalog and the *International Genealogical Index.* Through these branch libraries, members of the Mormon Church, as well as the public at large, can borrow duplicate copies of microfilm, which are obtained from the main library. In 1983 the branch libraries served more than 750,000 patrons in this fashion.

In addition to gathering and preserving source material, the Genealogical Society sponsored the first World Conference on Records and Genealogical Research at Salt Lake City in August 1969, and the second at the same place in August 1980. It also sponsors annual genealogical research seminars at Brigham Young University in Provo, Utah, which offers degree programs in genealogy.

As you continue to sharpen your genealogical skills, you will no doubt find that the three major types of genealogical libraries are indispensable for successful research. Unless you are fortunate enough to live near a great genealogical library, you will probably conduct most of your work at a nearby, medium-size facility. But even under these circumstances, you will still want to take advantage of the collections and services of the major genealogical libraries. Regardless of how far from Boston, Salt Lake City, or Washington, D.C., you reside, you will want to consider a membership in the New England Historic Genealogical Society because of the research services and lending library; to order various microfilms from the local Mormon branch library; and to check all ancestral surnames against the holdings of the New York Public Library, the Library of Congress, and the DAR Library.

COFFEY.

1. EDWARD COFFEY, son of Jeremiah Coffey, b. county of Cork, Ireland, Dec. 17, 1830 ; came to America, 1852. He m. Jan. 11, 1860, Hannah Corcoran, b. August 12, 1836, dau. of Patrick and Ellen (O'Connell) Corcoran. They res. in Boston a few years, removing to Plymouth, 1859. His industry has been rewarded, and by good citizenship he has earned the respect of his townsmen. Seven children.

    i.   JEREMIAH, b. July 8, 1861. unm. Res. in Plymouth until 1890, and is now a machinist in Baltimore, Md.

   ii.   JOHN, b. Dec. 8, 1862 ; was a bookkeeper in railroad office. He d. June 4, 1884.

  iii.   EDWARD, b. April 29, 1864. unm. Lived in Plymouth until 1890, when he removed to Boston. He is a machinist, B. & M. R.R.

  iv.   WILLIAM R., b. May 23, 1866. unm. A conductor B. & M. R.R. ; res. in Plymouth.

   v.   MARY, b. May 20, 1868 ; Plymouth High School, 1886 ; State Normal School, 1887 ; Sister M. De La Salle, Convent of Mercy, Manchester.

  vi.   DENNIS NOBLE, b. Oct. 18, 1871. d. June 27, 1875.

 vii.   ANNIE E., b. May 19, 1876. m. Herbert E. Jones (see).

Coffey family history information, from History of Plymouth (New Hampshire), Vol. II, *published in 1906. Compiled family histories often contain errors, especially concerning Colonial Period ancestors.*

Compiled Family Histories

A special word should be said about compiled family histories or genealogies. The heyday of these works was the period from the Civil War to the 1930s. Several thousand such monographs appeared in these decades. The compilers of these works usually labored conscientiously, but far fewer primary records had been printed, indexed, or gathered into a single convenient repository at that time. Thus, many mistakes, especially concerning Colonial generations, appear in the books.

The first American genealogists were often quite gullible in regard to English or Old World origins and coats of arms. In addition, since the northern half of the United States was prosperous during this period, most published genealogies concerned New England or Mid-Atlantic rather than southern families. The strength of these works is that they cover many nineteenth-century pioneers. Since the authors corresponded voluminously with other family members, these books are often amazingly complete and accurate for the nineteenth century. These works are particularly good for New England migrants to the Midwest, many of whom were still alive when the genealogies were written.

Many post-1930 genealogical scholars have written journal articles correcting the first several generations or the early sections of these genealogies. Various indexes and bibliographical guides to this periodical literature are discussed above and elsewhere in this book.

Remember that you will not make all of your genealogical discoveries in libraries. While library research will be a major part of your ancestral quest, you should combine it with visits to town halls, courthouses, state archives, and other record depositories. The best compiled genealogies are based on both primary and secondary sources. Library research is an important aspect of genealogical education, perhaps the most important, but it is only one aspect.

❧ *Pointers and Pitfalls* ❧

Using Library Resources

1. After you have exhausted family resources, turn to the library to continue your genealogical research.

2. If you go to a library with a major genealogical collection, start by getting an orientation tour or guide booklet.

3. Next, ask the librarian about any special features of the library's collection and any advice concerning the specific problems you are researching.

4. Be aware of any special conditions regarding use of the library's materials.

5. Try to visit libraries in localities where your ancestors lived.

6. If you can't, write to the reference librarian to request information. Always be brief and specific.

7. Genealogical collections can be divided into three basic groups: those found in small-town libraries or historical societies; those found in medium-size or major metropolitan libraries, which may have a separate genealogy research area; those found in large libraries with massive collections intended specifically to promote genealogical study.

8. Small-town libraries and historical societies offer unique and valuable resources such as county histories, local maps, local publications, histories of local institutions, and town vital records.

9. Librarians at town libraries can sometimes refer you to resources not found in the library itself.

10. Medium-size libraries include resources such as bibliographies, analytical indexes, genealogical compendia, and genealogical periodicals.

11. Thirteen of the largest genealogical libraries in this country are listed in this chapter. The two that offer the greatest range of materials and services are the New England Historic Genealogical Society and the Genealogical Society Library of the Church of Jesus Christ of Latter-day Saints.

12. Compiled family histories, published between the 1860s and the 1930s, are quite accurate for nineteenth-century information, although they contain many mistakes concerning Colonial generations. Since the 1930s, many journal articles have been written correcting data in these histories.

13. Compiled family histories focus mainly on New England and the Mid-Atlantic states and are particularly good in covering New England migrants to the Midwest.

CHAPTER FOUR

VITAL SIGNS

Birth, Death, and Marriage Records

Historical print depicting a scene from an Eastern European Jewish wedding.
The Bettman Archive, Inc.

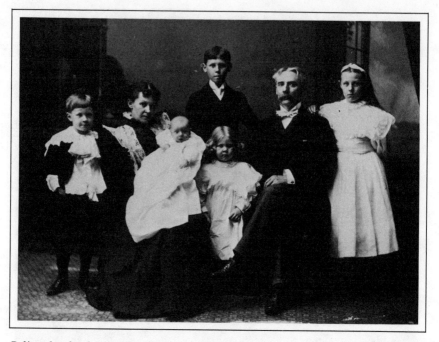

Believed to be the family of Henry T. Thurber, private secretary to President Grover Cleveland. Vital records can sometimes provide important data on nuclear family units. National Archives

 f all available primary documents, vital records offer the most immediate source of trustworthy genealogical information. By definition, vital records are official registrations of birth, marriage, and death, information that local and state governmental agencies are required by law to keep. They also often include data on parents. Over the years, the definition of vital records has been broadened to include church registers, cemetery inscriptions, and diary notations of the births, marriages, and deaths that occurred in a particular community. Most of the published vital records incorporate such unofficial information.

You must be wary, though, of accepting such information as fact. Even such highly touted sources as cemetery inscriptions can be misleading if interpreted incorrectly. In some volumes of published Massachusetts vital records, for example, it was customary to take the dates of birth from gravestones or calculate them from death dates listing ages, then add the data among the town births, whether or not the individual was actually born there. For instance, among the births in the published Natick, Massachusetts, vital records to 1850 is that of Albert C. Dearborn, born in November 1829. Next to his name, the key "GR 5" indicates that the record comes from his gravestone in the North Natick Cemetery. Albert died in Natick on July 15, 1902, age seventy-two years, eight months (hence the calculated date of birth). His official death record, however, filed with both the town and the state, lists his birthplace not as Natick but as Saco, Maine, and his parents as Thomas and Abigail (Merrill) Dearborn. This information is correct, for in the Saco vital records, among the children of Thomas and Abigail Dearborn recorded in 1842, we find the birth of Albert on November 4, 1829.

History of Vital Records

Of all the classes of documents available to genealogists, vital records are, curiously, among the most modern. Their history in the English-speaking world dates from the beginning of the Reformation, when the Church of England, following its break with Rome in 1538, instructed its individual parishes to maintain registers of baptisms, marriages, and burials. Despite this sixteenth-century origin, vital records were not uniformly required by statute or maintained as standard practice in either Europe or the United States until the nineteenth or early twentieth century.

The first laws requiring vital records in the American Colonies were passed in Virginia and the Massachusetts Bay. In 1632 the Virginia assembly decreed that the minister of each parish report annually to the court all baptisms, marriages, and burials in his jurisdiction. In 1639 the General Court of the Massachusetts Bay Colony required "that there be records kept of all . . . days of marriage, birth and death of every person within this jurisdiction." Legislation of a similar kind was soon passed by lawmakers in other New England colonies.

Although Virginia legislated the keeping of vital records as early as 1632, these laws were not generally enforced. This lack of concern reflects a problem with such records in the South until the nineteenth century. The failure to keep them in a systematic way during the Colonial period and after can be attributed to the high rate of geographical mobility that characterized the South during that era. Families often migrated four or five times, especially in the decades after the Revolution, always in search of new and productive land. Because the population was so unstable, legal instruments such as wills were not always used, and inheritance of property, though always a serious matter, occurred informally, often before the death of the father or grandfather.

Americans changed their attitude toward vital records only when they realized how useful these records could be for developing statistics concerning health and sanitation. Organizations such as the American Medical Association, the American Statistical Association, and the National Board of Health, all created during the middle decades of the nineteenth century, convinced federal and state leaders of the value of maintaining such records.

Massachusetts in 1841 became the first state to pass legislation requiring vital records to be maintained on a state level. The chart that follows provides a list of states and the dates when laws were passed requiring birth and death registration.

State	Death	Birth	State	Death	Birth
Alabama	1908	1908	Montana	1907	1907
Alaska	1913	1913	Nebraska	1905	1905
Arizona	1909	1909	Nevada	1911	1911
Arkansas	1914	1914	New Hampshire	1905	1905
California	1905	1905	New Jersey	1848	1848
Colorado	1907	1907	New Mexico	1919	1919
Connecticut	1897	1897	New York	1880	1880
Delaware	1881	1881	North Carolina	1913	1913
D.C.	1855	1871	North Dakota	1908	1908
Florida	1899	1899	Ohio	1909	1909
Georgia	1919	1919	Oklahoma	1908	1908
Hawaii	1896	1896	Oregon	1903	1903
Idaho	1911	1911	Pennsylvania	1906	1906
Illinois	1916	1916	Puerto Rico	1931	1931
Indiana	1900	1907	Rhode Island	1852	1852
Iowa	1880	1880	South Carolina	1915	1915
Kansas	1911	1911	South Dakota	1905	1905
Kentucky	1911	1911	Tennessee	1914	1914
Louisiana	1914	1914	Texas	1903	1903
Maine	1892	1892	Utah	1905	1905
Maryland	1898	1898	Vermont	1857	1857
Massachusetts	1841	1841	Virginia	1912	1912
Michigan	1867	1867	Washington	1907	1907
Minnesota	1900	1900	West Virginia	1917	1917
Mississippi	1912	1912	Wisconsin	1907	1907
Missouri	1910	1910	Wyoming	1909	1909

In early New England, it was often the custom to record births in family groups, usually one or two families per page in the record book. Sometimes the births would be listed shortly after they occurred, but usually they were recorded all at once (though sometimes before the couple stopped having children).

In the vital records of Corinna, Maine, we find recorded the births of the twelve children of Henry and Polly (Wiggin) Dearborn between 1801 and 1825. Only the youngest child, however, was actually born there. Examination of land and tax records shows that Henry and Polly had lived in New Durham, New Hampshire, from 1815 until 1825, and before that in Deerfield, New Hampshire. The vital records of these New Hampshire towns do not show the births of the older children born there. Therefore, the place where a birth is recorded is not always the actual place of birth.

Even if your family lived in a town where vital records were kept, their names still may not appear. Parents were generally responsible for making certain that their children's births were properly recorded. Some families carefully entered them in the family Bible, but failed to notify the town clerk. The town clerk might not have performed his duties carefully, or one or more of the town record books might have been lost over time. Any one of these causes might prevent you from finding vital records for your ancestor. Do not be discouraged if this situation arises. While vital records may provide the easiest proof of family relationships, such proof may also be gleaned from church records, wills, censuses, deeds, and various other documents as well.

Some Examples

Dr. Benjamin Dearborn was a young physician who lived in Portsmouth, New Hampshire, in the mid-1700s. Although the town of Portsmouth kept vital records, the records do not cover his family. Baptismal records reveal that by his wife, Ruth, he had two children, Ruth and Benjamin, baptized in the North Church in 1752 and 1754, respectively. Benjamin himself died in 1755, age thirty, as attested by his gravestone, which still stands in the North Burial Ground. Although we have no record of the marriage of Benjamin to Ruth either in town or church records, we know that she was the daughter of Dr. Nathaniel Sargent of Portsmouth, as she is specifically named in the latter's 1760 will. Thus, we have a basic record of Benjamin Dearborn and his family without recourse to vital records.

A much more difficult case is presented by Simon Dearborn of New Hampshire. Like Benjamin, his name never appears among the vital records of any town, but alternate records are not as easy to find in his case, nor do they provide as neat a solution. Simon was baptized in the Congregational Church in Greenland, New Hampshire, in 1743 (the exact date is not stated), son of Edward and Mary (Foss) Dearborn. We have no record of his marriage and know only that his wife's name was Margaret. In a deed dated June 22, 1770, he sold to his brother Thomas a parcel of property in Greenland that had been part of the estate of Edward Dearborn, his deceased father. Both he and his wife, Margaret, signed their "X" marks; the deed also tells us that Simon was living in Barrington, New Hampshire, at the time and was a joiner by trade. Two years later, then living in Epping, New Hampshire, Simon and Margaret signed their marks to a deed by which they sold one-eighth of his mother's right of dower to land in Greenland. Both of these deeds are recorded in Rockingham County, New Hampshire.

Simon and Margaret had moved to Middleton, New Hampshire, settling in the part that is now Brookfield, by 1783, when his name appears on several petitions. His name last appears in town records in mid-December 1786. At a town meeting the following May, it was "voted to take of the Widdow Margaret Dearborn's taxes for the years 1782, and 1783 and 1785 from the Constables." Obviously, Simon had died during the interim. His death is not recorded in the town, there is no extant gravestone, nor did he leave a will or administration. The last glimpse we have of Margaret is in the 1790 federal census, where at Middleton she headed a household of three females.

The placing of Simon and Margaret's children is even more problematic. There are no birth records for any offspring, but we can infer from various records that at least three grew to maturity. A John Dearborn appears in the 1790 census next to Margaret with what are apparently a wife and young son. He moved to Vassalborough, Maine, in 1796, where he dealt frequently in land records with a Henry Dearborn. As both men survived through 1850, we have an approximation of their ages from the census of that year. Perhaps the Eleanor Dearborn who married Joseph Cross at nearby Hallowell, Maine, is a sister.

From these examples, we have seen that even in New England, where vital records are profuse, many families are not covered by them. Tracing these families requires judicious use of other available records.

Portrait of little boy on a swing. Birth records can help you to identify an ancestor's offspring. Alison Scott

Consider an example involving vital records that at first seem almost too abundant. Let's say you are trying to discover the parents of your ancestor, Hannah Standley of Beverly, Massachusetts, who was married there on November 1, 1750 to Josiah Morgan. We see that there are three birth records that might fit:

Hannah Standley, dau. of William and Hannah, born 27 July 1724.
Hannah Standley, dau. of William and Ruth, bapt. 2 Sept. 1733.
Hannah Standley, dau. of William and Hannah, bapt. 23 Sept.
   1733.

In this case the last Hannah is the correct choice. To solve the problem, we have to look at the will of her grandfather, John Standley, who died in Beverly in 1758, which names among others his granddaughter, Mrs. Hannah Morgan.

Locating Vital Records

Generally researchers have two options when requesting vital records. They can write the state repository of vital records or obtain a copy from the appropriate agency at the town or county level. In most states the original is maintained at the state level, but a copy is also held in the town or county clerk's office. Very often you can obtain a copy faster by writing to the town or county simply because they have fewer such requests.

Because of recent restrictive state legislation, some vital records are not available at all unless you can prove that you are a member of the immediate family. In Massachusetts, for example, birth and marriage records are restricted after 1890 if the record involves an illegitimacy, adoption, or abnormal birth. Therefore, all birth and marriage certificates after that date must be screened by a clerk before the researcher is granted access.

If the vital records you seek were created since the state officially began to maintain such records, you should have little difficulty in obtaining a copy unless the original has been restricted for some lawful reason, usually involving illegitimacy or adoption. When requesting a vital record, as when asking for any other genealogical information, be as specific as possible and include any information that will help the clerk identify the correct individual. Try always to include, if known, the name, date, and place of the vital event you seek to document. A sample letter might read as follows:

Dear Sir,

Please send to me a copy of the full death certificate of Steven A. Ball who died in 1915 in Santa Ana, California. Enclosed is a check for five dollars to cover costs. Thank you for your attention.

Very truly yours,

Note that the letter asks for a copy of the *full* death certificate. An abridged or short version of the certificate will often omit information that is pertinent to your research.

Sometimes you will not have enough information to allow the clerk to identify the certificate you desire. You may have only a partial name, lack a precise birth or death date, or not know the residence. Do not let this discourage you. Identify the person you are seeking as completely as possible, and in your letter to the clerk, ask him to undertake a "search" of the records in his possession for all persons who seem to fit the description you provide. In your correspondence be sure to be brief, clear, and courteous.

Whether you are seeking the certificate of a person for whom you have full name, date, and place information, or are asking the clerk to undertake a general search, it is important to include with your request a cashier's check or money order (try to avoid sending personal checks

Father and daughter portrait. The search for vital records often involves writing to a town or county clerk. Ben Watson

because some clerks will not accept them) that approximates as nearly as possible the reasonable costs of the search and photocopying charges. Always enclose a self-addressed stamped envelope.

A major challenge for genealogists is locating vital records that may have been collected in the nineteenth century before the passage of state laws. Except in the New England states, such data was maintained very unevenly, with records existing in some towns and counties but not in others. Happily, during the 1930s the Works Progress Administration (WPA) employed scholars to make a "List of Vital Statistical Records," which became available in the 1940s. This work, which is now part of most major genealogical library collections, contains a thorough reporting through 1943 of the location of vital records (including church records) at the town or county level. It provides important information on the methods by which vital data was kept in the various localities and also when particular churches moved or stopped keeping records. Forty states participated in this WPA project, but Alaska and Hawaii (not then states), Connecticut, Delaware, Maine, Maryland, Ohio, Pennsylvania, South Carolina, and part of Vermont did not.

Other indexes exist for some of these latter states. Connecticut, for example, has the Lucius Barnes Barbour Collection of town vital records through 1850. The original card slips are available at the Connecticut State Library in Hartford. Microfilm copies of the Barbour Collection are in many major genealogical libraries. For Delaware, birth records for the period 1861 to 1913, death records from 1855 to 1910, index cards for baptisms from 1759 to 1890, and index cards for marriages from 1730 to 1850 are available at the Hall of Records in Dover. For Maine, a vital records index is available at the Maine State Library in Augusta (and the

A 1929 wedding portrait — today a family treasure. Clarissa Silitch

Maine Historical Society in Portland). It covers the Colonial and National periods to 1892. This index incorporates the records of eighty towns; for seventeen of them, vital record volumes have been published by the Maine Historical Society. There is also a *Bride's Index* to Maine marriages for the period 1895 to 1953.

For Maryland, indexes are deposited in the Hall of Records in Annapolis covering births from 1801 to 1877 and deaths from 1865 to 1880 in several counties. For Vermont, an index to vital records from the early period extending through 1955 is available at the secretary of state's office in Montpelier.

Also note that more than two hundred towns in Massachusetts have published vital records. These cover the early period through 1850 and occasionally later. For Rhode Island, the James N. Arnold Collection of vital records for 1636 to 1850 runs to twenty-one published volumes, and a recent new series by Alden G. Beaman (containing vital data reconstructed from miscellaneous sources) consists of nine volumes. Many New Hampshire town records extending well into the nineteenth century have been gathered and indexed in a collection at the State House in Concord.

Although most published vital records are to be found in New England, a few exist in other states. The federal government has prepared a helpful guide to vital statistics in the United States — *Where to Write for Vital Records*, U.S. Dept. of Health and Human Services Publication No. (PHS) 82-1184, which can be obtained free by writing to the United States Government Printing Office, Superintendent of Documents, Washington, DC 20204.

Content and Inaccuracies

Of records generated by the three types of vital events, the death certificate is often the most useful to genealogists because it contains important information on two generations of a family. A death certificate usually includes the following data: the deceased's name and age; date, place, and cause of death; physician's name; birthdate and birthplace of deceased; place of residence; marital status; whether a veteran; place of burial; names of undertaker; name of informant; occupation of deceased; name and sometimes birthplaces of the deceased's father and mother.

On marriage certificates, you will typically find this information: woman's maiden name; place and date of marriage; presiding minister; names of witnesses or bondsmen (often these are relatives); ages, birthplaces, and current residence of bride and groom; parents of bride and groom (not common outside New England).

Birth certificates usually include name and sex of newborn; time and place of birth; names of parents; ages and places of birth of both parents.

Because so much genealogically pertinent information is contained in vital records, and because they are usually "primary" sources, we sometimes forget that even they are subject to error. Like any genealogical source, they should be used with caution. For example, common names often present a problem; you may have some difficulty obtaining the correct marriage certificate for a couple with names such as William

Brown and Mary Smith. Another problem has to do with the validity of the data represented on a vital record. A person completing a marriage certificate may lie about his age or use a fictitious name.

On a death registration the accuracy of the record is entirely dependent on the informant. If the informant is a close relative, say a spouse, sibling, or child, you can be reasonably sure of the accuracy of the record. On the other hand, if the informant is a neighbor or acquaintance, there is less assurance of accuracy. On the death record of Lucy F. (Woodcock) Rea, who died in Andover, Massachusetts, in 1905, age eighty-eight years, five months, five days, it is stated that she was born in Marshfield, Vermont, daughter of Ebenezer Woodcock (born Ohio) and Hannah Day (born Chelsea, Massachusetts). In fact vital records show that her father was born in Needham, Massachusetts, in 1773 and her mother in Winchendon, Massachusetts, in 1779.

To take another example, Amos. F. Dearborn's death record states that he was the son of Andrew and Mary (Veazie) Dearborn and that they were born in Bedford, New Hampshire, and Germany, respectively. Although Mary's birth record has not been found, she certainly wasn't German. The informant on the death record was Mary's daugher-in-law, and perhaps to her Veazie sounded like a German surname.

You should be especially suspicious of documents that are incomplete. Too many "unknowns" on death certificates raise a serious question about the validity of the remaining information. Finally, it should be noted that vital records that predate the state's system of record registration usually do not include the names of informants; thus we must depend on the accuracy of town clerks and transcribers.

Where to Start

Where should you begin your examination of vital records? Start with yourself. Your birth certificate may well reveal an unknown fact or two about your parents' names, address, or former occupation. Next, obtain copies of the birth and marriage certificates (or death certificates if they are deceased) of your parents. These records should identify grandparents, and your grandparents' vital records should identify their parents, and so on for several generations, or as long as vital data continues to be available for your family. Although most researchers discover some gaps in the vital records of their American ancestors, it is often possible to trace three or four generations almost solely from these sources.

A horse-drawn funeral. Death certificates are usually the most informative vital records. The Bettman Archive, Inc.

Vital records also contain information that will help you add interest and color to biographies of your ancestors. You can often extrapolate occupations, causes of death, residence, longevity, and education from other kinds of primary sources, notably probate data, but nowhere can you learn this information as easily as from certificates of birth, marriage, and death.

As we enter the final fifteen years of the twentieth century, it is useful to remember that vital records have been officially maintained in many states for more than a century. Probably most Americans could trace their ancestry through these records alone for at least three generations. Those with Colonial New England ancestry might well trace it through vital records for five, eight, or even ten generations, although they should, of course, confirm their findings with other data. Clearly vital records deserve full exploitation.

❧ Pointers and Pitfalls ❧

Birth, Death, and Marriage Records

1. Vital records are records of birth, marriage, and death, which offer the most immediate source — though not the only source — of trustworthy genealogical information.

2. The earliest vital records kept by churches and town clerks are often incomplete and sometimes inaccurate.

3. Not until the nineteenth or twentieth century were vital records uniformly required by statute in the United States.

4. Researchers can seek copies of vital records from state offices or at the town or county level. The latter usually produce faster results.

5. Sometimes there are restrictions on access to vital records, especially for persons not in the subject's immediate family.

6. When writing to request vital records, be as specific as possible and be sure to request full — not abbreviated — certificates.

7. If you must ask for a search, be brief, clear, and courteous.

8. Send a cashier's check or money order to cover the cost of any work you request.

9. You can use the WPA's "List of Vital Statistical Records" to help you locate vital records collected before uniform statutes were applied. The U.S. government guide *Where to Write for Vital Records* is also helpful.

10. Of the three types of vital records, death certificates usually contain the most data.

11. Even though they are primary sources, vital records often contain inaccuracies.

12. Too many "unknowns" raise questions about the validity of the information in a vital record.

13. Start your vital records examination with yourself and work backward through each generation of your family.

CHAPTER FIVE

RELATIVE REVELATIONS

Church Records

All Saints Church
Peterborough, N.H.

Barbara Smullen

Meeting House of the West Parish Church, Barnstable, Massachusetts. Dave Lawlor

F or areas outside New England and periods before state-mandated registration of births, marriages, and deaths, the best sources for vital data are church records. Among the oldest types of genealogical information, they are frequently also the most reliable. In Europe sacramental records kept by the Catholic Church date from the Middle Ages, and for the Protestant Church from the Reformation. Jewish synagogue records date from the mid-seventeenth century. In America church records were regarded as official only for a brief period in Colonial Virginia, when the clerics of the "established" Anglican Church were authorized to perform marriages.

Ecclesiastical registers are accurate because the recording priest was usually present at or near the time of the event. Of course, ministers sometimes neglected to keep daily records and had to reconstruct them later. Such retrospective entries undoubtedly contain errors. In addition, church registers might not always agree with birth and death records. A baptism or christening or a burial might occur several days (or in the case of baptisms, weeks or even years) after birth or death. The value of ecclesiastical registers lies not only in their general accuracy, however; where official records were destroyed or never kept, they are often the only available substitute.

Several types of church records are valuable to genealogists. The most fundamental are baptismal (or christening), marriage, and burial records. In addition to these, churches may have information on the admission and removal of members, certificates of membership, communicant lists, letters of transferral, lists of ministers and church officials, and notations of disciplinary actions. These latter sources contain little vital data, but should provide much additional biography.

Depending on the time period and the church, baptisms, marriages, and burials may be recorded either chronologically, as part of the on-going business of the congregation, or in special membership rosters. Quakers, for example, usually maintained separate books for vital events. Baptists, on the other hand, often mixed this data with other entries. As the nineteenth century progressed, more and more congregations began using separate rosters to register vital events.

When using church records, examine everything available for the entire period of your family's association with the congregation. If you look only at baptism, marriage, and burial entries, you will miss whatever other information is buried in business or disciplinary proceedings. Note also entries for other families with the same surname. Especially in nineteenth-century rural towns, these records may refer to cousins.

Figuring out Where to Look

Before using church data at all, you must know each ancestor's religion. Clues to religious affiliation can come from several quarters. First, there is the family's current affiliation. Until recently, American Catholics, Jews, Lutherans, and Episcopalians have tended to adhere to their own faiths, and many families of almost all denominations have belonged to the same church for several generations. Intermingling of religion has become noticeable in the twentieth century, as men and women have migrated to all parts of the country and have made contact with or married into religious faiths different from those of their parents. While religious intermarriage was less common in the past, it did occur, and you should bear this in mind when conducting your research.

Clues to your family's religious convictions are often recorded in personal papers. Look carefully through any diaries, journals, correspondence, or obituaries in your family's possession. Wills are also an excellent source, for our forebears often left something to their church.

By his will dated November 16, 1956, and filed in the courthouse of the Regional Municipality of Durham (Canada), Joseph Earl Dearborn of Oshawa, Ontario, left St. Gregory's Catholic Church a bequest for masses to be said for him and his mother. Thanks to this clue, Joseph's gravestone (and that of his wife) was located in the cemetery adjacent to St. Gregory's Church in Oshawa.

If you can find a wedding or funeral notice in a local newspaper, the name of the presiding clergyman will also indicate the family's religious affiliation. The *Columbian Centinel* of January 22, 1834, had the following announcement: "In this city, [Boston, Massachusetts, where the *Centinel* was then a leading newspaper] on Thursday evening, Rev. M. Lindsay, Mr. Andrew Dearborn was maried to Miss Mary Jane Veazie." A perpetual calendar shows that the marriage took place on the sixteenth. The 1834 Boston city directory lists Rev. Lindsay as pastor of the First Methodist Episcopal Church on North Bennet Street in Boston. Undoubtedly, Dearborn or his bride was associated with this parish.

In addition to an ancestor's religion, we must know the actual church or parish he attended. Once we know his religion and residence, finding the right church is often easy and may well be the "first" church of that denomination in the community. Knowing that your ancestor was a Congregationalist, that he lived in Providence, Rhode Island, and that there was a First Congregational Church there, the next step is to determine whether the congregation still exists. If it does, contact the present minister and ask whether the records are still in the church's possession. If they are not, the minister is likely to know where they have been deposited. Many congregations with Colonial origins have placed their early records in a nearby historical society or an archives organized by the denomination. For instance, the records of Trinity Church, Boston, recently published by the Colonial Society of Massachusetts, have been deposited in the New England Historic Genealogical Society in Boston. Many early sacramental records of Catholic parishes in the Archdiocese of Boston have been deposited at the archdiocesan archives.

If the local church no longer exists, check with the local historical or genealogical society. The records may be deposited somewhere in the city. If not, the librarian of the local society may know their location or how to determine it. Of course, you may, like many other genealogical enthusiasts, know neither the religion nor residence of your ancestors. In that case, the following brief outline of American church history may prove helpful.

American Church History

Religious groups in Colonial America followed both regional and ethnic patterns. In New England, the dominant church was the Congregational. Other significant groups were Baptists, Presbyterians, and Quakers, who were strongest in Rhode Island and on Cape Cod and Nantucket. Nearly all religious faiths were represented in New England by the time of the Revolution.

The more diversified denominations and sects of the middle colonies were derived as often from continental Europe as from the British Isles. In New York, Pennsylvania, and Maryland, the predominant churches were the Dutch Reformed, Presbyterian, Lutheran, German Reformed, Catholic, and Society of Friends. Sectarian groups included Mennonites, Amish, and Moravians (Brethren). Many New Jersey residents (especially those of New England origin) were Congregationalists. During the eighteenth century, the middle colonies underwent a sizable evangelical revival; major beneficiaries were Baptists and Methodists.

In the southern colonies, the Church of England was an established religion until the American Revolution. Later reorganized as the Protestant Episcopal Church, it continued to attract many members, especially among the wealthy. During the seventeenth century, the South was religiously the most homogeneous region in the Colonies; during the eighteenth century, as thousands of families from the middle colonies moved into and beyond the Shenandoah Valley, this homogeneity quickly dissolved. Upland Virginia, with many Scots-Irish, was strongly Presbyterian. By 1800 the southern backcountry was populated by a potpourri of Quakers, Moravians, Presbyterians, and Baptists.

In the nineteenth century, religious life in America became even more varied. In addition to the religious groups of Colonial origin described above, larger American cities such as New York, Boston, and Chicago also received many Catholic and Jewish immigrants. Irish immigration, begun in the 1830s, became a tidal wave with the potato famine of the 1840s. By 1860 these new Irish Americans numbered several million. As a result, many traditionally Protestant communities such as Boston became heavily Catholic. The Catholic Church was reinforced in the late nineteenth and early twentieth centuries by a great influx of immigrants from southern and eastern Europe. Italians, Poles, Lithuanians, and others from Europe were joined by numerous French Canadians and Portuguese from the Azores. Leadership in the Catholic Church was provided largely by the Irish and Germans.

In addition to the burgeoning Catholic Church, the Jewish religion became a major force in American life, especially in large urban areas such as New York City. During the Colonial era, probably not more than a few hundred Jewish families lived in Rhode Island, New York City, Philadelphia, and Charleston, South Carolina. Largely Sephardic or Iberian in origin, they are well covered genealogically by Rabbi Malcolm Stern in *First American Jewish Families: 600 Genealogies, 1654-1977*, 1978. By 1900, however, several million Jews and many synagogues were located in the major eastern cities alone.

Protestants continued to immigrate to America in large numbers after the American Revolution. They came mostly from the British Isles, Northern Germany, and Scandinavia. After the Civil War, for example, more than twenty million Swedes and Norwegians settled largely in the northern Midwest. Nearly all were Lutherans or Reformed Lutherans.

Certainly one of the more successful ways to determine the religious background of your ancestors, whether they arrived in the Colonial period, the nineteenth century, or recently, is to know their ethnic and national origins in Europe or elsewhere. In general, if an ancestor was from the British Isles, his religious heritage was either Anglican, Presbyterian, Methodist, Quaker, Congregationalist, or Catholic; if from France, he was likely to be Catholic or French Huguenot; if from Flanders or the Netherlands, Catholic, Dutch Reformed, or Anabaptist; and if from the Scandinavian countries, Lutheran or Reformed Lutheran. Immigrants from northern Germany were often Lutheran, while those from southern Germany tended to be Catholic. Rhineland immigrants were often members of a "Pietist" sect, as were settlers from Switzerland. In America these Pietist groups became known as Mennonites, Amish, and Moravians (Brethren). Many late nineteenth- and early twentieth-century immigrants from eastern Europe, especially Poland and Russia, were either Catholic or Jewish.

Each of these national groups and churches developed its own methods of keeping records. A review of these methods should tell us what genealogical information we can expect from them.

Catholic.

Catholic Church records at the parish level are generally available if requested. The most important of these records are sacramental, relating to baptism, eucharist, confirmation, matrimony, holy orders, and the anointing of the sick and dying. The most genealogically valuable concern baptisms and marriages. Baptismal records are kept in standard fashion and include the following information: date of baptism (sometimes including the date of birth); the child's name; his or her parents' names, often including the mother's maiden surname; the names of the sponsors or godparents of the child; and the signature of the officiating priest. Since most priests preferred to enter baptismal and marriage records in English or the native tongue of the congregation, these registers are easy to use; even those in Latin followed a traditional format.

Catholic marriage registers are maintained in separate volumes and generally

A carving of the type found on Catholic, Episcopal, and some other churches. Yankee

include date, names of the bride and groom, names of two official witnesses, and the signature of the officiating priest. Like baptismal entries, these registers are created at the time of the event, so access is first by date and then by the surname of the husband. Occasionally, additional information contained in marriage registers also proves useful. For example, if one of the parties was non-Catholic, he or she was required to sign an oath promising to raise any children as Catholics. Some priests would note the places of birth or origin of the bride and groom.

The other sacramental records are not so genealogically useful, but are still worth examining. First communion records, sporadically kept, include only the date and names of the communicants. Confirmation records are maintained at the diocesan level, since this sacrament is administered by the bishop. They list only the children being confirmed, usually at age thirteen. Records of the ordination of priests are kept by the ordaining bishop and retained as part of the archives of the seminary and diocese.

Unfortunately, records of the anointing of the sick and dying, along with death and burial registers, have not been maintained systematically. Where they exist, burial records include date of burial, name of the deceased, date of death, age at death, whether penance and the eucharist were received, and the signature of the officiating priest. Since most dioceses have Catholic cemeteries, burial registers are frequently part of the cemetery records, distinct from the archives of the parish.

Researchers interested in Catholic forebears should also be aware of the business, administrative, and other papers deposited at the chancery of the diocese. These materials can frequently fill gaps in parish records. For example, chancery offices often keep copies of the wills of benefactors of the diocese or its agencies. Many fraternal and cultural associations and groups organized by the Church, as well as local Catholic associations such as parish holy name and altar societies, may keep records. Finally of note is the plethora of material provided since the mid-nineteenth century by the Catholic press. Most dioceses have a Catholic newspaper, and much of its coverage of individual parishioners is genealogically valuable.

When searching for Catholic records, remember that most sacramental records, especially baptismal and marriage registers, belong to the parish. Many early sacramental records have been deposited in diocesan archives, but many others have not. Still, the best place to begin your search is the diocesan archives. In addition to much sacramental data, this facility may have records of the bishops and chancery administration, as well as early registers of Catholic schools and orphanages. Approximately one-quarter of the 167 dioceses in the United States have established archival programs, and major Catholic archives can be found in most major American cities, including Boston, Baltimore, Philadelphia, Chicago, and Los Angeles.

Nineteenth-century engraving of the Episcopal Church at Brookline, Massachusetts, published in Ballou's Pictorial Drawing-Room Companion. *Yankee*

Episcopal.

Like its Catholic counterpart, the Protestant Episcopal Church in America has maintained careful records. Before organizing as an American denomination, the Episcopal Church was a locally controlled part of the Church of England, or Anglican Church. English Anglicans sent missionaries here under the aegis of the Society for the Propagation of the Gospel in Foreign Parts (SPG). These priests were supervised by the

Church of England. The SPG archives — mostly reports, minutes, and correspondence — are deposited in England. Several major university libraries in the United States, including the University of California at Los Angeles and the University of Texas at Austin, own microfilm copies.

Episcopal canon law on the national and diocesan levels requires pastors to maintain certain kinds of church records. For example, canon law stipulates that "every Minister of this Church . . . records in the Parish Register all Baptisms, Confirmations, Marriages, Burials, and the names of all Communicants within his Cure." It also requires that every priest maintain lists of those "who have received Holy Baptism; and a list of all persons who have received Confirmation . . . the names of those who have died in the past year or those who have been removed by letter of transfer . . . those whose domicile is unknown, and . . . those whose domicile is known but inactive." At the diocesan level, instructions to priests are even more detailed. Thus the Virginia diocese requires that "every minister shall keep a record of all communicants and all baptisms, confirmations, marriages and burials . . . specifying the name, age or the date of birth, the sponsors or witnesses, and, in the case of infants, the parents, of each person baptized; the names of persons confirmed, and by what Bishop; the names, ages, and residences of persons married, and the names of at least two witnesses; the names and ages of persons buried; and the date and place of every rite respectively."

Unlike American Catholic parish registers, which are almost without exception found either in the parish or chancery archives, the sacramental records of the Episcopal Church are scattered. More recent records may be outside the Church altogether, deposited in a historical society or state archives. Christ Church, Philadelphia, has retained possession of its vestry minutes and registers, dating from the Colonial era when the church was run by the SPG. These registers include baptismal data for six children of Dr. Joseph Strong (1770-1812), the Connecticut-born great-great-great-great-grandfather of Diana, Princess of Wales. The Diocese of Virginia, however, has deposited all its early records in the state library at Richmond. Likewise, Trinity Episcopal Church in Boston has deposited its records with the New England Historic Genealogical Society. It is usually necessary to obtain permission from the parish priest to consult Episcopal registers for genealogical purposes. This guideline applies whether records are maintained in the parish or diocese or are deposited at a secular institution.

The official archives of the Protestant Episcopal Church, called the Library and Archives of the Church Historical Society, are located in

Austin, Texas. At the historical society are, among other collections, the minutes of the House of Bishops, the House of Deputies, and the General Convention's joint commissions. Records of the church's missionary activities since 1820 are also deposited with the historical society and are catalogued as Domestic and Foreign Missionary Society Papers. Unfortunately, the Church Historical Society was not designated as the official Episcopal archives until 1940, so many official business and private papers of bishops are widely scattered in various repositories throughout the country.

Lutheran.

Like its Anglican sibling, the Lutheran Church has also existed in America since earliest Colonial times. The first known Lutheran service was held in 1619 at Port Churchill, on the Hudson Bay, in present-day Canada. By 1637 Lutherans lived along the Delaware River, and in 1648 they were also in New Amsterdam. Their greatest concentration, however, was in eighteenth-century Pennsylvania.

The combination of antiquity and decentralized authority in the Lutheran Church has caused Lutheran records to be even more widely scattered than Episcopal registers. Given the almost complete autonomy of local churches, records of the congregation were often kept in the home of the pastor or another church official. Such decentralization was not reversed when the Concordia Historical Institute in St. Louis, Missouri, was created as a depository for Lutheran archives nationwide.

Lutheran Church records divide into three categories. The first are registers of baptisms, confirmations, marriages, and funerals. The second are monthly or quarterly meeting records of individual congregations, especially covering business and disciplinary actions. The third category is unique: Lutheran "member profiles" contain data on an individual's service to the church and may also refer to education, work experience, and special abilities.

In general, you will find Lutheran parish records at the local level. If a congregation has been dissolved, its files and papers may be deposited at the Concordia Historical Institute in St. Louis. The archives there also include biographical data on ministers and other church professionals; early nineteenth-century Lutheran immigration records; some family Bibles, hymnals, and devotional literature; and biographical works pertaining to Lutheran families in America.

Congregational Church in Fitzwilliam, New Hampshire, erected in 1818. Yankee

Congregational.

Congregational Church records date from the 1630s. Congregationalism dominated New England throughout the Colonial period, but many nineteenth-century churches became Unitarian, and a few became Baptist. In the twentieth century, Congregationalists are most often affiliated with the United Church of Christ.

The Puritans of New England founded the Congregational Church. Basing their faith on the Bible and writings of early Calvinist preachers, they chose to immigrate to New England rather than endure the "popish" practices of the Anglican Church. The more radical Puritans, known as "separatists," left the Church of England entirely and founded Plymouth Colony in 1620. The less radical group hoped to reform the Anglican Church from within by creating a model community in the New World to serve as a "beacon light" to the old. Their immigration began in 1630 when John Winthrop led a large fleet to Boston. Within a decade the Puritan population of New England exceeded twenty thousand.

Until the nineteenth century, the Congregational Church was an "established" church in New England, supported by township taxes. Ministers were employed by the town, and meeting houses were for government as well as church business.

Congregational records are of two types, township and church. The township or parish (usually but not always the same), not the church, was the legal entity. In the nineteenth century, this situation sometimes led to major community divisions when some church members chose to remain orthodox Congregationalists, while a majority of the parish opted for Unitarianism.

Church records kept by the town were usually financial in nature and included lists of ratepayers (taxpayers). The records of Congregational churches themselves include baptisms and later, marriages, church meetings, and membership rolls. Only the children (or later, grandchildren) of church members were baptized and then not necessarily at birth. Marriages were not recognized as a sacrament by Congregationalists, so early marriages will not appear in Congregational Church records. By 1700, however, many Congregational ministers were performing marriages, and these were generally recorded. It is unusual to find a Congregational death or burial record, but ministers sometimes listed members who died during the year. The following entries from the Congregational Church of Kingston, New Hampshire, are typical:

1742: May 2d John Carter and Judith his Wife Ownd the Convenant.

1743: April 24: the Ch'h being Stopd after Divine Service Voted that Sara Weed Widow Orlando Weed & Sarah his Wife Eliza. & Dorothy Weed & Dorothy Hoit Upon their desire to be dismissed from their relation to this Church and recommended to the Communion of the Ch'h in South Hampton where they dwell.

Lords day October 7th 1744 Ruth Brown formerly Morrill A Member of this Church having been guilty of the Breach of ye 7th Commandment Made Publick Confession of it before th Ch'h & Was by An United Vote received to their Charity & Communion Again.

Congregational membership records sometimes contain the notation "deceased" or note that a member was either received "by letter" from another church or granted such a letter before moving to another community. These records also include disciplinary actions taken against individuals in the congregation. If a man and woman had a child too soon after marriage, they would be forced to confess the sin of fornication before the congregation. In such cases, the approximate dates of marriage will be noted — and sometimes the bride's parents as well.

The Congregational Library in Boston usually knows the location of specific records. For Massachusetts Congregational and Unitarian churches, check Harold Field Worthley, *An Inventory of the Records of the Particular (Congregational) Churches of Massachusetts Gathered 1620-1805.*

Quaker.

Many Americans have Quaker ancestry through families originating in Rhode Island, New Jersey, Pennsylvania, North Carolina, or Cape Cod and Nantucket in Massachusetts. Of all religious groups represented early in the American Colonies, Quakers probably left the most comprehensive records.

The Society of Friends organized its activities into a series of meetings — five-year meetings, yearly meetings, quarterly meetings, monthly meetings, and meetings for worship. For genealogists the most important was the monthly meeting, when the business of the congregation was transacted. Monthly meeting records include entries for births, marriages, and deaths, requests for admission or letters of transfer, disciplinary actions, and declarations of intent to marry.

Quaker meeting records differ markedly from records of other faiths, most notably in the absence of baptisms and ministers. Quakers did not believe in baptism, "hireling" pastors, or tombstones. Fortunately, they substituted birth for baptismal data and maintained careful marriage and death registers.

A young Quaker couple who wished to marry had to "pass meeting." This two-to-three-month process involved appearances by the young couple before respective men's and women's committees to request permission to marry, and final approval by the monthly meeting. Once the request was granted, the minutes of the monthly meeting would record that the couple was "left at liberty to consummate their marriage according to the good order of Friends."

The marriage certificate itself is genealogically invaluable. Signed by *everyone* present at the ceremony, it was given to the couple; today, where they exist, these certificates are treasured family heirlooms.

Because Friends frowned upon erecting tombstones, they were expected to keep careful death and burial records. These are frequently more detailed than those of any other faith. Death records often note burial place, residence, and informants (persons with whom the deceased last resided). Burial records are precise, often including an exact description of row and plot.

Some of the most comprehensive Quaker records are membership transferrals from one meeting to another. Mr. Willard Heiss, probably the foremost living authority in this field, cites an example from the 1969 *World Conference on Records and Genealogical Seminar:*

In 1836 Stephen Thomas of Deep River Monthly Meeting, Guilford Co. [North Carolina], made a request to the monthly meeting for a certificate of removal. This removal was for himself, his wife Sarah, their family, and to be addressed to New Garden Monthly Meeting, Indiana. A committee was appointed, investigations into his affairs were made (he had no debts or legal obligations) and a certificate was issued.

A couple of months later Stephen Thomas presented this certificate to New Garden Monthly Meeting, Wayne Co., Ind. It was accepted and recorded. Stephen and his wife, Sarah, had been named in the Deep River Record, but it isn't until New Garden, that we learn the "family" consisted of two children — Henry and Martha. Stephen and his son, Henry, are recorded in the men's minutes. If the women's minutes were lost, we might have lacked information on the daughter, Martha. In many cases the complete certificate is recorded in both sets of minutes.

Early Quakers kept two sets of minutes: those for men and those for women. As you can see from this example, both sets should be examined whenever possible.

Experienced genealogists are often delighted to find new Quaker ancestors solely because most Quaker records have been either published or are readily available in two central depositories, an ease of access unique among American church records. Any Quaker research should begin with William W. Hinshaw's, Thomas W. Marshall's, and Willard Heiss's *Encyclopedia of American Quaker Genealogy*, in 7 vols. Volume 1 includes meeting records for North Carolina, South Carolina, Georgia, and Tennessee; volume 2 has those for New Jersey and Pennsylvania; volume 3, for New York City and Long Island; volumes 4 and 5 for southwestern Pennsylvania, Ohio, and one meeting in Michigan; volume 6 for Virginia; and volume 7 for Indiana. New England Quaker records, deposited at the Rhode Island Historical Society in Providence, are, unfortunately, unpublished.

The central repositories of Quaker records are Swarthmore and Haverford colleges, both near Philadelphia. The Friends Historical Society at Swarthmore contains genealogical data; the library at Haverford, biographical material. In addition to the just-mentioned Rhode Island Historical Society, other depositories include Guilford College, Guilford Courthouse, North Carolina, and Whittier College in Whittier, California (for southern and western Quakers, respectively).

Methodist and Baptist.

Among denominational archives so far discussed, Methodist and Baptist Church records, widely scattered, are frequently the least genealogically valuable. The Methodist Church in this country dates from the middle 1700s, when its founders, the Englishmen John Wesley (1703-1791) and his brother Charles Wesley (1707-1788), visited the Colonies. They were followed by another founder of Methodism, George Whitefield, who made several missionary trips to America before the Revolutionary War. The American Methodist Church separated from the Protestant Episcopal Church and spread widely in the following five decades.

Until at least 1860, and sometimes thereafter, its ministers were "circuit" preachers who traveled from church to church. A circuit typically required four weeks and early ministers were required to change circuits every three to six months. With so much movement, church records were, of course, difficult to maintain. In addition, early Methodist ministers regarded such data as their personal property and were likely to carry it in saddlebags rather than leave it with individual congregations.

American Methodism radiates from three centers — New York, Philadelphia, and Maryland. The records in Maryland are the least well preserved because it was the most rural of the three areas. None survive from before 1790, and few from before 1840. For New York and Philadelphia, the situation is only slightly improved.

After 1840 printed record books containing sections for memberships, marriages, and baptisms were used, albeit irregularly and mostly in cities. No death records were maintained in the Methodist Church until 1900. In those record books that survive, one can find information concerning membership, baptisms, and marriages.

Membership information consists mostly of names and marital status. Few include addresses unless in large cities before 1850. Marriage dates, maiden surnames of wives, and dates of admission were included for about half the entries. Baptismal records show birthdates and names of parents, whenever the person baptized was a child. Birthplaces of those baptized were seldom noted. Even less information is available on people who were baptized as adults. Marriage records include the ages of the man and woman, occupation of the man, and sometimes residence.

Today there are three major repositories of Methodist records. In the New England area, extant Methodist records are housed at the Boston University School of Theology. Records of the mid-Atlantic region are maintained at the Historical Society of the Philadelphia Conference of the Methodist Church at Old St. George's Church. Southern Methodist records are deposited at the American Associaton of Methodist Historical Societies, Lake Junaluska, North Carolina. In the Baltimore-Washington area, some material dating from 1913 (or earlier) is in the custody of the Baltimore Conference Historical Society; copies are available at the Hall of Records at Annapolis.

Baptist Church records are perhaps least useful of all. Inconsistently kept, they were often regarded as the personal property of the minister. Because the Church practiced "adult baptism," ministers often omitted baptismal data and simply noted when an individual was accepted as a member of the Church.

For Baptists especially you should examine all available records, including business data. By doing so, you may find that an ancestor was active on committees, taught Sunday School, was the subject of disciplinary action, or changed churches by means of a letter of recommendation from the minister.

For the highly decentralized Baptists, it is best to visit the individual church whose records you seek. If that church has been closed or dissolved, however, begin your search by inquiring at the local historial society. Records of some dissolved churches can be found at either the American Historical Library, Rochester, New York, or the North American Baptist Archives, Sioux Falls, South Dakota. Other early data is gradually being acquired by historical societies. For example, the Baptist records of Swansea, Massachusetts, recently bought from a dealer and donated to the New England Historic Genealogical Society, date from the 1660s and document the founding of the second Baptist church in Massachusetts. Long considered lost, this small volume was in private hands for more than two centuries.

Jewish.

As with many Protestant churches, Jewish synagogue records have been the responsibility of individual synagogues. Their completeness varies accordingly. The Jewish population in America is basically divided between Jews of Spanish and Portuguese origin, known as Sephardic Jews, and those of German and Eastern European origin, known as Ashkenazic Jews. Before 1700 Jewish families were living in New York City and Newport, Rhode Island. During the eighteenth century, Jewish settlements were established in Savannah, Georgia; Charleston, South

Carolina; Richmond, Virginia; Philadelphia and Lancaster, Pennsylvania; and Montreal, Canada. All these groups were Sephardic and based their religious practices on those of Portuguese synagogues of Amsterdam and London.

Synagogue records include minute and account books, communal or congregational histories, and registers of birth, circumcision, bar mitzvah, confirmation, marriage, and death. Unfortunately, there was often no well-established policy for maintenance of such records, and they sometimes fell into the possession of the record-keeper himself, rather than remaining with the synagogue.

In looking for synagogue records, it is best to begin with the synagogue itself. In addition, you should contact the American Jewish Historical Society, 2 Thornton Road, Waltham, MA 02154, and the American Jewish Archives, 3101 Clifton Avenue, Cincinnati, OH 45220. Both repositories have important primary and printed materials, notably biographical works, congregational histories, and early synagogue records.

Mormon.

Like Baptists and Jews, Mormons do not baptize infants. Yet Mormons have unquestionably the best church records in America and probably anywhere else. This excellence is due to the religious significance the Church attributes to genealogical research necessary for the rebaptism of all known ancestors of its members.

The basic records created by the Church of Jesus Christ of Latter-day Saints cover blessing, baptism and confirmation, marriage, ordination to the priesthood, and death. Infants receive a "blessing" soon after birth. The official record includes the child's name and birthdate, the names of the parents and their birthplaces, and the date of blessing. Mormons baptize their children at age eight, or if the person is an adult, soon after he or she is received into the Church. Confirmation follows almost immediately. Mormon marriage records include standard data about husband, wife, parents, and witnesses. The Mormon Church also generates a unique set of data known as ordinations to priesthood offices. These records document the progression of the male population in the various offices of the Church and add other biographical details. Finally, the Church of Jesus Christ of Latter-day Saints maintains careful death records and has begun the practice of consolidating after his death all records generated by any Church member during his lifetime.

In addition to records generated by participation in the life of the

Church, the Church of Jesus Christ of Latter-day Saints asks its members to trace their ancestors in all lines for at least four generations and to submit this work, in the form of family group sheets, to the Genealogical Society Library in Salt Lake City. The result of earlier requests for members to trace their entire known ancestry, an archive developed between 1942 and the late 1960s, is also at the GSL in Salt Lake City. It contains many errors copied from bad sources, but thousands of useful clues as well.

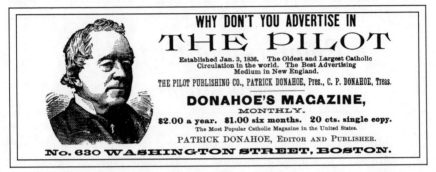

An advertisement from the 1891 Boston Directory *for* The Pilot, *a Catholic newspaper still published today. NEHGS*

Denominational Newspapers.

Worth noting, too, are the various nineteenth-century denominational newspapers, which usually carried marriage and obituary notices. These notices have no geographical restrictions and are often much more detailed than those in the secular press. *The Morning Star,* a weekly newspaper published in Dover, New Hampshire, was sponsored by the Free-Will Baptists, a small sect concentrated mainly in northern New England. The following obituary, for the issue of Wednesday, April 15, 1863, is typical:

Died in Markesan, Wis. March 12, of diphtheria, after an illness of five days, CHARLES P. DEARBORN, in the 32nd year of his age, Mr. D. was born in Gilmanton, N.H. where he remained until he was about twenty-one years of age; he then went to Lowell, Mass., and while there he gave his heart to God and united with the F.W. Baptists . . . . From years ago he came to Markesan. . . . He has left a wife, an aged mother, several brothers and sisters. . . .

It should now be apparent that a wide spectrum of church records is available to genealogists in this country. Some have been generated by various religious practices, others through organizations and activities related to particular churches. In numerous ways, these church records complement and extend the nation's official vital data.

Pointers and Pitfalls
Church Records

1. Church records are among the oldest and frequently most reliable sources of genealogical information. They are especially good for vital data outside the New England area and prior to state-mandated records.

2. The most helpful church records concern baptisms (or christenings), marriages, and burials, but be sure to check *all* records from the period during which your ancestor was associated with the church.

3. Church records are arranged either chronologically as part of overall church proceedings or in special membership rosters.

4. To determine your ancestor's religious affiliation, seek clues in the family's present affiliation and in personal papers such as wills.

5. If the church your ancestor attended still exists, contact the current minister to learn the location of the church's archives. If the church no longer exists, contact the local historical or genealogical society.

6. See the sections in this chapter on specific denominations for advice on how to locate records within the church of your ancestor.

7. Nineteenth-century denominational newspapers can provide information on marriage and obituary notices.

CHAPTER SIX

UNRAVELING THE PLOT

Cemetery Records

Cherub's face on a gravestone. Yankee

Main gate of the Mt. Auburn Cemetery, Watertown, Massachusetts, 1859. Yankee

Cemetery records are a major boon to genealogical research. Some memorials to the dead predate recorded history; burial records, often on the tombs themselves, exist from antiquity forward. In Colonial America burials were recorded by churches, and as you drive through the countryside today, you can find cemeteries in almost every community.

Different types include the churchyard cemetery, probably the most traditional and often adjacent to a place of worship; public cemeteries, maintained by cities, towns, and counties; family burial plots, a distinctive feature of rural New England and the rural South; state and national cemeteries, which honor our war dead; and private garden cemeteries such as Mount Auburn in Cambridge, Massachusetts, filled with ornate statuary and sculpture, especially popular among wealthy families of the nineteenth and early twentieth centuries. Early Catholic graveyards often contain lots set aside for transients (i.e., persons unable to purchase lots), poorhouse residents, and similar persons. Few American cemeteries are "reused" each generation, as in Europe, or turned into parks. The gravestones in our cemeteries have been designed to survive several hundred years.

Cemetery records probably exist for at least a few ancestors of most living Americans. Although our nation has been more inclined than many to bury its dead in permanent cemeteries, most gravemarkers for our earliest ancestors — our Colonial and early nineteenth-century forebears — do not survive. A major cause of this lamentable situation is cemetery neglect. As early as 1800 the Reverend William Bentley of Salem, Massachusetts, described the graveyard in Portsmouth, New Hampshire, as "an ancient graveyard in the greatest confusion and tho' the monuments of the best families are to be found in it, they are in the utmost neglect."

Until at least the 1920s the dead in Philadelphia were buried in temporary vacant lots over which the city later expanded. More recently, cities such as Los Angeles have relocated cemeteries to make room for skyscrapers or highways. Thousands of reburials were necessitated in Massachusetts by the creation of the Quabbin Reservoir, which flooded the towns of Greenwich, Enfield, Prescott, and Dana. Currently plans are underway to remove the graves in the old Yuba City Cemetery in Yuba City, California. No burials have taken place there for many years, as the available plots were filled long ago. The area is to be made into a public park, but it is uncertain whether the gravestones will be relocated or simply discarded. Sometimes a cemetery must be moved even in rural areas. About a decade ago the damming of the Patoka River in southern Orange County, Indiana, forced the builders to relocate an entire cemetery to a dry site up the hill.

Southerners, because they lived far apart, often buried the dead on their farms. In time and with new owners, these gravesites were often neglected, obliterated, or "lost." Many nineteenth-century pioneers died en route to the West and were buried either along the trail or at sea. Some of our ancestors, victims of natural or manmade disasters, lie only in mass burial grounds.

Such attrition is inevitable, but it should not discourage you from searching for an ancestor's grave. Many cemeteries have survived, and you can find burial records in numerous public and church offices. If your ancestors lived in America before 1800, you are likely to discover useful cemetery data for at least a few of them.

To use cemetery records, the genealogist must first locate where his ancestors lived and died. Begin by asking relatives where their siblings, parents, and grandparents were buried. Next comb diaries, journals, and newspaper obituaries. Death certificates frequently indicate places of burial, as do funeral homes and church records, but you must know the place of death (at least the state), the funeral home, or your ancestor's church to use them. If you suspect that an ancestor was buried in a family cemetery, not a public or church facility, you will probably have to determine the exact location of his house or farm. Land records in the county courthouse or old local maps might help you to locate home sites. (Land records are covered in detail in chapter 8.) Topographical sheet maps provided by the U.S. Geological Survey, available from many sporting goods stores, indicate the locations of many rural cemeteries.

Recording Inscriptions

Once you know the state, county, and (when pertinent) the town where your ancestor was buried, the next step is to find the gravestone and make a permanent record of the inscription. There are three ways to record epitaphs. The first and preferred method is to photograph the stone. A second possibility is to make a rubbing of the stone's face. The third option is a careful transcription of the inscription.

Photographing.

Before photographing a stone, your first task is to clean it. Using a soft bristle brush, such as a toothbrush or potato brush, carefully remove all dirt or moss. Do not use chemicals, detergents, or stiff brushes, as they might damage a deteriorating stone. You may also need a trowel or grass clippers to remove dirt or grass around broken or sunken stones. Do not try to remove lichen by physical means. The plant's roots may extend into the stone's crevices and could cause the stone to crumble if removed.

For best results you should photograph a gravestone in bright sunlight. Overcast or hazy weather may cause the camera to produce a foggy image of the inscription. Do not photograph the stone in snow; reflected light lessens contrast. Additionally, the sun and stone should be at sharp angles. To photograph when the sun is shining squarely on the tombstone increases the chance of a poor image.

If these methods do not result in a sharp image of the inscription, rub a wet sponge over the stone's surface. This will darken the face while leaving the lettering dry and distinctive. To produce greater contrast, a companion may hold a mirror or flashlight and shine the light sideways across the inscription.

Detail of the ornamental gravestone of Susanne Jayne, who died in 1776 in Marblehead, Massachusetts. NEHGS

Rubbing.

Rubbing is another means of obtaining a permanent record of an inscription. A rubbing may not capture the inscription as precisely as a photograph, but it can be used to illustrate your genealogy or be framed and displayed in your home.

To do a rubbing, you need thin paper through which you can readily feel the face of the stone with your fingers. For practice you can use newsprint or shelf paper, but you should do permanent rubbings on good-quality rice paper or sketch paper of high rag content, both available at art supply stores. Next you need a supply of colored wax cakes. It is all right to practice rubbing with school crayons, but such soft wax smears easily and should not be used for a final rubbing. Use instead a hard wax with high pigment content. You should also have a roll of masking tape, a small bristle brush, and a cardboard mailing tube for storing completed rubbings and extra sheets of paper.

Once you have selected a stone to rub, clean it with the bristle brush, then attach the paper to the face, securing it on all four sides with masking tape. Be sure that the paper is free of wrinkles and stretched tightly over the stone. If the paper shifts during the rubbing, a blurred image will result. Rub lightly using the flat side of the wax. Rub in the same direction, and work gently at first so that color does not smear across areas that should remain white. When you have completed coloring the area to be rubbed, go back and darken it to suit your taste. To complete the rubbing, buff the wax with a cloth or paper bag. Finally, remove the paper from the stone, identify it by the person's name and the cemetery, and carefully slip it into your cardboard mailing tube. Note that some cemeteries do not permit rubbings, and others require that you obtain prior permission.

An example of unusual gravestone design. The marker is for Major Lemuel Hide at Hockanum Cemetery in Hadley, Massachusetts. NEHGS

Transcribing.

The third method of obtaining a permanent record of a gravestone is to prepare a transcription of the lettering. This is the fastest and easiest way. Transcribing must be done with the utmost care, however, so as not to drop a word or line, invert numbers, or simply misread. Try to copy the inscription exactly as it appears on the stone. Use slashes to indicate the ends of lines, and identify with a question mark placed inside brackets any word or letters about which you are uncertain. Note the following example from a stone in the Mount Auburn Catholic Cemetery in Watertown, Massachusetts:

Erected by Nancy O'Donnell/in memory of/her beloved brother/Michael O'Donnell/died Aug. 23 1872/age 60 yrs/A native of Culdaff/County Donegal/Ireland.

You should be especially cautious when recording transcriptions chiseled in marble, for this kind of stone tends to dissolve more readily than slate and is especially susceptible to acid rain. When you encounter such erosion, remember that it may render the numbers 3 and 5 indistinguishable and reduce 4s to 1s.

Your final task in transcribing a gravestone is to identify its location in the cemetery. First select a permanent landmark in the cemetery, perhaps the entry gate, and number the rows from that point. Then number the stone within its row. Thus you may record your ancestor's gravestone as number 18 in row 23.

Information from Gravestones

The inscription on a gravestone or marker can produce much valuable information. In addition to the year, some stones indicate the month, day, and sometimes even hour of death. Just as commonly, many stones list the person's age in years, months, and days. In the Johnson cemetery in Limington, Maine, for example, you can find a marker for Jacob Dearborn, who died September 15, 1861, age fifty-eight years, eleven months, and seventeen days. From this inscription it is possible to determine a precise birthdate. Not all gravestone inscriptions are accurate, however, especially those erected long after the event. To determine birthdates from a gravestone if the death date and age are noted only in years, simply subtract one from the other. Always indicate in your notes, however, that the birth year is approximate and calculated from a gravestone (*b. ca. 1657, calc. from age on g.s.*).

For persons born before but dying after 1752, remember to take into account the eleven-day calendar change of that year. This requires a little explanation. In 1582 Pope Gregory XIII, in order to eliminate ten extra days that had gradually crept into the Julian calendar since it was established by Julius Caesar in 46 B.C., ordered that the extra days be dropped. He also decreed that henceforth the new year would begin January 1 instead of March 25. For almost two hundred years, England, as a Protestant nation, stubbornly resisted this change, although many Englishmen and American Colonists informally followed the new, more scientific calendar. Before the introduction of the Gregorian calendar, it is more difficult to tell the year of birth of a child born in the months of January, February, or March. Was the baby born in the old or new year? In England and her colonies, this led to a system of "double dating." A child born in January 1702 (using the Gregorian calendar) would be recorded as born in January 1701/2 by the parents, reflecting both the Julian and Gregorian calendars. This practice continued in the British colonies until England formally adopted the Gregorian calendar in 1752.

Gravestones sometimes note the exact birthplace of an immigrant ancestor. For example, in the Mount Auburn Catholic Cemetery in Watertown, Massachusetts, is a "Francois Peirrot, born Feb. 9, 1817 at Deneuvre Meurthe, France, died Jan. 3, 1862 at Boston, Mass." Another stone reads "Julia Boyle, died May 14, 1864, aged 56 yrs. A native of Omeath, parish of Carlingford, County Louth, Ireland." The gravestone of a husband and wife buried in Morse Corner's cemetery in Corinna, Maine, provides the birthdates of both: "Mr. Henry Dearborn, born in Deerfield,

N.H. May 11, 1780, died Sept 1, 1862" and "Mrs. Polly wife of Henry Dearborn, born in New Market, N.H. May 15, 1778, died Feb. 11 1866."

Tombstone inscriptions may also name a last or former husband. The following example is from the Congregational churchyard in Kittery, Maine:

> Lawrence, Lydia E., w. Col. John L. Lawrence, dau. the late John Emery of York, ME. d. May 22, 1861, aged 78 yrs. Mrs. Lawrence's first husband was the late Capt. John Follett, whose mortal remains are interred here by hers.

In this case, not only are Lydia's two husbands listed, but her father is also.

Children's gravestones frequently name parents, as in an inscription from the Bartlett family burial ground in Eliot, Maine: "Susan Bartlett, daughter of Capt. William and Mary H., died Jan. 4, 1848, aged 4 das."

In addition to age and family information, useful biographical data may also be inscribed on tombstones. One extraordinary example comes from a Fogg family plot also in Eliot, Maine:

> William. To my dear father from his affectionate son and sole surviving member of the family J.S.H. Fogg, M.D., Boston, 1862. William Fogg son of John and Abigail Fogg born Nov. 3, 1790 died Sept. 13, 1859. He lived honored and beloved and died lamented by all his townsmen. He represented Eliot in the State Legislature in 1825, 26, 34 and was town clerk 11 years, town treasurer 6 years, selectman and justice of the peace for many years, appointed postmaster by President Monroe he held the office through six successive administrations. William Fogg married 1st Betsey D. Hill June 16, 1821 2d. M.P. Moody Aug. 30, 1846. Children by 1st wife Son B. & D. May 16, 1822. Ann R.B. Jan 12, 1824 D. Aug. 10, 1843. John S.H.B. May 21, 1826. Grad. Bowdoin College 1846 M. Sarah F. Gordon July 11, 1850. Joseph William B. Feb 18, 1829 D. Mar 2, 1829. William A.B. May 21, 1832 D. Sept. 19, 1857.

Memorials were sometimes erected to persons not buried in the lot. In the Bunker Hill Catholic Cemetery in Charlestown, Massachusetts, for example, you find the following:

In memory of/Mary Rohan/who died Feb. 19, 1832/aged 43 years./ A native of Kilcash, County of Tipperary, Ireland. She was the wife of John Rohan/of Mulinagluph who died/Sept. 16, 1818, aged 30 years./ This stone was erected by Edw. & Mary Rohan as a tribute of respect to their memory. / May they rest in peace. Amen//

The arrangement of gravestones may provide important clues to family relationships and even social status. Sometimes a central marker is surrounded by individual headstones for each family member. Adjacent or nearby graves may be those of relations, and the proximity of tombstones is often the first clue of kinship. When investigating the burial place of an ancestor, look also for graves elsewhere in the cemetery of people who share your family's surname. In a Dearborn family plot in Maplewood Cemetery in Barnes, Kansas, is the gravestone of one William W. Dearborn, born May 3, 1877, died December 11, 1926. A Marie S. Dearborn, 1872-1935, is buried in the Skovgaard lot in another section of the cemetery. A look at county marriage records explains the mystery: William W. Dearborn and Marie Skovgaard were married at Trinity Lutheran Church in nearby Greenleaf on July 18, 1896.

Finally, we should note that gravestone inscriptions often reveal much about an ancestor's opinions, religious beliefs, and wit. Captain John Loveland, who died in 1776, addresses his offspring:

My children and Grandchildren all
Death here to you aloud doth call;
Your earthly father is now dead,
and you're survivors in his stead.
Remember you must die also,
And to the dust must shortly go;
See then you walk in wisdom's road
Till you're prepared to dwell with God.

Another, Adam Crandall, 1733-1820, contemplates his judgment:

> This stone stands but to tell ye place
> Where his dust lies not what he was
> When saints arise yt day will show
> The part he acted here below.

In a more humorous vein:

> After having lived with her said husband
> upwards of sixty-five years, she died in the
> hope of resurrection to a better life.

Or:

> Reader, pass on! Don't waste your time
> on bad biography and bitter rhyme;
> For what I am this crumbling clay insures,
> And what I was, is no affair of yours.

Keep in mind that the information on the gravestone, particularly the dates, may be incorrect. The gravestone of James Dearborn, a Revolutionary War soldier, who is buried in Davis Meeting House Cemetery in Effingham, New Hampshire, states that he died November 29, 1843. However, his obituary notice in *The Morning Star* (Dover, New Hampshire) appeared in the issue of January 11, 1843, and states, "Died in Effingham, N.H. Nov. 29, 1842, of old age brother James Dearborn, aged 87 years and 10 months . . . ."

It is often the custom now to carve only birth and death years, not full dates, on monuments.

Gravestone detail — a winged cherub. Yankee

Cemetery Caretaker Records

Almost as valuable as gravestone inscriptions are the records in the custody of the cemetery's caretaker, who may be a church sexton or clerk or the superintendent of a public cemetery. Such records usually include the location of each grave and date of burial; the purchaser of each lot and frequently the present owner(s) and his or their relationship to the purchaser; and records of payment for upkeep. Caretaker records are often more complete than gravestones and can include, in addition to the usual information about death date and lot number, the date and place of birth, names of parents, name of spouse, and names and addresses of survivors. When visiting a very large cemetery, it is not practical to search casually for an ancestor's gravestone; first check the caretaker's records, if only to determine the location of the family plot.

All too often stones have been removed by caretakers, stolen, or mutilated beyond recognition. Others have been "swallowed" by the ground and can be recovered only through archaeological excavation. In these cases, you can only hope that the sexton's or caretaker's records will supply the missing data.

Writing to Cemetery Caretakers

Always try, as suggested earlier, to obtain copies of cemetery records in the custody of the caretaker. Purchase, burial, and upkeep records are rarely transcribed, so you will have to write directly to the person in charge of the cemetery. Many large urban cemeteries have full-time staff and careful records and will often answer inquiries by mail.

Be as specific as possible in letters requesting information from a caretaker. Include a self-addressed envelope and enclose a check for, say, five dollars to cover the cost of the search and photocopying expenses. The letter might read as follows:

Dear Sirs,

Would you please check your records to determine whether a Nathaniel Cardell was buried in Mount Auburn Cemetery. It is believed that he died sometime in the 1880s, at approximately age 67.

In addition, please send me any information on the original and subsequent owners of the lot. Enclosed is a self-addressed stamped envelope and a check for five dollars to cover costs.

Very truly yours,

Sources of Transcribed Inscriptions

"Cemetery hopping" can be time-consuming and expensive; it can also require many vacations. If visiting the cemetery where your ancestor is buried is not feasible, you should try to determine whether another genealogist or organization has copied the cemetery's inscriptions. You can also write to the sexton or cemetery superintendent asking for a copy of records that refer to your ancestor, but expect some delay in the reply.

Fortunately, epitaphs in many American cemeteries have been copied, and some have been published. Many more inscriptions have been transcribed locally and given to local libraries and genealogical and historical societies. In a few instances, when massive numbers of epitaphs have been transcribed, microfilm copies are available in the nation's largest genealogical libraries.

Those cemetery inscriptions that have been published appear for the most part in genealogical journals and newsletters and in the publications of local historical societies. Many cemetery inscriptions from New

England have appeared in *The New England Historical and Genealogical Register*. Other genealogical journals that have devoted considerable space to cemetery inscriptions include *The New York Genealogical and Biographical Record, The National Genealogical Society Quarterly, The Connecticut Nutmegger, The Genealogical Magazine of New Jersey, The Virginia Genealogist, The Kentucky Genealogist,* and *The South Carolina Magazine of Ancestral Research*. Many regional genealogical societies publish cemetery records in newsletters or special publications. For a guide to these organizations, see Mary Keysor Meyer's *Directory of Genealogical Societies in the U.S.A. and Canada*, which notes all publications sponsored by the listed societies. For example, the Skipworth Historical and Genealogical Society in Oxford, Mississippi, has published two volumes of *Lafayette County Cemetery Records* and sponsors a local newspaper column titled "Ancestor Tracking."

Typescript or handwritten cemetery inscriptions far outnumber their printed and microfilmed counterparts. Unfortunately, no comprehensive catalog to this scattered and unpublished data is yet available. The massive typescript inscriptions prepared over several decades by DAR chapters are available at the NSDAR library in Washington, D.C., and pertinent volumes are usually deposited in local genealogical societies or libraries as well.

Several societies formed in recent decades are dedicated to the recording of gravestone inscriptions, the study of gravestone art, and the preservation of ancient cemeteries. For example, the Maine Old Cemetery Association (MOCA) was founded in 1969; through 1980 its members had transcribed the epitaphs in more than twenty-five hundred cemeteries. Available in typescript volumes at the Maine State Library in Augusta, these transcriptions are also found on microfilm (two series totaling ten reels) in various large libraries. MOCA members have also prepared a surname index to this massive project that includes more than two hundred thousand names. A similar Vermont Old Cemetery Association (VOCA), organized in 1958, has encouraged the transcription of cemetery records in that state.

In Massachusetts an Association for Gravestone Studies (AGS) was founded in 1977. Its statement of purpose notes that "early grave markers are important as memorials, as historical and genealogical documents, as art objects, and as material expressions of cultural attitudes." Dedicated to the preservation of ancient cemeteries, AGS also publishes *Markers*, a scholarly journal covering the early history of gravestone art and various related topics.

The Prince Edward Island Heritage Foundation in Charlottetown has transcribed all tombstones in the province and entered this data in an alphabetized surname card catalog. This file also contains entries from census schedules, obituaries, and business directories.

Nearly all genealogical and historical societies, and even many public libraries, have some transcribed cemetery inscriptions for their area. Many can be found at major state libraries and historical societies and in larger genealogical society libraries. For example, at the Connecticut State Library in Hartford is deposited the Hale Collection of Connecticut cemetery records. As head of a Works Progress Administration (WPA) project during the 1930s, Charles R. Hale supervised the transcription of tombstones in more than two thousand Connecticut cemeteries. These records were merged into a single master index of individual names. You can find other massive collections of New England cemetery inscriptions at the Rhode Island Historical Society in Providence, the New England Historic Genealogical Society in Boston, and the New Hampshire Historical Society in Concord.

Outside New England, you can find important collections of cemetery records at the New York Genealogical and Biographical Society in New York City; the Library of Congress, the National Genealogical Society, and the DAR Library in Washington, D.C.; the Western Reserve Historical Society in Cleveland; the Allen County Public Library in Fort Wayne, Indiana; the Newberry Library in Chicago; the Latter-day Saints (LDS) Library in Salt Lake City; and the Los Angeles Public Library.

The microfilming of the MOCA's cemetery transcription project has already been mentioned. The Mormons have microfilmed the Hale Collection, and you can obtain copies through LDS libraries. In addition, the New England Historic Genealogical Society recently microfilmed and offers for sale its Corbin Collection, which includes epitaphs from numerous towns in western Massachusetts, as well as Connecticut, New Hampshire, Rhode Island, Iowa, and Ohio. This fifty-five-reel collection is now available in at least twelve major U.S. libraries, more than half of which are outside New England.

An Ideal Example

In the best of all possible worlds, we could easily obtain all records concerning the death of an ancestor. These documents would include a gravestone inscription, burial records (from a local sexton or a cemetery caretaker), death certificate, and possibly a newspaper obituary and church or funeral home records. Altogether these materials would yield the person's name, residence, age at death, cause of death, birthplace, occupation, and parents' names and birthplaces.

One glorious example that almost matches this ideal is now in print. *Gravestone Inscriptions from Mount Auburn Catholic Cemetery, Watertown, Massachusetts* edited by Marie E. Daly, published in 1983, sets a new standard by including not only cemetery inscriptions but also abstracts of death certificates and burial records and notes. The following is an example:

Gravestone (GS): Michael O'Donnell died Aug. 23, 1872 age 60 yrs. A native of Culdaff, County Donegal, (a) Erected by Nancy O'Donnell in memory of her brother.

Burial Records (BR): Michael O'Donnell, Aug. 25, 1872 60 yrs. family GR135 R5 West.

Death Certificate (DC): Michael O'Donnell of 100 Endicott Street Boston, (b) a widowed bootmaker, died of Pneumonia, Aug. 23, 1872 age 60 yrs. His parents Hugh and Ellen O'Donnell, were born in Ireland.

vol. 249 p. 169.

(a): Culdaff is a mountainous parish pop. 5,995 in 1831, located 6 miles northwest of Moville on the Inishowen Peninsula, vol. 1 p. 550.

(b): 100 Endicott Street was located on the corner of Cooper Street diagonally across from St. Mary's rectory in the North End of Boston.

Finding and recording cemetery records may be one of the most enjoyable aspects of tracing your ancestors. By visiting cemeteries you can see the towns or counties where your ancestors lived. For many people, photographing or rubbing gravestones becomes a lifelong hobby. Numerous individuals have expanded their own research to make copies of all inscriptions in cemeteries they visit. The results are many of the typescript and handwritten inscriptions now available to researchers in libraries across the country.

❧ *Pointers and Pitfalls* ❧
Cemetery Records

1. There are several types of cemeteries, including churchyard, public, family, state, national, and private garden.

2. Cemetery records probably exist for at least a few ancestors of most living Americans.

3. Numerous factors have damaged the availability of cemetery records, including cemetery neglect and relocation.

4. Determine where your ancestors are buried by interviewing relatives and checking sources such as death certificates, obituaries, diaries, and journals.

5. Make a permanent record of your ancestor's gravestone by photographing, rubbing, or transcribing it.

6. Be careful to transcribe exactly and watch for changes in an inscription caused by aging of the stone.

7. Keep in mind the eleven-day calendar change of 1752 when calculating dates.

8. Information on gravestones might include inaccuracies, particularly concerning dates.

9. Cemetery caretaker records can also be very helpful, especially when a gravestone has been lost or no longer exists.

10. Many epitaphs have been copied or transcribed and placed in local historical societies and public libraries. A few major collections of transcriptions can be found in large genealogical libraries.

CHAPTER SEVEN

PROBING PROBATE

Wills, Inventories, and Other Documents

Section of an early will. NEHGS

P robate records, which include wills, inventories, letters of administration, and guardianships, are essential tools of genealogical research. They are especially valuable because the focus of probate is the family; beneficiaries named in a will are usually a spouse, children, grandchildren, in-laws, or siblings. Nowhere else, except perhaps in vital records and deeds, is proof of family relationship established with equal precision.

In addition to genealogical details, probate documents tell much about the living arrangements, wealth, family attitudes, religious beliefs, education, literacy, and civic mindedness of our ancestors. More than any other type of historical document (except, perhaps, a diary or autobiography) probate records are a "window" through which we can catch an intimate glimpse of our ancestors' family relationships and lifestyles. Sometimes these records will reveal the affection and generosity family members felt toward each other. In other cases, bitter feelings predominate, as in the 1763 will of Samuel Payne of Suffolk County, Massachusetts, who hoped that his "bad" wife would inherit as little as possible: "I give to the woman that lives with me called my wife, called Ruth Payn so much of my Estate as she can git by law & no more for she is a very imprudent & bad woman, & hath hurt my Estate many hundreds of pounds by giving and selling out of my house things that did not belong to her. I know she doth not deserve any of my Estate & I hope she will not get much of it."

Probate records divide into two basic categories: those of people who died testate — that is, leaving wills — and those of people who died intestate, leaving no written instructions as to how their property should be distributed at death. We shall first examine wills.

There are three basic types of wills. The first, known as the "attested" will, is prepared for the testator. In Colonial days this was often done by local magistrates, and in recent times by lawyers. The second, called a "holographic" will, is actually written by the testator himself. Finally there is the "nuncupative" will, deathbed wishes communicated to and recorded by a witness present at the bedside. All three types must be signed by witnesses. Of the three types, the attested will is the most common, although in the Colonial and Early National periods you can find some holographic wills and a few nuncupative ones as well.

Interpreting an Early Will

It will be useful here to examine, in some detail, an early will that contains many features typical of the wills of its time. We have selected for closer study the attested will of Ebenezer Jaquith, a third-generation member of an ancient New England family originating in Charlestown, Massachusetts.

In the name of God Amen I Ebenezer Jaquith of Willmington in the County of Middlsex and Common Wealth of Massachusetts Yeoman Being aged but of a Disposing Mind and Memory calling to mind the Mortality of my Body and knowing that it is appointed for all men once to Dye: Do make and ordain this Writting to be my Last Will and Testament that is to say Principaly and first of all I Give and Recommend my soul into the hand of God that gave it and my Body Recommend to the Earth to be Buried in Decent Christian Burial at the Discretion of my Executor here after Named; as touching Such Worldy things and Estates as it hath pleased God to Bless me with all in this Life, I give and Dispose of the Same in the following manner and form and first of all my will is that all my Just Debts and funeral Charges be paid.

Imprs To my son Ebenezer I give and Bequeath the Sume of Eighty Dollars to my Son William I give and Bequeath the Sume of Five Shillings to my Son Thomas I give and Bequeath the Sume of Eighty Dollars to my Son Isaac I Give and Bequeath the Sume of Six Shillings, to my Daughter Rebecahs heirs I Give and Bequeath the Sume of Twelve Shillings to each one to my Daughter Betsee heirs I Give and Bequeath the Sume of twelve Shillings to Each one I give and Bequeath to my Daughter Patty the Sume of one hundred Dollars I give and Bequeath to my Daughter Bettey the Sume of one hundred Dollars I give and bequeath to my Son Joshua all my Real and personal Estate that I shall die seized of lying in willmington or Else whear with buildings on the same Excepting the East End of the Dwelling House with Convinent Room in the Seller I Give and bequeath unto Mary my wife

So long as Shee Remains my widdow to be well Supportd and taken care of bouth in Sickness and health and in case of Death whilst remaining my widdow to be buried in Decent Christian burial by my son Joshua Whoum I make sole Executor of this my Last will and Testament who is to pay to my sons Ebenezr William Thomas and Isaac and to the heirs of my Daughters Rebeca and Bettey the same with in given and bequeath to Each of them with in three years from my Deceas I ordain this my Last will and Testament in wittness where of I have hear unto Sett my hand Seal this Ninteenth Day of November in the Year of our Lord one thousand Seven hundred and Ninty in the fifteenth year of your ammerican Independance.

Signed Sealed Pronounced and Delivered
In Presents us

Reuben Butters   Ebenezer Jaquith
James Jaquith
Andrew W Duncklle

Observe that the will begins with the testator identifying himself by name, place, and title or occupation (yeoman, i.e., farmer). By reading just the first few lines, we discover basic facts about residence and social status. A word of caution: for many people who wrote wills at an advanced age, their last place of residence was often with a son or daughter in a community sometimes distantly removed from where they lived most of their adult lives and raised their children.

After identifying himself, Ebenezer employs standard language that declares the testator's competency to dispose of his estate, professes his reverence for God and concern for his immortal soul, and instructs his executor to give his body a decent burial. To this point the language reads almost like a formula. But as you read many such opening statements, it becomes apparent that some people seize the opportunity provided by a will to dwell at some length on their religious beliefs. When they occur, such dissertations offer unique access to some of our ancestors' deepest personal feelings.

Following preliminary statements, the testator arrives at the fundamental purpose of the will: to instruct his executor how his property is to be distributed among his heirs. Here, of course, the will reflects the present condition of the testator's family and can give clues as to provisions made previously for children (especially married children) not mentioned in the will.

We can make several inferences about Ebenezer Jaquith and his family based on the instructions in his will. Note first that the children were not all favored to the same degree. Among the sons, only Joshua, the youngest, was given any real estate. How can we explain this? Wasn't it customary for early American families to give the bulk of their real estate to the eldest son, a practice known in European countries as primogeniture? The answer to this question is no. If a father died intestate, some colonies and states stipulated by law that the eldest son was to receive a "double portion," and many early American families did give double portions to the eldest son. But primogeniture was practiced only rarely, even in the South where statutes favoring it sometimes lasted into the early nineteenth century. Rather, most early American families followed the rule of "partible" inheritance, dividing real estate somewhat evenly among sons (but not always including daughters).

Did Ebenezer follow the rule of partible inheritance? His will states clearly that he wishes to give all his "Real and personal Estate . . . in willmington or else whear" to his youngest son, Joshua. What we must remember is that Ebenezer's will is undoubtedly not telling the whole story. Perhaps many years earlier he gave substantial amounts of real estate to his four older sons, Ebenezer, William, Thomas, and Isaac. This possibility can easily be checked through land records for Middlesex County (the legal mechanism for transferring land in this way was a "deed of gift"). Indeed, as it happens, Ebenezer had two families. Joshua, a child of his third marriage, was born sixteen years after Isaac, his next youngest son (by his first wife). Often additional research will be needed to give you a clear understanding of information found in a will.

What does Ebenezer's will tell us about his daughters, Rebecah, Betsee, Patty, and Bettey? First, it seems clear that Rebecah and Betsee are married with children and have already received a dowry or "portion" from their father, since he leaves only twelve shillings to each of their "heirs." Local vital or church records will probably include the marriages of these daughters, as well as the births of their children if they married locally. Patty and Bettey are each left one hundred dollars, substantial money for that day. Does this mean that the latter were still unmarried at the time of their father's death, and Ebenezer intended this to be their dowries? Probably. Later marriage records would tend to corroborate this hypothesis.

Upon first reading, perhaps you are shocked by Ebenezer's regard for his wife. After a life together during which she bore him several children, Ebenezer sees fit to leave his wife only "the East End of the Dwelling House with Convinent Room in the Seller," and only "So long as shee Remains my widdow." He does, however, order his son Joshua to see that his wife is "well Supportd." In fact, Ebenezer's provision for his wife was typical of early American households and may be seen as generous. Widows were seldom given real estate outright by their husbands, although they were often given personal property such as household items. As in this case, a widow got the "use" of part of the estate during her lifetime or until remarriage. Many widows married shortly after the deaths of their husbands. (An important exception to this practice was the property a woman inherited or owned before her marriage. Usually it was informally understood between husband and wife that the latter would retain control of her "dowry." Often this understanding was formalized in an "antenuptial" agreement, sometimes mentioned in wills.)

Most of the conclusion of Ebenezer Jaquith's will, like the beginning, is a standard formula. Note, however, the unusual patriotic statement "in the fifteenth year of ammerican Independance." Following his signature are those of three witnesses — Reuben Butters, James Jaquith, and Andrew W. Duncklle. Witnesses could not be beneficiaries, but were often relatives. In Ebenezer's case, Reuben Butters and James Jaquith were nephews.

Confusing Terms in Wills

From our examination of Ebenezer's will, its centrality to any genealogical investigation of his family is obvious. It is equally clear, however, that the will may leave out vital genealogical information or even cause some confusion. We have no way of knowing from this document whether Mary was his first or a later wife (in fact, she was his third). He refers to three of his daughters, Betsee, Patty, and Bettey, by what we assume are diminutive nicknames. While we can infer that the two older daughters married, Ebenezer mentions neither their husbands nor their surnames. We must remember, too, that some family members — especially deceased children who died without heirs or offspring who have already received their inheritance — may not be mentioned in the will at all.

Confusing terms also abound in Colonial documents, although not in Ebenezer Jaquith's will. For example, senior and junior now denote father and son. In the seventeenth and eighteenth centuries, however, those terms meant "elder" and "younger" and were often applied to cousins or unrelated neighbors with the same name. The terms "in-law," "cousin," "brother," and "sister" are major problems also. "In-law" might be used in the modern sense of the husband or wife of a testator's sibling or child, but it could just as easily refer to a stepchild. In 1718 Lydia Locker of Salem, Massachusetts, gave to "my two daughters-in-law Merium Hascoll and Susanna Dow. . . all my moveables and person-all Estate." In fact, these daughters-in-law are the children of her *former* husband, John Hill, by his *former* wife! Donald Lines Jacobus, probably the greatest American genealogist of the twentieth century, talks thus of the problems associated with the term "cousin":

The term "cousin" is perhaps the one which is most puzzling to the untrained searcher. It was applied loosely to almost any type of relationship outside the immediate family circle. It was most frequently used to denote a nephew or niece, but it could be applied to a first cousin or more distant cousin, or to the marital spouse of any of these relatives, and sometimes to other indirect connections who were not even related by blood. The first guess should be that a nephew or niece was meant; if this also proves impossible, it may require long and profound study to determine just what the connection was. This applies, generally speaking, to the use of the term in the Colonies prior to 1750. No definite and exact date can be fixed, for the terms nephew and niece gradually supplanted cousin to denote that form of relationship . . . .

Jacobus also lists various possibilities for "brother" and "sister":

[W]hen a man writes in his will "my brother Jones" and "my sister Jones," he may be referring to his own sister and her husband, to his wife's sister and her husband, or to his wife's brother and that brother's spouse.

Other Notes on Wills

When a will is admitted to probate and "allowed," it is said to be "proved" or "probated." Customarily it is presented for probate shortly after the testator's death, usually from within a few days to a month or so. Occasionally there will be a long delay between the time when the testator signs his will and the time, after his death, when it is presented for probate, as in the case of the immigrant Godfrey Dearborn's will, to which he made his "D" mark at Hampton, New Hampshire, on December 14, 1680. His son John did not present the will for probate until May 10, 1711, more than thirty years later. The delay led to an unusual complication: by 1711 one of the witnesses to the will, Mehitable Dalton, had died, and it became necessary for her son, Philemon Dalton, to attest to her signature.

Sometimes a will contains unexpected but welcome information. The will of George Standley of Beverly, Massachusetts, mariner, dated July 24, 1694, and filed in Essex County, tells us that he was still active in his trade:

     I George Standley of Beverly in ye County of Essex in ye province of ye Massachusets bay; being by gods providence bound to Sea . . . .

The will of his neighbor, Jeffrey Thistle of Beverly, dated October 29, 1675, is even more informative:

     In the name of God Amen. The last will and Testament of Jeffrey Thissell at Abbotsbury in ye County of Dorsett in old England but at p'sent in New England being in perfect health and Memory but being bound to sea . . . .

One final point on wills: sometimes they suggest a former residence, which can lead to proof of parentage, information extremely useful to the researcher.

Intestate: When There Is No Will

What if a person died "intestate" without leaving a will naming heirs? Who inherited the property, what are intestacy records, and how are such records useful to genealogists? Intestacy law in early America was based largely on English precedent. But although primogeniture prevailed by law in English intestacy cases, that practice did not always prevail in America. In the New England colonies (except for a period in Rhode Island), as well as in Pennsylvania and Delaware, "partible" division of real estate among all children, with the eldest son receiving a "double portion," was the law in intestacy cases. In many of the other colonies, especially in the South, although primogeniture was the law, partible inheritance again was often the custom.

When a person died intestate, his property was administered by the court according to state or colonial statutes and customs of the time. Once the court (usually the county court) was informed that an individual of sufficient property had died intestate, it appointed an administrator, someone who would oversee the preparation of an estate "inventory" of real and personal property and work with the court in determining beneficiaries.

Intestacy records can sometimes prove as genealogically valuable as wills and often contain additional information. For example, death dates are often contained in intestacy records, especially those prepared after 1800. In intestacy cases involving large amounts of money or property, numerous "heirs," hitherto unknown, may surface to claim their share of the estate. Such persons must prove their kinship to the deceased, and those persons determined by the court to qualify as beneficiaries are listed in a document generally called the "order of distribution."

Along with orders of distribution, other records in the file may be equally useful for tracing kinships. Occasionally these papers tell more than the will itself. For example, Jasper Rea of Andover, Massachusetts, in his will filed in Essex County in 1899, left all his property to his wife Lucy. The petition for probate, however, adds the names and addresses of his five children: Jasper P. Rea of Snohomish, Washington, Mary E. Blood of Andover, Lucy A. Putnam of Vineland, New Jersey, Charles P. Rea of Andover, and Alice R. Dearborn of Andover. Often the ages of individuals are given as well.

If a person dies intestate and leaves neither spouse nor children, his or her property would be inherited by the nearest living blood relatives, usually siblings or parents. If any of the siblings due to inherit the intestate's property have already died, then the siblings' children inherit their parent's share *per stirpes*, that is, they divide equally among them the share that their parent would have received.

Let's look at a few examples of how this practice works. In the petition for administration of the estate of Emma A. Dearborn of Green Island, New York, who died on October 24, 1902, filed in Albany County, we find the following list of heirs:

Name	Address	Relationship
Jay Dearborn	Brentwood, NH	brother
George W. Dearborn	Epping, NH	brother
George H. Miller	Epping, NH	nephew[1]
Emma Hill	Milton Three Ponds, NH	niece[1]
Gilbert Dearborn	New Lebanon, NY	nephew[2]
George Dearborn	Lebanon Springs, NY	nephew[2]
William Dearborn	Lebanon Springs, NY	nephew[2]
Dewitt C. Dearborn	22 Second Ave., Troy, NY	nephew[2]
Ella Bristol	Torrington, CT	niece[2]
Frances Eldridge	Beverly, MA	grand-niece[3]
Ida Barker	Peabody, MA	grand-niece[3]
Ella Gearling	Amsterdam, NY	grand-niece[3]
James Dearborn	4 Ingalls Ave., Troy, NY	grand-nephew[4]
Warren C. Dearborn	3117 7th Ave., Troy, NY	grand-nephew[4]
Charles Dearborn	3117 7th Ave., Troy, NY	grand-nephew[4]
Fannie Millington	117 Paine St., Grand Is., NY	grand-niece[5]
Laura Millington	117 Paine St., Grand Is., NY	grand-niece[5]
Josiah Millington	117 Paine St., Grand Is., NY	grand-nephew[5]
Mary Millington	117 Paine St., Grand Is., NY	grand-niece[5]
John Millington	117 Paine St., Grand Is., NY	grand-nephew[5]
Guy Dearborn	E. Haverhill, NH	nephew[6]
Henry F. Dearborn	E. Haverhill, NH	nephew[6]
Nella Wheeler	E. Haverhill, NH	niece[6]

[1] child of Susanna (Dearborn) Miller, deceased sister
[2] child of Louis C. Dearborn, deceased brother
[3] child of Charles Dearborn, deceased (son of Louis C. Dearborn, deceased brother)
[4] child of John Dearborn, deceased (son of Louis C. Dearborn, deceased brother)
[5] child of Elizabeth (Dearborn) Millington, deceased (daughter of Louis C. Dearborn, deceased brother)
[6] child of Henry F. Dearborn, deceased brother

From this one document, we learn the names of more than twenty relatives of Emma Dearborn. Note that the nieces, nephews, grandnieces, and grandnephews are listed only if their parent who would have shared in the inheritance has already died.

Sometimes the amounts of money received by heirs in the division of an estate allow you to discover the degree of relationship from the fraction of the total received. In the estate of Eleanor M. Dearborn of Portsmouth, New Hampshire, who died intestate in Rockingham County, unmarried and without issue in 1855, the inventory of $133.01 was divided as follows:

Orrin C. Hodgdon	Milton, NH	$ 3.69
Mary Hodgdon		
Nathan Chapman	Milton, NH	7.39
Abigail Chapman		
Joseph Dearborn	Biddeford, ME	22.17
Joseph Dearborn	Milton, NH	7.39
Nathaniel Dearborn	Milton, NH	22.17
Thaddeus Spear	Gardiner ME	22.17
Herman Stinson overseers of the poor		
George W. Willey	Milton, NH	22.17
Abigail M. Willey		
Thomas Dearborn	Clinton, ME	22.17
Nathan Chapman	Milton, NH	3.69

The amounts $22.17, $7.39, and $3.69 represent one-sixth, one-eighteenth, and one-thirty-sixth, respectively, of $133.01. From this it follows that Eleanor had six siblings and that apparently five of them were living as of 1855. The smaller fractions tell us that a deceased sibling left three children, of whom two were living, and two grandchildren. (When married women were involved with legal matters, it was customary for their husband's names to appear with theirs; thus Mary Hodgdon, apparently a grandniece of Eleanor Dearborn, was the wife of Orrin C. Hodgdon.)

Special Administrations, Bonds, Inventories, and Guardianships

Two special types of administration deserve further mention. The first of these, administration *cum testamento annexo* (administration with the will annexed; usually abbreviated adm. c.t.a.) occurs if a testator in his will fails to name an executor or if the executor fails or refuses to act. The administration is carried out by the court, however, as if by an executor. The other special case is known as an administrator *de bonis non* (abbreviated adm. d.b.n.). This case occurs when the executor of a will or an administrator resigns or dies before fully settling the estate. In such cases, another individual, often a relation, petitions the court for letters of administration *de bonis non*, which convey to him the power to settle the estate.

One of the more common documents found in processing an estate is a bond. By this document the administrator (called the "principal") agrees to pay the court a fixed amount of money, usually twice the estimated value of the estate, if the obligations involved in settling it are not properly discharged. Two sureties, or bondsmen, are named as well. Quite commonly the principal, and often one or both of the sureties, are relatives of the deceased. Although the duties of the executor and administrator are virtually identical, one of the chief differences between the two is that an executor does not have to be bonded. Bonds are found much more often than lists of heirs. While they do not provide as much genealogically useful information, they are often helpful in establishing family relationships.

Another important probate document for both testate and intestate cases is the "inventory," a detailed list of the deceased's real and personal property. Even more than wills, inventories let the family historian peer into the lives of his ancestors and examine their standard of living. (Keep in mind, however, that many inventories reflect a person's wealth in old age when much property has already been given to children.) The reader can infer the size of a "homestead" and other properties, determine whether his ancestor died wealthy or in debt, and almost move from room to room, noting the value of beds, chairs, rugs, quilts, silver, and pewter. If the ancestor was an artisan or merchant, the inventory will detail the contents of his store or shop; if a farmer, it may count his cattle and bushels of wheat. Books, highly valued before the mid-nineteenth century, are often noted.

Inventory lists suggest much about an ancestor's beliefs and interests. Although primarily focused on the material culture of the American family, many inventories contain surprising genealogical details. Sometimes they provide an actual date of death. You can often glean clues to family relationships from the names of persons who owed the deceased money. Significant moneylending within families occurred frequently before 1900, and loans still outstanding at death are often recorded by name and amount in a person's inventory.

The following, a portion of the estate of John Crummell of Charlestown, Massachusetts, prepared on December 25, 1661, demonstrates many of these features:

ESTATE OF JOHN CRUMMELL OF CHARLESTOWN
(Middlesex Probate Docket No. 5325)
25th dec: 1661

An Inventory taken of the goods and chattells and Lands of John Crummell deceased

impr: in Loose wampam peage at 12 a peny 02-03-09
It. 27 dozen of knives at 2s 6d pr doz: 03-07-06
It. 22 dozen of auls at 12d pr dozen 01-02-00

chamber

2 beds filled with wooll and one fether bolster and 2 old blankets
06-09-00
It. 2 spininge wheels 9s and one pillion 12s 01-01-00

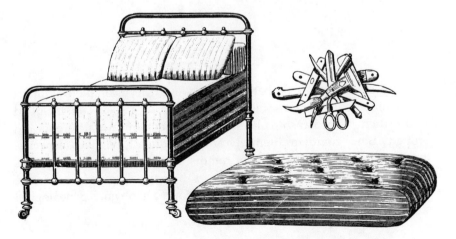

in the hall

     It. one silke Neckcloth 00-05-06
     It. his waring aparill 08-15-00
     It. in money in his purse 00-19-09
     It. 2 chests 10s and 17 peeces of pewter 02-08-00
     It. 2 brass kandlestiks 5s and 2 tinn driping pans 00-08-00

abroade

     It. one pr oxen at 13£ 13-00-00
     It. 6 cowes at 4£ 10s per a cow 27-00-00
     It. 2 heifers 1 Year old and the vantage 06-00-00
     Thomas Williams his servants time 05-00-00
     It. 4 old gunns 03-00-00
     It. in furrs: of sevrall sorts aprized by mr Tinge and mr Atkinson
        82-13-06
     a debt due from Abraham Parker 01-00-00

this inventory was taken by us whose Names are hereunto subscribed by order from the creditors of John Crummell diseased which is done acordinge to or best discretions as witness our handes:

(signed) John Parker
       William Flitcher
       Jacob Parker

    Any discussion of probate records would be incomplete without mentioning that in most states "guardianship" papers are included among them. Guardianship files sometimes mention natural parents and property. Since guardians themselves were frequently relatives (especially court-appointed supervisors of minors under fourteen; older minors could choose their guardians), records of their appointments and, when they survive, of their later reports to the court are obvious genealogical sources.

Locating Probate Materials

With few exceptions, probate is handled in the United States at the county level. Usually the county courts, especially in New England, maintain both the original papers and a transcription in separate volumes prepared by a clerk of the court. The transcriptions are frequently easier to read and access than the files containing the original papers. Transcriptions, however, especially for the Colonial era, should be used with caution, as copying errors were common. In addition, not everything was copied. Receipts, for example, were often thought dispensable. For signatures, however, they are invaluable. Despite the inconvenience to the court clerk in retrieving the original file, and the frequently poor quality of the microfilm, it is always preferable that you consult the original files.

Probate records are often indexed alphabetically by the name of the deceased (or by the name of the ward for guardianships). These indexes, usually unpublished, include year, name, case, and probate number. The following example is a small portion of the index to Suffolk County, Massachusetts, probate records:

Year	Name	Case	No.
Quigley			
1865	Bernard	administration	46625
1884	Bridget	administration	71224
1888	Bridget	administration	79928
1876	Catherine	guardianship	58599

The number in the far right column is known as the "docket number"; always use it when requesting a copy of any original probate file from a county clerk/court.

If you wish to consult the volumes of transcribed documents, it is frequently necessary to use the docket number and to refer to another set of indexes, this time arranged chronologically, by docket number. These indexes, which are not available in all states but generally exist for New England, are maintained in the clerk's handwriting and refer to the volume and page number where the probate document has been transcribed. Again, remember that the transcribed volumes are often inaccurate and sometimes incomplete. At the same time, however, important probate documents may be missing from the actual file, in which case you should consult the transcribed volumes as well.

Unfortunately, most probate indexes list only the testate, intestate, or guardian. Only in a few states are beneficiaries indexed as well. Several southern states are notable exceptions. Of course, published probate records usually have an every-name index, which would include names of beneficiaries.

What is required to obtain probate information? First, you must know the county or other court probate district where your ancestor resided and where the estate was probated. With this information, you may write directly to the court (or visit in person) and request the pertinent documents. Usually a straightforward letter that includes the full name of the testate or intestate, the docket number if known, and other information such as date of death and residence will be sufficient. The letter might read as follows:

Dear Sir:

It is my understanding that Robert J. Morse of Boston, Massachusetts, left an estate that was probated in Suffolk County, Massachusetts, sometime in the late nineteenth century. Please forward a copy of any probate documents that exist on this person in your court and bill me for any charges. Enclosed is a self-addressed stamped envelope. Thank you in advance for any assistance you can give me in obtaining these records.

Sincerely yours,

While it was customary for a probate to be filed with the court in the county of the deceased's residence, there may be occasions when it was filed elsewhere, as in the case of Richard Dearborn, a subsistence farmer who died intestate at his home in Hartford, Oxford County, Maine, in 1861. The administration was filed in Franklin County, Massachusetts. In the petition for administration dated August 14, 1871, Joseph Dearborn of Hartford, son and only heir of the deceased, petitioned that Damon A. Cheney, a creditor, be appointed administrator. The bond, the only other document in this case, shows that Cheney lived in Orange, Franklin County. Because of the long delay between Richard's death and the settling of the estate, it seems that the family was allowing matters to slide until forced into action by a creditor who wanted money owed him.

Paper money from the Bank of Tennessee — perhaps once part of a probate settlement.
NEHGS

Since Cheney probably initiated the process, possibly after bringing civil suit, the administration was filed in his home county rather than in that of the deceased.

A state-by-state list of the court districts that are responsible for probate records in the United States can be found at the end of this chapter.

Finally, a significant amount of early probate material, especially for New England, has been published and is readily available in most research libraries. In particular, the early probate records for New Hampshire and New Jersey have been published in *New Hampshire Provincial and State Papers* and *Archives of the State of New Jersey*. Important works for Massachusetts and Maine include *The Probate Records of Essex County, Massachusetts (1635-1681); Suffolk County Wills: Abstracts of the Earliest Wills Upon Record in Suffolk County, Massachusetts; The Probate Records of Middlesex County, Massachusetts, 1647-1664* (forthcoming); *Plymouth Colony Probate Guide: Where to Find Wills and Related Data for 800 People from Plymouth Colony, 1620-1691; Maine Wills, 1640-1760;* and *The Probate Records of Lincoln County, Maine: 1760-1800.*

Much probate material has been published in various genealogical journals, especially *The New England Historical and Genealogical Register*. Equally important, the library of the Church of Jesus Christ of Latter-day Saints has microfilmed many early probate records and indexes in this country and in other nations as well. You may consult these records at the main library in Salt Lake City or at one of the many branch libraries located throughout the United States and Canada.

Alabama — county courts (but check for additional courthouses located in cities other than the county seat)

Alaska — judicial districts at Juneau, Nome, Anchorage, and Fairbanks

Arizona — county superior courts

Arkansas — county circuit courts

California — county courts

Colorado — county courts

Connecticut — probate district courts (but probate records to 1850 are deposited at the Connecticut State Library)

Delaware — county register's courts; contact the Hall of Records in Dover for early probate records

District of Columbia — Register of Wills, 5th and E Streets NW, 20001

Florida — county judge's courts

Georgia — courts of ordinary

Hawaii — circuit court of the island

Idaho — county courts

Illinois — county probate courts (in counties of more than 70,000) or county courts

Indiana — district or county courts

Iowa — district courts in each county

Kansas — county probate courts

Kentucky — county courts

Louisiana — parish district courts

Maine — county probate courts

Maryland — county registers of wills

Massachusetts — county courts

Michigan — county probate courts

Minnesota — county probate courts

Mississippi — county chancery courts

Missouri — county probate courts

Montana — county district courts

Nebraska — county courts

Nevada — county courts

New Hampshire — county probate courts. Note that probate materials for the period 1635 to 1771 are published in the *New Hampshire State Papers*.

New Jersey — probate materials for the period 1682 to 1817 are published in the *New Jersey Archives*; the originals to 1804 are deposited in the secretary of state's office in Trenton. For later materials contact the county courts.

New Mexico — county courts

New York — county surrogate's courts

North Carolina — county superior courts

North Dakota — district courts

Ohio — county probate courts

Oklahoma — county courts

Oregon — county courts

Pennsylvania — county registers of wills

Rhode Island — town probate courts

South Carolina — county courts

South Dakota — county courts

Tennessee — county courts

Texas — county courts (but for larger counties, contact the probate court)

Utah — county district courts

Vermont — district courts (microfilm copies of probate records to 1850 deposited in the office of the secretary of state, Montpelier)

Virginia — county circuit courts

Washington — county courts

West Virginia — county courts

Wisconsin — county courts

Wyoming — county courts

❧ *Pointers and Pitfalls* ❧

Wills, Inventories, and Other Documents

1. Because they often list many family members, probate records, including wills, inventories, letters of administration, and guardianships, are genealogically invaluable.

2. Probate records are categorized as testate, for persons who left a will, and intestate, for persons who did not.

3. Caution: Many people who wrote wills at an advanced age were living far from the place where they had spent most of their adult lives and may have already given away much of their property.

4. A will can reveal much about an ancestor's religious convictions, family relations, and other personal matters.

5. Often a will does not tell the whole story, and a researcher must seek answers from other sources.

6. Caution: Confusing terms abound in Colonial documents.

7. Wills sometimes suggest a person's former residence, and this can lead to further genealogical discoveries.

8. In intestacy cases, primogeniture was often the law but partible inheritance the custom.

9. Intestacy records are sometimes just as valuable as wills and can contain information not found in wills.

10. Inventories can provide a detailed look into an ancestor's standard of living and a "tour" through his property.

11. It is best to refer to original files rather than transcriptions for probate records because the latter often contain errors.

12. When requesting probate records, provide as much information about the subject as possible: name, date of death, residence, and docket number when known.

13. While it is customary for a probate to be filed in the county of the deceased's residence, it may be filed elsewhere.

14. A significant amount of probate material has been published, especially for New England.

CHAPTER EIGHT

READING BETWEEN THE BORDERLINES

Understanding Land Records

Hawaiian cowboys, 1899. National Archives

A receipt for real estate, signed by Joseph Avery at Orleans, Massachusetts, January 21, 1824. Such receipts are sometimes discovered among old family papers. NEHGS

Land records, which locate our ancestors in a particular time and place, are fundamental to genealogical research. In a society where most families owned land and most areas kept land records, often voluminous, land records frequently document migrations that all other records have missed by identifying a family's origin or later whereabouts. Sometimes, too, land records state many kinships, thus allowing us to sort local individuals with common surnames into family groups. Because these records are often well maintained from the origins of the community and because family inheritance is sometimes reflected in the records, many genealogists turn first to land records in their search for family information.

To most of us, land records mean "deeds," usually deposited in the county courthouse. Although deeds are undoubtedly the most important land conveyances used by family historians, "patents," or "first deeds," which document the initial transfer of land from government to individual (or state, railroad company, or other corporate body), precede them. Because considerable personal information was sometimes required to obtain land from our colonial and national governments, these patents are a major genealogical resource. A short history of them is thus in order.

From Public to Private:
Early Land Transfers

From the 1600s until well into the twentieth century, the colonies and the federal government found numerous ways to distribute land to the American people. Land was given as an inducement or reward for military service, offered as a reward for immigrating or sponsoring the passage of others, given to settlers in disputed territories such as Florida or Oregon, and sold cheaply. Obtaining land from the government, however, was never simple. In early New England, for example, only inhabitants of a town were eligible for land grants. Often the grant depended on a willingness to live on the land and cultivate it. In the National era, as per the land act then in force, a person had to provide evidence of military service, marriage, or citizenship.

In the Colonial period, land records and the patterns of land distribution often reflected the original aims of the colonizer. The founding fathers of New England wanted to establish Christian commonwealths consisting of well-ordered townships. This was achieved, in part, by carefully controlling the distribution of land. Rather than grant land to individuals, colonial legislatures generally preferred to give land to groups of proprietors who would promise to organize a town and build a school and a church. An example of this practice is the decision of the Connecticut General Court to grant land for the settlement of Norwalk, in 1650:

Nathaniel Ely and Richard Olmsted in the behalfe of themselves and other Inhabitants of Hartford, desired the leave and approbation of the Courte for the planting of Norwaake, to whome an answer was returned in substance as followeth: —

That the Courte could not but, in generall, approve of the endeavors of men for the further improvement of the wildernes, by the beginning and carrying on of new Plantacons in an orderly way; and leaving the consideracon of the just grounds of the proceedings of the petitioners to its propper place, did manifest theire willingness to promoate theire designe by all due incouragment, in case theire way for such an undertaking were found cleare and good and provided the numbers and quality of those that ingage therein appeare to bee such as may rationally carry on the worke to the advantage to the publique wellfare and peace; that they make preparations and provisions for theire owne defence and safety, that the country may not be exposed to unnecessary trouble and danger in these hazardous times; that the devisions of the lands there to such as shall inhabitt, bee made by just rules and with the approbacon of a Comittee appointed for that end by this Courte, or to bee rectified by the Courte in case of aberrations, and that they attend a due payment of their proportions in all publique charges with a ready observation of the other wholesome orders of the Country.

In return for a land grant, proprietors were required to undertake certain obligations. An example of these is found in the charter granted to the 117 proprietors of the new town of Chester, New Hampshire, dated May 8, 1722:

1st That every Proprietor build a Dwelling House within Three years and Settle a family therein and brake up three Acres of Ground and Plant or Sow the Same within four years and Pay his proportion of the Town Charges when & So often as occasion Shall require the Same.

2dly That a Meeting House be built for the Public Worship of GOD within the Said Term of four years.

3dly That upon the Default of any Perticular Proprietor in complying with the Conditions of this Charter upon his Part Such Deliquent Proprietor Shall forfeit his Share to the other Proprietors which Shall be Disposed of According to the Major Vote of the sd Com'oners at a Legall Meeting.

4ly That A Proprietors Share be reserved for a Parsonage another for the first minister of the Gospel Another for the benefit of the School . . . .

Frequently such grants by Colonial governments of New England created townships six miles square, a pattern that would later be adopted by the federal government in settling the public domain. Note that the Connecticut Court counseled the petitioners to establish "just rules" for the "devisions of the lands."

Once land was given to the town (or to a group of proprietors who owned the land separately), the grantee could decide who would, in the future, be given or allowed to purchase parts of the original grant. Following an initial division to provide land for the first proprietors and their families, subsequent divisions would occur through the years so that sons and grandsons could also have land in the town. Sometimes five or six such divisions would occur over a century or more before the entire township became private property. These divisions were recorded in the proprietary records, which often list each grantee and the amount of his grant. Note that the original town meeting and proprietors' records are usually deposited today in the local town clerk's office. Many such records have been compiled on microfilm and are available at the Church of Jesus Christ of Latter-day Saints Genealogical Society Library in Salt Lake City.

Land grants were handled differently in the mid-Atlantic and southern colonies than in New England. Speculation — buying land to sell it later at a profit — was a primary motivating factor in land exchanges in these regions, so there was less control of the distribution of property through corporate bodies. Grants and sales directly to individuals were common practice. These grants ranged in size from fifty acres given to most immigrants to Virginia, to tens of thousands. A few individuals, mostly court favorites of King Charles II, received lands directly from the British government, then sold or leased them to settlers or other speculators. Land offices in these colonies processed applications for land patents, and their records are now often housed at state archives. Legislative and court proceedings also contain evidence of land transactions. Many records of these proceedings, especially those for Georgia, South Carolina, Virginia, Pennsylvania, and New York, have been published and are readily available in most large research libraries.

After the Revolution, the Colonies were gradually transformed into a nation and began to explore and settle the vast territory beyond the Appalachian Mountains. Many veterans received land on the western frontier, especially in New York, the Ohio Valley, Kentucky, and Tennessee. The Louisiana Purchase of 1803, the Mexican War of the 1840s, and several later land purchases, most notably Alaska, put the American people in possession of a continent stretching from the Atlantic to the Pacific and Arctic Oceans. The federal government assumed control of this "public domain" and insisted that settlers surrender their Colonial claims. Public lands grew. The entire land area of thirty states belonged for a time (usually before statehood) to the federal government.

Bounty Land.

The first distribution of the public domain was in the form of "bounty land." The practice of granting land in return for military service has a long Colonial history. New Englanders received tracts as early as the 1670s, in return for service in King Philip's War, 1675-1676. Some of this land was still being distributed to heirs of these soldiers in the 1720s and 1730s.

Beginning at the time of the Revolution, bounty land was offered as an inducement to military service, and between 1842 and 1844, land was given as a reward for it. Thus soldiers who fought in the War of 1812, the Indian Wars, and the Mexican War were eligible to apply for a land "warrant," which they could then "surrender" at the appropriate land office for a patent, which entitled them to take possession of their land. Bounty land was offered in present-day New York, Pennsylvania, Ohio, Kentucky, Tennessee, South Carolina, and Georgia for the American Revolution, and in present-day Illinois, Missouri, and Arkansas for the War of 1812. Beginning with the Mexican War, warrants were redeemable at any federal land office. Note that most land warrants were "assignable," meaning they could be sold to another person. Many soldiers chose to sell their warrants rather than settle on the offered land.

One soldier from the War of 1812 who received a bounty land warrant was Asa Dearborn of Vassalborough, Maine. Dearborn served as a substitute for William Gardiner, enlisted as a private in Captain Daniel Wyman's Company, Massachusetts Militia. Records show that he enlisted on September 12, 1814, and was discharged twelve days later. For this service he received bounty land warrant #63229-160-55 (63229 is the warrant number, 160 is the number of acres received, and 55 indicates that the warrant was received under the Act of 1855). That Asa lived in the Vassalborough area all his life and died in neighboring Augusta in 1859 seems to indicate that he sold his warrant.

Because so many soldiers assigned their warrants to others, the warrants themselves are not very useful in tracing ancestors who served in the military. Of immense genealogical value, however, are the bounty land warrant applications. The soldier and his family had to qualify for a bounty land warrant much as they had to qualify for a military pension. The veteran was required to prove his identity and document his military service. A widow and other heirs had to prove their relationship to a parent or husband who qualified for a bounty land warrant. Thus the bounty land warrant application files may contain marriage certificates, the testimony of neighbors and friends, and other personal evidence. These files are deposited at the National Archives together with pension applications. They have been indexed as part of the *Index of Revolutionary War Pension Applications in the National Archives*, National Genealogical Society Publication No. 40. Files of other wars are not as well indexed. Copies of pre-Civil War bounty land warrant applications can be obtained through the mail by using National Archives Trust Fund

(NATF) form 26. Copies of this form are available from The National Archives, Washington, DC 20408.

Other Land Records.

Other categories of land records deserve brief mention here before our discussion of the Homestead Act of 1862. Beginning in 1800, it became possible to buy land on credit from the federal government at $2 per acre. In 1820 purchases on credit were eliminated, but the price per acre was reduced to $1.25. This price held through 1908. If a pioneer ancestor acquired land in this fashion, the purchase may be documented in either a "credit entry file" or a "cash entry file." Of particular interest in these files is the final certificate issued when the purchase was completed. A final certificate normally shows name and place of residence of entryman as given at the time of purchase, date of purchase, number of acres in the tract, description of the tract (subdivision, section, township, and range), a summary of the payments made, and a citation to the record copy of the patent in the Bureau of Land Management. Note that the National Archives possesses a master three-by-five card index, alphabetically arranged by the name of entryman, to the cash entry files for Alabama, Alaska, Arizona, Florida, Louisiana, Nevada, and Utah.

"Donation entry files" also contain information of genealogical value. These files concern land granted to individuals who settled in the territories of Florida, Oregon, and Washington during the 1840s and

Turning over the first sod on the homestead. Few if any records were kept during the early years of settlement in frontier regions. National Archives

1850s. The size of the grant was based on marital status and date of settlement. Settlers were required to be U.S. citizens. Donation files include date and place of birth, date and place of marriage if applicable, and proof of citizenship for naturalized persons. The Oregon and Washington files have been fully indexed, and both the files and index are available on microfilm from the National Archives. For Florida, the master card index mentioned above has references to files containing final certificates.

The family researcher should also be aware of a category of land records at the National Archives known as "private land claims." Covering the period 1789 to 1980, these files contain the papers of individuals (or their descendants) who, having received grants from foreign governments, were applying for patents from the federal government to obtain clear title to their land. Many English, French, and Spanish families affected by the American Revolution, the Louisiana Purchase, or the Mexican War found themselves in the nineteenth century having to prove that they had been legally granted land by the English, Spanish, Mexican, or French crown. The proof in these files sometimes includes wills, deeds, and marriage certificates. Many records relating to individual claims have been transcribed and published in *American State Papers, Public Lands*. A consolidated index to these records was published under the title *Grassroots of America*, edited by Philip W. McMullin. For private claims in the period from 1826 to 1876 see *Reports of the Committee on Private Land Claims of the Senate and House of Representatives*, 2 vols. (45th Cong. 3rd. sess. Misc. Doc. 81, serial 1836).

Homestead Act.

Homestead entry files are of special interest. Commencing with the Homestead Act of 1862, American citizens or those who were intending to become citizens could receive 160 acres of land from the federal government for only a small filing fee. Land under this act was generally available until 1934 (although some was granted as late as 1983). Before an individual could receive title to his 160 acres, he had to become an American citizen, to live on the land for five years, and to "improve" it somehow during that time. Homestead files thus include testimony by the claimant and witnesses that these conditions of settlement had been met. The claimant's testimony includes his name, age, and place of birth, the date when the land was first settled, the number and relationship of the family members, and a legal description of the property. If the homesteader was not born in the United States, the file often contains a copy of his naturalization papers. More than half of those who initially filed for a homestead grant did not complete the conditions of settlement. Nevertheless, these initial files often contain much the same information as is available in the files of successful applicants. They will at least locate your ancestor in a certain time and place.

Locating Patents and Application Files

How can you retrieve the application files, as well as the patents, should you wish to examine them? As noted above, papers relating to several land acts are published or available on microfilm, and some indexes exist as well. For the great bulk of land patents and application files, especially those relating to the Homestead Act, the process of identifying an ancestor's papers is complex. It is perhaps best understood by reviewing the method by which the federal government distributed land to individual citizens.

Beginning with the ordinances relating to the Northwest Territory in the 1780s, the federal government developed a careful process by which an individual obtained a piece of the public domain. Modeled on the New England township system, it involved several steps. The federal government first extinguished any prior (and especially Indian) claims on the land. The land was then surveyed and laid out in townships six miles square. Once the land was surveyed, the federal government opened a local land office to process petitions from individuals, or entrymen, seeking public land in that area. Land offices maintained two key documents — a tractbook and a platbook — which are essential in identifying the location of an ancestor's land. Tractbooks contain a description of each entry arranged by township and range. Platbooks provide a visual representation on a map of the land description entered in the tractbook.

Let's look more closely at how an ancestor's property would be depicted in a platbook. According to the federal rectangular land survey system, each territory opened for settlement had to have a "principal meridian line" running north and south and a "base line" running east and west. Using these two coordinates, the territory would be divided into "ranges" and "townships," and each township into sections. There were thirty-six sections in each township, each section being one square mile (640 acres). The vast majority of settlers acquired ownership of a fraction of a section. Knowing the correct meridian line is essential to finding the township where an ancestor settled. Note that some states have more than one meridian line. Below is a graphic illustration of this rectangular survey system established by the federal government.

(A)

3rd Principal ▷ Meridian	4th Principal ▷ Meridian	5th Principal ▷ Meridian	△ Base Line

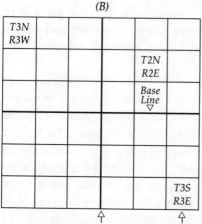

(B)

T3N R3W					
				T2N R2E	
				Base Line ▽	
				T3S R3E	

5th Principal Meridian   Township 3 South,
                            Range 3 East

(C)

6	5	4	3	2	1
7	8	9	10	11	12
18	17	16	15	14	13
19	20	21	22	23	24
30	29	28	27	26	25
31	32	33	34	35	36

Section 34
Township 3 South
Range 3 East

(D)

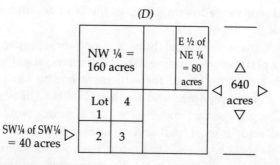

Section 34, Township 3 South, Range 3 East, 5th Principal Meridian

In locating the "legal description" of an ancestor's property, work from large to small: first find the correct principal meridian and base line; then the range and township; and finally the section and your ancestor's piece of land. The legal description begins with his land and expands to the principal meridian. Thus "E½ NE¼, Sec. 34, T3S R3E, 5th P.M." would be the legal description found in the tractbook of the hypothetical property sketched in the diagram on page 142: "The east half of the northeast quarter of Section 34, Township 3 South, Range 3 East, 5th Principal Meridian."

Once the homesteader, or entryman, had completed the conditions of settlement, his file was sent from the local land office to the General Land Office (GLO) in Washington, D.C. If this application was approved, the GLO issued a patent (first-title deed) to the individual, who in turn would often record it in the local county deed book. Many GLO records, including some of the tractbooks, have been transferred to the Bureau of Land Management (BLM). But all completed homestead application files are deposited in the National Archives. Family historians are obviously most interested in the homestead case files because of the genealogical data they may contain. The problem, however, is that you must have the legal description of an ancestor's land to identify the case file, since they are arranged by acts, state, land district, and thereunder, numerically. If you cannot obtain the legal description by other means, you must obtain it from the tractbooks or patents deposited in the appropriate BLM office. (See *Guide to Genealogical Research in the National Archives*, p. 215, for a complete description of the BLM offices.)

Sometimes it is possible to obtain a legal description of an ancestor's property without consulting a tractbook or patent. Check first to see whether the patent was registered in the local county deed book. Sometimes you can ascertain a legal description from a historical atlas. These historical atlases are often called platbooks because they feature land ownership plat maps. Some atlases are included as part of the "subscription" county histories so popular in the late nineteenth century. Researchers can sometimes determine the township and range number where their ancestor homesteaded from population and mortality schedules. With the township and range number, you can determine the tract location by consulting in the BLM only the entries covering that particular township.

For an extensive discussion of federal land patents, together with various invaluable indexes, see also Clifford Neal Smith's *Federal Land Series: A Calendar of Archival Materials on the Land Patents Issued by the*

United States Government, with Subject Tract and Names Indexes. When completed, this set will certainly be the authoritative treatment of its subject.

Deeds

Once an individual obtained a patent or first-title deed to his property, he could then convey it to another party. Although there are numerous instruments by which land can be conveyed from one party to another, including wills and lease agreements, the most common method is the deed (or "fee simple" of English common law). Deeds are extremely valuable documents for the genealogist. Along with census, probate, and vital records, they are the "bread and butter" of genealogy because of the family relationships they often reveal. So voluminous, in fact, are seventeenth- and eighteenth-century deeds that they might well be considered the best single genealogical source for Colonial America.

Before the Civil War, most free American families aspired to land ownership, and most American men acquired some land in their lifetime. Thus, while probably far less than half of this population either left wills or is mentioned in probate records, well over half is recorded in deeds. For this reason as well, deeds are probably a truer indicator of wealth than wills or inventories. Wills usually indicate a man's wealth only in old age, after he may by "deed of gift" already have given much of his property to his children. Deeds, on the other hand, often allow us to chart the economic cycle of an individual throughout his lifetime. They might tell us when a man was first given property by his parents; how much he bought and sold during his lifetime; and when he began to give property to his own children.

A closer look at a few deeds will tell us more specifically what we can expect to learn from them. Note that when an individual is the recipient of property, he is called the "grantee"; when he is the seller or giver, he is called the "grantor."

A Deed from the Colonial Period.

We will first examine portions of a deed from the late seventeenth century. Note first that both the grantor and grantee are identified by name, place, and occupation (Edward Rawson was secretary of the Massachusetts Bay Colony from 1650 to 1686). Edward Rawson's wife is identified as well, although her maiden name is not included. She was Rachel Perne, niece of the immigrant Dr. John Greene, of Warwick, Rhode Island. Wives' names are not always mentioned in deeds, but they were frequently listed when property was given to children or if land originated in the wife's family.

∽⊙∾

> To all People to whome this present Deed of Sale Shall Come Edward Rawson of Boston in New England gent. and Rachell his wife send greeting Know Yee that the sd Edward Rawson with the free and full Consent of his sd wife . . . .

Next we see the "consideration" that the buyer, in this case John Pynchon, paid for the land. In cases of gifts to children, the consideration was often a statement of affection. Thus in 1707 Henry Dearborn of Hampton, New Hampshire, gave two half-shares of land in the West Division in Hampton "for & Consideration of the Natural Affection and Fatherly Love and good will which I have and do bare unto my well Beloved Son in Law Philemon Blake and my Daughter Sarah Blake and now wife of the sd Philemon Blake" (New Hampshire Province Deeds, 82:419). In a more luminous case, Edward Strode deeded his son Jeremiah a plantation in Berkeley County, Virginia, in 1773 in consideration of "one grain of corn at Christmas if demanded."

∽⊙∾

> . . . for and in Consideracon of the sume of One Hundred Seauenty pounds currant money of New England to him in hand well and truly paide before the Sealeing and delinery of these presents by John Pynchon of Boston aforesd Mercht. the receite whereof he doth hereby acknowledge and himselfe therewith to be fully Satisfied and Contented . . . .

Next there is a careful description of the land in terms of location and size. For tracts bought and sold in public land states, the description reflects the rectangular survey system and is expressed in subdivision, section, township, and range. In older states land was often measured in terms of rods, poles, and perches (1 pole = 1 rod = 1 perch = 5½ yds = 16½ ft), and the boundaries were defined by distinctive landmarks and adjacent features.

Note that Rawson's deed mentions the abutting property owners. Such information is especially valuable for reconstructing the family relationships of neighbors. Not only did kinsmen often settle near each other, but many parts of early towns were often known by a family name such as "Brownsville" or "Smithdale." Where many individuals with the same surname lived nearby, land records often help genealogists sort them into separate family clusters.

[Rawson] Doth giue grant bargaine sell alien enfeoffe and Confirme unto the sd John Pynchon his heires and asignes for euer A peece or pcell of land scituate and being in Boston aforsed Viz. all the remainder of that parcell of land which Lately belonged to the dwelling house of him the sd Edward Rawson he haueing disposed of the whole into seuerall house lotts; which peece or pcell of land fronteth northerly and is bounded by the Lane or high way (lately laide out through the land which was the sd. Edward Rawsons) Leding from the broad streete into the Comon or trayning field and measureth in breadth next the sd. lane One hundred fforty and two foot be the same more or less and is bounded on the east by the land of the sd John Pynchon and on the South or reare in part with the land of Arthur Mason and in part with the land of Ephrraim Pope measuring on that side One hundred forty and four foote be the same more or Less and is bounded on the west with the land of Jacob Jesson Togeather with all his propriety in the sd Lane . . . .

Finally note that three dates are given in this deed — those of execution, acknowledgment, and recording. The first, in the text itself, indicates an exact time when all mentioned facts were as described and all contracting parties were living. On the second date (in this case the following day), the grantor acknowledges before witnesses that these signatures were authentic and voluntary. The final date indicates when the deed was publicly recorded. These dates, especially the last, are genealogically important. Sometimes many years lapsed between the time when the grantors signed the deed and the grantee (who was responsible for recording it) finally had it entered in the town or county deed book. Sometimes it was not recorded until an heir wished to sell the land many years later and needed to establish clear title. Thus a deed might appear in the record book decades after the grantor had died, and because grantor/grantee indexes are arranged, in the main, chronologically, you may have to search the entire index.

... In Witness whereof the sd Edward and Rachell Rawson haue to these presents put there hands and Seales this second day of June in the year of our Lord god One thousand Six hundreded Seuenty and ffiue 1675 p Edward Rawson and a seale

Signed Sealed & Deliu d. in
presence of us possession
of the aboue granted prem-
isses being giuen to Con-
tent
Willm: Hubbard
John Holyoke
Recorded & compared 3d. of 7br: 75

June 3d 1675 mr. Edward
Rawson acknowledged
this Instrumt. his act &
deed Before mee
John Pynchon Assist.

p ffree Grace Bendall Record r.

The above-cited Dearborn-to-Blake deed was executed on February 4, 1706/7, acknowledged on March 24, 1706/7, and recorded on October 29, 1765; Henry Dearborn himself died on January 18, 1724/5. (An explanation of the slashes in the dates appears in chapter 5 in the discussion on cemetery records.)

Multiple-Grantor Deeds.

Some deeds contain a gold mine of information. One type is the "multiple-grantor" deed in which children of a deceased parent join in selling inherited property. Thus in 1720 the children of Jeremiah Neal, Sr., sold land that had been "late in ye possession of our father."

KNOW ALL MEN by these presents That we Jeremiah Neal Junr. Housewright & Robert Neal Marriner & Hannah my wife and Charles Hooper & Hannah my wife formerly Hannah Neal Daughter of Jeremiah Neal Senr. & Abigail Neal Spinster all of Salem in ye. County of Essex in ye. Province of ye. Massachusets Bay in New England and Mercy Neal and Deborah Neal both of Boston in ye. County of Suffolk in ye. Province aforesd. Spinsters Daughters also of ye. sd. Jeremiah Neal Senr. all which Six viz — Jeremiah Neal Junr. Robert Mercy Abigail & Deborah Neal & also Hannah Hooper formerly Hannah Neal as aforesd. are all children of ye sd. Jeremiah of his late wife Mary and ye Grandchildren of Robert Buffam late aforesd. Deced . . . for and in Consideration of ye. Sum of forty five pounds to us in hand well and truly paid by Benjamin Lynde of Salem aforesd. Esqr. about five acres of land at Castle Hill in Salem "bounded northerly with Colo John Turner and ye said Benjamin Lyndes land, southerly on land late of William Beam Decd. and also all that our part of Marsh Land on ye Westerly Side of ye Creek that passes through ye now Castle Hill bridge lying S:Easterly from ye sd. bridge & bounded Westerly with ye. Stone wall or Salem Commons fence Northerly with Robert Wilsons part of marsh land Easterly with ye sd. Creek and Southerly with ye late John Hill Deced's part of Marsh Land Contains about one Quarter of an acre of Land more or less both which parsells of Upland & Marsh were late in ye posession of our father Jeremiah Neal Senr. aforesd. who hath given up all his right & Title & posession in & unto all & every ye. premises unto his two Sons ye. sd. Jeremiah Neal Junr. & ye. sd. Robert Neal by a firm Deed of Release or Quit Claim as by ye sd. Deed may more fully appear."

[Signed and sealed with signatures or marks by all grantors and necessary witnesses]

Fractional Deeds.

In some instances multiple-grantor sales are recorded in several "fractional" deeds rather than singly. Thus in the deed below, Ann Curtice sells "one eleventh part" of a piece of land in Salem, Massachusetts.

Ann Curtice wife of William Curtice Junr. late of Salem in the County of Essex deceased sells for 60 pounds Old Tenor to Ezekl Marsh Junr. of said Salem, Husbandman "all my Right and interest being one eleventh part of and in All that piece of land situate in said Salem, Containing in ye whole about thirty acres . . . , and is bounded as follows Viz. Southerly on ye road or highway then Easterly & Southerly on land of Ensign John Proctor, then easterly on land of Thos. Needham, then Northerly Easterly & Southerly on land of ye sd Ezekl Marsh, and on every other part on land of ye sd Thos Needham to ye road aforesd . . . with one eleventh part of ye buildings thereon standing, & of ye Priviledges there belonging."

Witnesses:

John Epes
Joseph Epes

her
Anna **A** Curtis
mark

(Essex County Deeds 96:63, dated 27 Dec. 1748; acknowledged 28 March 1749; recorded 20 Aug. 1751.)

When you encounter a fractional deed, be alert for other deeds immediately preceding and following that also pertain to fractions of property sold to the same grantee. Through the grantor/grantee indexes, you should be able to locate all eleven elevenths of the land. By doing so, you will learn the name of Ann's siblings and discover that they are the children of Thomas Gould of Salem Village (Danvers), Massachusetts, deceased, intestate. This deed is useful, too, because it is a reminder of the laws of inheritance as practiced in Colonial New England. When a man died intestate, his widow, if there was one, was entitled to a life interest in one-third of the estate. The remainder was divided among the surviving children (or their heirs), with the eldest son obtaining a double portion. The fact that the Gould estate was divided into eleven pieces indicates that there were ten children in the family.

Quitclaim Deeds.

It should be noted that "quitclaim" deeds were sometimes used in lieu of wills to settle estates. In a quitclaim deed, an heir can transfer whatever rights he may have to a piece of property. Below, the grantors John Callum and William Coman of Providence, Rhode Island, disposed of property outside the county in which they resided:

John Callum and William Coman, both of Glocester in the County of Providence in the Colony of Rhode Island and providence plantations, yeomen, Joseph Coman, Benja. Coman and Richard Coman, all of Providence, etc., yeomen, and John Bennit of Scituate in the county aforesaid, yeoman, in consideration of £10 curent money of New England quitclaim to "Our Brother Caleb Callum of Salem", Essex County, Mass. Bay Colony, carpenter, "All Our right title Interest and Claime of in and to all ye estate that did belong unto our Hond. Mother Elizabeth Comman decd. lying and being in ye Town of Kingsale in ye County of Cork in Ireland" etc.

Witnesses:
Elisha Knowlton
Nathan Place

John Callum & a Seal
William Comon & a Seal
Joseph Coman & a Seal
Benja Coman & a Seal
Richard Coman & a Seal
John Bennet & a Seal

In this case, the deed points to the European origins of the family. Mention of previous residence is more common in reverse situations, when a deed recorded in County A shows a grantor, now a resident of County B, disposing of his real estate in County A. This migration pattern is illustrated when grantor Levi Dearborn, then of Pennsylvania, arranged (by granting power of attorney to his son William) to sell his property in New Hampshire:

"Know all men by these presents that I Levi Dearborn late of the town of New Castle in the County of Rockingham and State of New-hampshire but now of the borough of Dundaff in the County of Susquehanna and State of Pennsylvania, farmer, have made, constituted and appointed, and by these presents do make constitute and appoint, and in my place and stead, put and depute my trusty Son William

Dearborn of the same Borough of Dundaff my true and lawful Attorney for me and in my name, place and stead to grant, bargain and sell all that farm, tract or parcel of land, now owned by me, situate in the aforesaid town of New Castle . . . ."

Levi Dearborn (L.S.)

Deeds Instead of Probate.

Keep in mind that it was not unusual for individuals to convey their real and personal estate to one of their children during their lifetime in return for lifelong care and maintenance, thus making probate of the estate unnecessary. As a rule, this practice was more common among the less-well-to-do who lived in rural areas. Whenever your ancestor is not listed in the local probate index, check grantor deed indexes to determine whether he "deeded away" his property during his lifetime. The following, from New Hampshire Province Deeds, 21:220 (dated August 13, 1714; acknowledged August 31, 1714; recorded July 8, 1735) is typical:

Henry Derburn [Dearborn] of Hampton, farmer, "for & in Consideration of ye Natural Affection & fatherly love wch I have & do Bear unto my Belovd Son Henry Derbun" of Hampton, for diverse good causes "more pticularly yet my sd Son Henry Derbun take Care & Maintain me & my Wife during Each of our Natural Lives with Al things Needful for us or Either dureing our Natural Life both In Sickness & In Health & also be at ye Charge of a Decent Burial for Each of us & paying al such Debts as shal be owing or Contractd by me or my sd Wife In our life time . . . ." hereby give and grant all my real and personal estate except what I have already disposed of in writing and what I have given to my three daughters of household goods mentioned in a deed of gift bearing even date.

Witnesses: /s/ Henry H Derbun (seal)
John Derbun
Elisha Smith

Locating Deeds

One advantage in using deeds is that they are generally well indexed. Indexes are divided between grantors and grantees, but do not usually include every name mentioned in the document. Multiple-grantor deeds, for example, are likely to be indexed by the name of each mentioned grantor followed by "et al." Indexes are generally arranged in chronological series and within that series, alphabetically by surname or the first two letters of the surname. A few public land states are not indexed by individual at all but rather by subdivision, section, township, and range. In such cases it may be necessary to obtain this information from another source, such as a historical atlas in a county history or "mugbook."

Except for Connecticut, Rhode Island, and Vermont, where deeds are usually housed in the town or city clerk's office, copies of deeds can be obtained by written request from the clerk of the county court (or sometimes county register of deeds). Large genealogical libraries may have copies of the grantor and grantee indexes for nearby counties. Many land records of the Colonial period and nineteenth century have been microfilmed by the Church of Jesus Christ of Latter-day Saints and are available in Salt Lake City or through the Mormon branch libraries. Some Colonial deeds, from New England especially, have been transcribed and published.

Family portrait in front of the family home. Christa Patterson

An example of an early land deed. Land records can sometimes help you track down a "missing" ancestor. NEHGS

Tax Records

Taxes were levied on both real and personal property throughout the United States at both the state (or colonial) and local level. In New England, the most genealogically useful tax rolls are those kept by towns; elsewhere those kept by counties fill this role. In addition to taxes on property, a head or poll tax was commonly levied on males twenty-one and over. Usually they were excused from paying this tax after reaching age sixty.

Tax records have several uses. Because they were taken annually, they provide regular glimpses of your ancestors between census years. Also, a large percentage of the adult male population is listed. Even those who owned only personal taxable property, but not real estate, appear.

Tax rolls are usually set up as a series of columns headed by the items to be taxed, with the man's name to the left. The columns are filled in with the amount of the tax or acreage, or they are left blank if not applicable. By comparing tax rolls for the same person over a number of years, you can develop a fairly detailed profile of your ancestor's economic status.

Let's look at an example. Henry Dearborn appears in the town of New Durham, Strafford County, New Hampshire, about 1816, when his name is listed on the annual tax rolls. From Strafford County deeds 86:291 we see that Henry Dearborn of Deerfield, Rockingham County, yeoman, purchased for $1,071.87 from John and Lemuel Roberts, 85¾ acres of land in lot 2, 1st division in New Durham. Examining the annual entries for his name from 1816 to 1825 (the last year his name appears), we get the following data:

While the figures change slightly in the different columns from year to year, all of Henry's acreage is in lot 2, 1st division. Between 1821 and 1824 he is taxed for 58½ acres, but in 1825, for his last listing, he is taxed for only one poll and one horse. By comparing the 1824 and 1825 tax rolls for all those who owned land in lot 2, 1st division, we find that a Samuel Davies and a Betsey Pearl appear in 1825 as owning 29½ and 29 acres, respectively, while the acreages of all other landowners remained constant. Thus it appears that Henry sold his land to these two individuals, even though there are no recorded deeds to that effect.

While the individual tax records tell us relatively little about an ancestor, they can be quite helpful when used cumulatively or in conjunction with other sources. At the very least, they allow us to locate an ancestor in place and time and often to identify his neighbors. Tax lists

Inh's. Names	Town Tax £ s d	Poll Tax £ s d	Real Estate £ s d	Personal Estate £ s d	Sum Total £ s d
Arms Moses			1 12 1		1 12 1
Avery Amos	1 1 10				1 10 · ·
Blodget Abraham	1 1 10			12 3	2 2 3
Butler James	1 1 10			11 8	2 1 8
Boardwell Eleaz'r	1 1 10	3 1 11	1	6 3	5 18
Boardwell Enoch	1 1 10	2 6 8	1	2 6	4 19 2
Boardwell Gideon	1 1 10	2 · 7		11 4	4 1 11
Boardwell Job	1 1 10	1 17 4		10 ·	3 17 4
Boardwell Reuben	1 1 10	1 5 8		8 9	3 4 5
Boyd John	1 1 10	2 4 2	1	9 9	5 3 9
Boyd William	1 1 10	12 10		8 2	2 11 ·
Boyd David	1 1 10	15 9		7 7	2 13 4
Boyd Samuel	1 1 10	1 12 8		17 6	4 · 2
Belding Daniel	1 1 10	2 · 3		4 7	3 14 10
Burdick John	2 3 ·	3 6 7	1	16 2	7 19 9
Bates Edward	1 1 10	4 1		8 2	2 2 3
Bates Martha	· · ·	16 4		7 ·	1 3 4
Bates Jonathan	1 1 10	1 1 4		18 8	3 10 ·
Bates, Martha Guardian to					
Robbert Bates		· 4 1			· 4 1
Bates Moses		· 3 ·			· 9 ·
Colman Job	1 1 10	12 10		5 10	2 8 8
Cobb Elisha	1 1 10	1 8		5 10	3 3 10

A tax list for Shelburne, Massachusetts, 1779, showing amounts paid for poll tax, real estate, personal estate, and sum total. NEHGS

are usually the major basis for "reconstructed" censuses.

In summary, we should stress again that land records — both patents from the government and deeds between private parties — rank with probate and vital records as primary sources of genealogical information. Not only do they help us document an ancestor's changing residence, they also reveal many kinships. And they are a major source of data on the economic and social status of many of our forebears.

❧ *Pointers and Pitfalls* ☙
Understanding Land Records

1. Land records can help you trace elusive ancestors who migrated frequently during the century following the Revolution.

2. Patents, or first deeds, document the earliest transfers of U.S. land from government to private ownership.

3. Bounty land, given in exchange for military service, was offered by the government for almost two centuries starting in the 1670s. Bounty land warrant applications are extremely informative genealogical documents.

4. Other documents pertaining to government land grants or sales include final certificates from cash or credit entry files, donation entry files, and private land claims.

5. Homestead entry files from the period of the Homestead Act (1862-1934) are also valuable genealogical documents.

6. Identifying an ancestor's land records can be a complex task. It requires some understanding of the government's method of dividing the parcels of land it distributed.

7. Deeds can reveal the economic cycle of an ancestor's life and help reconstruct family and neighbor relationships.

8. Multiple-grantor deeds, fractional deeds, and quitclaim deeds can reveal data such as names of children and place of family origin.

9. Sometimes an ancestor conveyed property to his children in exchange for care in old age, thereby eliminating the need for probate. This makes some land records even more valuable.

10. Deeds are usually well indexed.

11. Except in a few New England states, deed copies are available from the county clerk's office.

12. Tax records, which list property owners and landowners, can be particularly helpful when used in conjunction with other resources.

CHAPTER NINE

TALLYING TO THE CAUSE

Using Census Records

A 1940 census taker in Alaska. National Archives

The Cherokee Strip in Oklahoma Territory, 1893. National Archives

s already noted, the century from the Revolution to about 1875 is unquestionably the most difficult in American genealogy. The nation was in flux, in part because much new territory was opened for settlement. The great westward migration was encouraged by the Northwest Ordinance of 1787, the Louisiana Purchase of 1803, the War of 1812, and the Mexican-American War of the 1840s. It was common for nineteenth-century families to move four, five, or six times, constantly in search of better land and opportunity. Families raced into wilderness areas to stake claims well in advance of the county court system and official record-keeping. With so much movement and often little government, far fewer records than genealogists would like exist for our pioneer forebears. The major exception is the federal census.

The federal census did not, of course, always catch in its net every family living in nineteenth-century America; but few families were so mobile or lived in such remote places that they were not recorded at least once. Few records available to present-day researchers are as comprehensive, standardized, and informative as the census.

The Federal Census: History and Examples

Although some earlier county or colony-wide censuses survive, the federal census of 1790 was the first document in this country, indeed in the world, that attempted to record the population of an entire nation. This national "head count" was mandated by the Constitution. Its original purpose was the apportionment of the House of Representatives.

Although the census was at first intended to count only the population, it was later used for other purposes. In 1810, for instance, a manufacturers' schedule was prepared, listing owners, companies, and goods. In 1840 pensioners from the American Revolution or other military service were listed by name and age. Mortality schedules were maintained from 1850 through 1880.

Each successive census asked for more information. The first six censuses listed only heads of household. Other family members, servants, boarders, slaves, etc., were identified only by sex and age group. Each family was entered on a single line of the schedule. While the pre-1850 censuses do not name every household member, they at least identify the family's residence each decade. If your ancestors lived in areas not covered by vital records, pre-1850 federal censuses can fill many gaps or corroborate other evidence.

Let's look at an example. Jacob Dearborn was born in Orrington, Maine, where town vital records include his marriage to Hannah Rooks on May 4, 1797. Penobscot and Hancock county deeds naming both Jacob and Hannah consistently call him a blacksmith and prove that he was in Bangor in 1818 and moved to Kilmarnock by 1823. The deeds also show us that this particular Jacob Dearborn (there was another in the same area) was living in Orrington until at least 1810. With this information, we can now easily identify him in the census:

Orrington, Hancock County, Maine — 1800
Jacob Dearborn   1 male under 10
                      1 male 26-44

Orrington, Hancock County, Maine — 1810
Jacob Dearborn   2 males under 10   2 females under 10
                      1 male 10-15   1 female 26-44
                      1 male 26-44

Bangor, Penobscot County, Maine — 1820
Jacob Dearborn   1 male under 10   2 females under 10
                      1 male 10-15   1 female 10-15
                      1 male 16-18   1 female 16-25
                      1male 16-25   1 female over 44
                      1 male over 44

Kilmarnock, Penobscot County, Maine — 1830

Jacob Dearborn	1 male 15-20	1 female 10-15
	1 male 50-60	1 female 20-30
		1 female 40-50

Kilmarnock, Penobscot County, Maine — 1840

| Jacob Dearborn | 1 male 60-70 | 1 female 60-70 |

An analysis of Jacob's household in these five censuses makes it possible to reconstruct the family, keeping in mind that any of the unnamed individuals might be boarders, servants, or not at all related.

The 1800 census shows Jacob living alone with a young son. Where was Hannah? As stated above, we know from other records that she lived well into the 1800s, and this is borne out by the later censuses, so we can only attribute her absence to a lapse on the enumerator's part.

In the 1810 census we find Jacob and his wife with five children — three sons and two daughters. It appears that the eldest son (in the 10-15 category) is the same as the one enumerated with Jacob in 1800. In 1820 we again find Jacob, his wife, and the same five children, plus three additional ones born within the past decade. Note that by comparing the ages of the older five children in the 1810 and 1820 censuses, we can estimate their ages with greater precision. By 1830 the family has shrunk to Jacob, his wife, and three children. The other children either have reached adulthood and moved away or have died. Two things worth noting in this year are that Jacob's wife is reported to be in a younger age bracket than she should be and that there have been no new births in the family in the past decade — which is logical when you consider the parents' ages. By 1840 the family is further reduced to just the elderly Jacob and his wife. Even though we have no vital records for Jacob's family with the exception of his marriage record, we can reconstruct his family and follow its progress fairly accurately based only on census records and having no names other than that of the head of household.

As you can see, the numbers and ages of unwed individuals within a family may not remain consistent from one census to another. Nevertheless, it is often possible to reconstruct at least the outline of an early nineteenth-century family from pre-1850 census data alone.

The federal census of 1850, redesigned by Lemuel Shattuck, shifted the focus of data from families to individuals and thus revolutionized census information generally. A native and historian of Concord, Massachusetts, a gifted physician, founder of the American Statistical Society, and designer of the 1845 Boston census upon which the 1850 federal census was modeled, Shattuck believed that census data could be used to improve public health. The 1850 census thus records the name, age, and birthplace (usually only a state) of every household member. Known as the first modern census, it truly "pulls back the curtain" on our mid-nineteenth-century forebears. From earlier censuses, we could only speculate, for example, that a male listed as between ages 10 and 15 was a son of the household head. From the various names, ages, and birthplaces in the 1850 census, we can infer most family relationships.

The following family, living at Holland, Orleans County, Vermont, is a typical example:

Name	Age	Sex	Occupation	Value of Real Estate	Birthplace
Hiram Dearborn	58	M	Farmer	$1,000	NH
Polly Dearborn	57	F			NH
Joseph	14	M			VT

Another milestone in census information was reached in 1880. One column added to the census form asked the relationship of each member of the household to its head; two other columns told the birthplace of the parents of each individual. Young men and women known only by approximate age in censuses prior to 1850, or by name, age, and birthplace between 1850 and 1870, were finally identified in 1880 as children of household heads. Those members of a household who were not related to its head were now identified as servants or boarders. And with known birthplaces of parents (almost always states or countries), national derivations and even the identification of likely forebears from earlier censuses become much easier to discern. One word of caution: while the 1880 census establishes the relationship of family members to the head of the household, it does not indicate the relationship to the wife of a male head of household. Some of his children may be her stepchildren, especially if the wife is considerably younger than her husband. Remember, too, that these listings need not include all children. Married sons usually have established their own households; some may be away at school or college; and some may be living with other families.

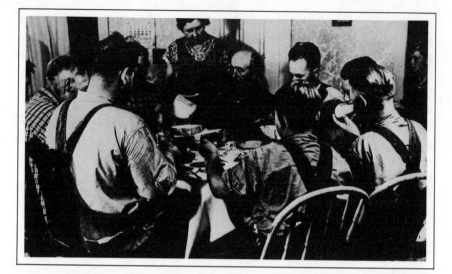

Farm hands at dining table, 1939. Early census data for a migrant worker ancestor might be included under the employer's name or family group. National Archives

Let's consider a few examples. Looking again at Holland, Vermont, this time for 1880, we find that the Joseph Dearborn who was enumerated as a boy of fourteen with his parents thirty years before is now living with his brother William (listed as head of a household adjacent to Hiram's in 1850).

Name	Race	Sex	Age	Rel.	Mar. Stat.	Occup.	Birthplace	F	M
Dearborn, William	w	m	67		mar.	farmer	NH	NH	NH
Dearborn, Harriet	w	f	54	wife	mar.	keeping house	VT	QUE	QUE
Dearborn, Joseph	w	m	44	bro.	sing.	farmer	VT	NH	NH
Chandler, Mary	w	f	23	serv.	sing.	servant	VT	PA	QUE

In the 1900 census we find the family of Lorenzo P. Dearborn, a traveling salesman, boarding in a hotel in Janesville, Rock County, Wisconsin. The columns in the following chart represent, from left to right:

name, relation to head of household, race, sex, birth (month and year), age, marital status, length of marriage, number of children, number of children living, and birthplaces of the subject, his father, and his mother.

Dearborn, Lorenzo, P.	Bo.	w m	Dec. 1853	48	mar.	8		MA	VT	VT
Dearborn, Flossie S.	Bo.	w f	Dec. 1867	32	mar.	8	1-1	WI	NY	VT
Dearborn, Charles W.	Bo.	w m	Sept. 1884	15	sing.			MO	MA	WV
Dearborn, Whitcomb D.	Bo.	w m	Sept. 1894	15	sing.			WI	MA	WI

Because this family was living in a hotel, they are listed as boarders; we are not told how they are related to the hotel proprietor or to each other. We can, however, determine several facts. As of 1900, Lorenzo and Flossie had been married for eight years, and she was the mother of one child, then living. Presumably this would be Whitcomb, as the places of his parents' births match those of Lorenzo and Flossie (note that his age is given as fifteen — he was actually five). Charles could have been Lorenzo's child by an earlier wife, but subsequent research proved that he was actually Lorenzo's nephew.

Sometimes relatives we find in successive censuses do not "age" at the proper rate. Such kinsmen may not know their true age or may reduce it for reasons of vanity. Often, however, another member of the family who provided this information to the enumerator was merely guessing.

Alfred Squires Utley, "famous fiddler of the Western Reserve." Census records from certain years reveal data about an individual's economic and occupational status in life. NEHGS

One example is the family of Daniel Dearborn of Maine; its entries in the 1850, 1860, and 1880 censuses are as follows:

1850 Census, Maine, Kennebec County, Gardiner

Name	Age	Sex	Occupation	Birthplace
Daniel Dearborn	41	m	tanner	ME
Mary Dearborn	32	f		ME
Daniel H. Dearborn	14	m		ME
Samuel Dearborn	12	m		ME
George F. Dearborn	6	m		ME
Charles E. Dearborn	3	m		ME
Mary J. Dearborn	18	f		ME

1860 Census, Maine, Piscataquis County, Monson

Name	Age	Sex	Occupation	Birthplace
Daniel Dearborn	55	m	farmer	ME
Mary A. Dearborn	43	f		ME
George F. Dearborn	15	m		ME
Charles E. Dearborn	13	m		ME
James T. Dearborn	9	m		ME
Sarah T. Dearborn	4	f		ME

1880 Census, Maine, Penobscot County, Lowell

Name	Relation	Race	Sex	Age	Birthplace F	M
Dearborn, Daniel		w	m	74	ME ME	ME
Dearborn, Mary N.	wife	w	f	64	ME ME	ME
Dearborn, James T.	son	w	m	29	ME ME	ME
Dearborn, Sarah T.	ad. dau	w	f	24	ME ME	ME
Dearborn, Thomas F.	g.s.	w	m	12	ME ME	ME
Dearborn, Annie L.	ad. dau. ch.	w	f	7	ME ME	ME
Miles, Leonard	ad. dau. ch.	w	m	2	ME ME	ME

In addition to the obvious age discrepancies, we learn from the 1880 census that Sarah T. Dearborn was an *adopted* daughter of Daniel and

Mary and that Annie L. Dearborn, age seven, and Leonard Miles, age two, were the adopted daughter's children.

Once you have located a particular family in several decennial censuses, you will find a wide variety of information about different family members, wealth, occupation, schooling, property, ownership, and migrations. Reuben G. Dearborn was born about 1832 in Switzerland County, Indiana, a son of Reuben and Rebecca Dearborn. The elder Reuben, a native of North Hampton, New Hampshire, married Rebecca Lee in Switzerland County in 1828, and is enumerated there in the 1830 census with one male 40-49, one female under 5 and one 20-29. Reuben Sr. died in the mid-1830s, intestate, and the widow remarried within a short time. The name of Dearborn does not appear in the 1840 census because Reuben and his older sister (the little girl in the 1830 census) probably were living with their mother, stepfather, or maternal grandparents, the Lees. The six census enumerations of Reuben Dearborn that begin in 1850 can be listed as follows:

1850 Census, Indiana, Switzerland County, Cotton Twp.

Name	Age	Sex	Race	Occupation	Value of Real Estate	Birthplace
David Lee	33	m	w	farmer	$4,000	IN
Jane Lee	32	f	w			OH
Charles Lee	9	m	w			IN
Margaret Lee	7	f	w			IN
Ann Lee	5	f	w			IN
Jane Lee	3	f	w			IN
David B. Lee	1	m	w			IN
Reuben Dearborn	18	m	w			IN
Ann Lee	73	f	w			NJ
Louise Livings	9	f	w			IN

1860 Census, Indiana, Crawford County, Jennings Twp.

Name	Age	Sex	Race	Occupation	Value Real/ Personal	Birthplace
Reuben Dearborn	27	m	w	farmer	$500/$428	IN
Sarah S. Dearborn	24	f	w			IN
David L. Dearborn	5	m	w			IN
Lewis C. Dearborn	4	m	w			IN
Rebecca Dearborn	2	f	w			IN

1870 Census, Indiana, Crawford County, Boone Twp.

Name	Age	Sex	Race	Occupation	Value Real/ Personal	Birthplace
Reuben G. Dearborn	37	m	w	farmer	-/$300	IN
Sarah J. Dearborn	35	f	w			IN
David L. Dearborn	15	m	w			IN
Lewis C. Dearborn	13	m	w			IN
Rebecca Dearborn	12	f	w			IN
Charles L. Dearborn	10	m	w			IN
Nancy Dearborn	8	f	w			IN
Mary Z. Dearborn	6	f	w			IN
Euseba Dearborn	3	f	w			IN

1880 Census, Kansas, Ness County, Eden Twp.

Name	Race	Sex	Age	Relation	Occupation	Birthplace	F	M
Dearborn, Ruben	w	m	48		farmer	IN	—	—
Rebecca J.	w	f	22	Dau.	keeping house	IN	IN	IN
Nancy	w	f	17	Dau.		IN	IN	IN
Drucilla M.	w	f	14	Dau.		IN	IN	IN
Useba	w	f	13	Dau.		IN	IN	IN
Hugh	w	m	6	Son		IN	IN	IN

1900 Census, Idaho, Washington County, East Weiser Precinct

Name	Rel.	R.	S.	Birth-date	Age	Mar. Stat.	Occupation	Birthplace	F	M
Dearborn,										
Reuben G.		w	m	Oct.1833	66	wid.	Ditch render	IN	VT	IN
Hugh C.	son	w	m	Apr.1877	23	sing.	Farm laborer	IN	IN	IN

1910 Census, Kansas, Ness County, Eden Twp.

Name	Rel.	S.	R.	Age	Mar. Stat.	Birthplace	F	M
Dearborn,								
Reuben G.		m	w	77	wid.	IN	VT	OH
Hugh C.	son	m	w	36	sing.	IN	IN	IN

A clear picture of this family emerges after a close examination of these records. In 1850 Reuben was living in an extended family. David Lee was his mother's younger brother, and Ann Lee, age seventy-three, was probably his grandmother. By 1860 Reuben had moved some miles down the Ohio River to Crawford County and acquired a wife and family. Note that he named his son for his uncle, and his daughter for his mother. By 1870 the family had grown by four more children, but financially Reuben seemed to be struggling. The next decade shows tremendous changes within the family. After the birth of the last child, Hugh, about 1874, the family moved from the forested hills of southern Indiana to the high plains of western Kansas. Apparently Reuben's wife died during this interim, and his two oldest sons, David and Lewis, probably left to seek their own fortunes. Reuben continued to make his home in Ness County for at least the next thirty years, although in 1900, curiously, we find him living in western Idaho, now definitely a widower, with his son Hugh.

Census Information and Indexes

To work easily with federal censuses, researchers should know how they are organized, to what extent they may be easy or difficult to use, which have been published, and what specialized guides and indexes are readily available. As suggested already, federal censuses are generally the most comprehensive records available to modern genealogists. Unfortunately, not all have survived. Nearly the entire 1890 schedule was destroyed by fire in 1921. The 1790 records for Georgia, Kentucky, New Jersey, Tennessee, and Virginia were burned during the War of 1812. Scattered other censuses have also been lost or destroyed. (For a complete list of lost schedules, see Val D. Greenwood's *The Researcher's Guide to American Genealogy*, pp. 143-153.)

Still, more than ninety percent of the U.S. federal census, 1790-1910, survives and is widely available. Only federal censuses through 1910 are open to the public. To protect the privacy of living individuals, censuses are restricted, i.e., "closed," for seventy-two years (thus the 1920 census becomes available in 1992). Anyone may request restricted census information about himself or his spouse. Immediate family members and legal heirs can request such data about the deceased.

Both in the original and on microfilm, census information is usually grouped according to state and county, which are arranged alphabetically. Towns or villages within a county are seldom arranged alphabetically, although all information from a single town or village usually appears together. Individual surnames never appear alphabetically, but occur in the order in which the enumerator visited households. Therefore, you must know the name of the individual you seek, the census year, and the state and county of residence to benefit from census records. Once you know this information, and if there are no printed indexes, you must proceed through listings of the county page by page, entry by entry, until your forebear appears.

The chart shows the various categories of information on the 1790-1910 censuses. Note especially the changes that began with the 1850 census.

Contents of Census Schedules, 1790-1840 and 1850-1910
1790-1840

Name of head of family and number of free white males (within specified age groups) and free white females (for 1790 only, age groups in each household were unspecified)

1790	1800	1810	1820	1830	1840

Number of free white females, within specified age groups, in each household

—	1800	1810	1820	1830	1840

Name of slaveowner and number of slaves owned by each owner

1790	1800	1810	1820	1830	1840

Number of male and female slaves, within specified age groups, owned by each owner

—	—	—	1820	1830	1840

Number of foreigners, in each household, not naturalized

—	—	—	1820	1830	—

Number of deaf, dumb, and blind persons, within specified categories, in each household

—	—	—	—	1830	1840

Name and age of each person receiving a federal military pension

—	—	—	—	—	1840

Number of persons in each household attending specified classes at school

—	—	—	—	—	1840

Immigrants leaving Ellis Island, 1907. The Bettman Archive, Inc.

1850-1910 (free inhabitants of each household)

	1850	1860	1870	1880	1885	1890	1900	1910
Name and age	1850	1860	1870	1880	1885	1890	1900	1910
Name of street and number of house	—	—	—	1880	1885	1890	1900	1910
Relationship to head of family	—	—	—	1880	1885	1890	1900	1910
Month of birth, if born within the year	—	—	1870	1880	1885	—	1900	—
Sex, race, birthplace, and occupation	1850	1860	1870	1880	1885	1890	1900	1910
Whether naturalized or whether naturalization papers had been taken out	—	—	—	—	—	1890	1900	1910
Number of years in the United States	—	—	—	—	—	1890	1900	1910
Value of personal estate	—	1860	1870	—	—	—	—	—
Value of real estate	1850	1860	1870	—	—	—	—	—
Whether home and farm free of mortgage	—	—	—	—	—	1890	1900	1910
Marital status	—	—	—	1880	1885	1890	1900	1910

Item	1850	1860	1870	1880	1885	1890	1900	1910
Whether married within the year	1850	1860	1870	1880	1885	1890	—	—
Month of marriage, if within the year	—	—	1870	—	—	—	—	—
Whether temporarily or permanently disabled	—	—	—	1880	1885	—	—	—
Whether suffering from acute or chronic disease	—	—	—	—	—	1890	—	—
Whether crippled, maimed, or deformed	—	—	—	1880	1885	1890	—	—
Time unemployed during the census year	—	—	—	1880	1885	1890	1900	1910
Whether deaf, dumb, blind, or insane	1850	1860	1870	1880	1885	1890	—	1910
Whether a pauper	1850	1860	—	—	—	1890	—	—
Whether a prisoner or a homeless child	—	—	—	—	—	1890	—	—
Whether a convict	1850	1860	—	—	—	1890	—	—
Whether able to speak English	—	—	—	—	—	1890	1900	1910
Whether able to read and write and whether attended school within the year	1850	1860	1870	1880	1885	1890	1900	1910
Birthplaces of father and mother	—	—	—	1880	1885	1890	1900	1910
Whether father or mother of foreign birth	—	—	1870	1880	1885	1890	1900	1910
Number of living children, if a mother	—	—	—	1880	1885	1890	1900	1910
Whether soldier, sailor, or marine during the Civil War (U. S. or Conf.), or widow of such person	—	—	—	—	—	1890	1900	1910

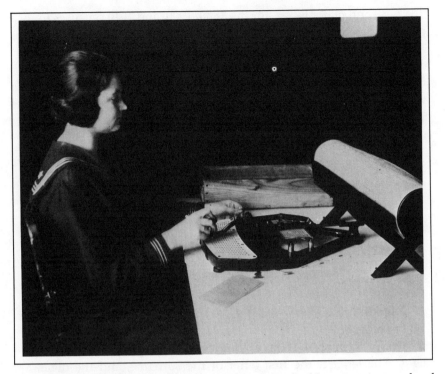

A Pantograph Punch machine of the type used earlier in this century to record and compile census data. National Archives

Number of years in present marriage

| — | — | — | — | — | — | *1900* | *1910* |

Number of children born

| — | — | — | — | — | — | *1900* | *1910* |

Mother tongue

| — | — | — | — | — | — | *1900* | *1910* |

Certain indexes and research methods make the census easier to use. All the surviving schedules of the 1790 census were published by the federal government in the early 1900s, with a single, indexed volume for each state. Later reprinted, these volumes are available in most research libraries.

A second major index, for the 1880, 1900, and 1910 censuses (only a partial index for 1880 and 1910), was completed by the Works Progress Administration (WPA) in the 1930s. This index, compiled on note cards deposited at the National Archives, follows the "Soundex system," which groups together surnames of the same or similar sounds but with variant spellings. To locate a particular surname, you must first find its Soundex code. The complete code chart is as follows:

Code	Key Letters and Equivalents
1	b,p,f,v
2	c,s,k,g,j,x,z,q
3	d,t
4	l
5	m,n
6	r

Note that the letters a,e,i,o,u,y,w, and h are not assigned Soundex code numbers.

In the Soundex system, a name is identified by a letter and three digits. The letter is the first letter of the surname, and the digits are determined by the chart above. When double letters or letters of equivalent sounds appear side by side in a name, they are coded only once, with a single number. A name with no Soundex numbers or with only one or two numbers is completed with zeros. Thus the name Eberhard would appear as E163 in the Soundex code, the name Lee as L000, the name Morse as M620, and the name Stanley as S354. A complete discussion of the Soundex system can be found in *Guide to Genealogical Research in the National Archives*, p.19.

The completeness of this index varies. For the 1880 census, Soundex entries include only those households containing a child age ten or under. The Soundex cards show the name, age, and birthplace of each member of such households, and there is a separate cross-reference card for each child age ten or under whose surname differs from that of the household head under whom he is listed. For the 1900 census, there is a complete Soundex index to all household heads with cross-reference cards for all persons with different surnames. For the 1910 census, there are microfilm Soundex indexes at the National Archives only for Alabama, Georgia, Louisiana, Mississippi, South Carolina, Tennessee, and Texas. Another indexing method, known as "miracode," has been used to develop indexes for Arkansas, California, Florida, Illinois, Kansas, Kentucky, Michigan, Missouri, North Carolina, Ohio, Oklahoma, Pennsylvania, Virginia, and West Virginia. There are no indexes for the remaining states and territories.

In addition to the indexes mentioned above, numerous state indexes have been published since the mid-1960s, especially for the 1800, 1810, 1820, 1830, 1840, and 1850 censuses. Accelerated Indexing Systems (AIS) of Bountiful, Utah, has published indexes of all extant federal censuses through 1850. (Plans to publish later indexes have been announced.) This series, unfortunately, is full of transcription mistakes. Nonetheless, we can find thousands of "lost" pioneer ancestors in it and infer many migration patterns. Some index series have been produced by other publishers as well.

Besides the AIS volumes, numerous privately published census indexes covering the period from 1800 through 1850 have appeared in the past two decades. Their accuracy is much higher than those produced by AIS. An extensive list of the best of these is found in appendix C.

City directories are also available for many cities and towns, especially in New England, the Mid-Atlantic states, and the Midwest. Most were published annually during the nineteenth century and are immensely helpful for identifying the towns or villages where your ancestors lived. City directories are arranged alphabetically by surname and contain each person's name, occupation, and street address. Since the federal census is alphabetized only by names of states and counties, city directories can save hours of searching. Once you know your ancestor's street address, simply scan the census schedules for the appropriate town until you reach the correct street. Only then must you read each name individually. When tracing ancestors who lived in very large cities, a search of city directories is even more essential. From street addresses, you can proceed to local ward and precinct maps and thus reduce the number of census pages you must examine entry by entry.

```
Feinberg Jacob, machinist, h. 2 Eaton pl. [53 Wall.
  "   Joseph, tinware and crockery, 58 Salem, h.
  "   Marks, peddler, h. 7 Margaret
Feinstein Morris, tailor, 39 Wall, h. 29 Pitts
Feiss Ferdinand, removed to New York city
Feist Otto, porter, h. 112 D
Feistkorn William E. student, bds. 72 Mt. Vernon
Feitel Franz H. clerk, 45 Hanover, bds. 3 Eden-
           st. ct.                        [st. ct.
  "   K. W. Mrs. magnetic physician, h. 3 Eden-
Felber Gustave A. salesman, 375 Wash.b.at Chelsea
  "   Mary Mrs. h. 4 Heath av.
  "   Otto, engraver, 3 Franklin, bds. 4 Heath av.
Felch Bros. shoe manufs. 121 Summer    [Natick
  "   C. H.  boots  and  shoes, 120  Summer, h. at
  "   Daniel, hostler, h. 1 Russell pl.
  "   Fred. R. lawyer, 5 Tremont, rm. 35, h. at
       Derry Depot, N.H.              [Myrtle
  "   George M. truant officer, 12 Beacon, h. 10
```

A section of a page from the 1891 Boston city directory. NEHGS

Special Data From Censuses

Beginning with the 1810 census, enumerators recorded socioeconomic data on what are called nonpopulation schedules. This data often concerned manufacturing, agriculture, or commerce, but also included military pensioners in 1840 and mortality schedules from 1850 through 1880. The names and ages of Revolutionary and other pre-1840 pensioners were published by the Department of State in *A Census of Pensioners for Revolutionary or Military Services; With their Names, Ages, Places of Residence . . . .* This work was reprinted by the Southern Book Company and by the Genealogical Publishing Company.

The mortality schedules for persons who died during the year before June 1 of the census years 1850, 1860, 1870, and 1880 included, among other data, name, age, sex, race, marital status, occupation, birthplace, and month and cause of death. The original mortality schedules were distributed to nonfederal repositories in 1918 and 1919, but in recent years the National Archives has acquired microfilm copies. You can find a chart showing which mortality schedules are available in *Guide to Genealogical Research in the National Archives,* pp. 14-16.

In addition to the decennial censuses since 1790, the federal government has also authorized several special censuses, most notably an 1885 head count in five states and territories — Colorado, Florida, Nebraska, New Mexico, and the Dakota territory. This census supplies the same

information as its 1880 federal predecessor, although in many cases enumerators listed only initials rather than full names.

Laws establishing states or territories usually provided for censuses also. These are especially useful for filling "gaps" in the decennial enu-

Young spinner in a cotton mill, 1910. The girl's age was uncertain when photographer Lewis Hine took this picture. Inaccuracies often crop up in the age category of old census records.

meration. For the location of these schedules, see *State Censuses: An Annotated Bibliography of Censuses of Population Taken after the Year 1790 by States and Territories of the United States*, compiled by Henry J. Dubester. A brief checklist of published state, special, and reconstructed censuses appears in appendix D.

Obtaining Census Records

As mentioned earlier, only censuses through 1910 are "open" to general research. To obtain information from open censuses, you must contact the National Archives in Washington, D.C. The National Archives will furnish duplicate copies of census pages from its 1790-1910 censuses, although its staff will not undertake research. To obtain a copy of a census page, give the state, county, enumeration district (for 1880, 1900, and 1910), volume number, and exact page on which a family is listed. No special form is required, but you should state this information clearly in a letter addressed to the National Archives, Washington DC 20408.

Microfilm copies of the federal census, which can be purchased from the National Archives, are widely distributed throughout the country, especially in its eleven regional branches, or National Archives and Records Centers. These branches (each of which has a copy of the entire series of 1790-1910 censuses microfilmed) are located in the following cities:

Boston, 380 Trapelo Road, Waltham, Ma 02154
  Serves Connecticut, Maine, Massachusetts, New Hampshire, Rhode Island, and Vermont.

New York, Building 22 — MOI Bayonne, Bayonne, NJ 07002
  Serves New York, New Jersey, Puerto Rico, and the Virgin Islands.

Philadelphia, 5000 Wissahickon Avenue, Philadelphia, PA 19144
  Serves Delaware, Pennsylvania, Maryland, Virginia, and West Virginia.

Atlanta, 1557 St. Joseph Avenue, East Point, GA 30344
  Serves Alabama, Georgia, Florida, Kentucky, Mississippi, North Carolina, South Carolina, and Tennessee.

Chicago, 7358 South Pulaski Road, Chicago, IL 60629
  Serves Illinois, Indiana, Michigan, Minnesota, Ohio, and Wisconsin.

Kansas City, 2306 East Bannister Road, Kansas City, MO 64131
Serves Iowa, Kansas, Missouri, and Nebraska.

Fort Worth, *(building address)* 4900 Hemphill Street,
(mailing address) P.O. Box 6216, Fort Worth, TX 76115
Serves Arkansas, Louisiana, New Mexico, Oklahoma, and Texas.

Denver, Building 48, Denver Federal Center, Denver, CO 80225
Serves Colorado, Montana, North Dakota, South Dakota, Utah, and Wyoming.

Los Angeles, 24000 Avila Road, Laguna Niguel, CA 92677
Serves Arizona, the southern California counties of Imperial, Inyo, Kern, Los Angeles, Orange, Riverside, San Bernadino, San Diego, San Luis Obispo, Santa Barbara, and Ventura; and Clark County, Nevada.

San Francisco, 1000 Commodore Drive, San Bruno, CA 94066
Serves Hawaii, Nevada (except Clark County), California (except the counties served by the Los Angeles branch), and American Samoa.

Seattle, 6125 Sand Point Way NE, Seattle, WA 98115
Serves Alaska, Idaho, Oregon, and Washington.

In addition to the eleven regional archives, various major libraries have also acquired all or most of the federal census microfilms. Complete sets are at the New York Public Library, the Miami Public Library, the Allen County Public Library in Fort Wayne, Indiana, and the Latter-day Saints Genealogical Society Library in Salt Lake City, among others. The Boston Public Library has 1790-1910 films for the six New England states, and the Houston Public Library has 1790-1880 films for the whole country. Even libraries in small towns often have complete 1790-1880 films for their counties.

In conclusion, we should emphasize that the census is at once an extremely valuable and frustrating document to use. Listing almost all American heads of household through 1840, and most individuals in the entire population thereafter, it includes millions of names and most of our nineteenth-century ancestors. But locating them is a challenge. Distinguishing among people of the same name; identifying the right state, county, and town; locating an index or combing hundreds of unindexed entries (in the 1860-1880 schedules especially); and reading many pages of nineteenth-century handwriting on microfilm all are problems you must overcome. Clearly, you should approach these records only when you know the name and at least the locale with some certainty. When you find ancestors in the census, however, the genealogical rewards are often great. Not only will you find lists of parents and children and their ages, but also clues about origins, wealth, and large family networks.

Census interview with a fruit and flower grower in Hawaii. National Archives

❧ *Pointers and Pitfalls* ❧

Using Census Records

1. Few records available to present-day researchers are as comprehensive, standardized, and informative as the federal census.

2. Although the first six censuses, from 1790 to 1840, identified only heads of households, they can fill many gaps in your research for the difficult period following the Revolution.

3. Starting in 1850 the census changed its focus from the family to the individual, making it a more valuable resource for genealogists.

4. In 1880, the census began stating the relationship of each household member to the head of household and listing the birthplace of the parents of each household member.

5. Caution: The 1880 census can cause confusion because it does not state the relationship of household members to the spouse of the household head. A wife much younger than her husband is often not the mother of all his children.

6. Some records from 1790 and most from 1890 have been lost, but more than 90 percent of all census records from 1790 to 1910 survive and are widely available. Census records are "closed" for seventy-two years except to immediate family members and legal heirs.

7. The chart in this chapter reveals what types of information are found in the censuses since 1790.

8. Individual names do not appear in alphabetical order in census records. Information is grouped by state and county.

9. Many indexes can make your use of census records easier.

10. City directories can help you locate information in census records more easily.

11. Several special censuses and special information on the regular censuses can provide valuable information, including data about mortality, military pensions, and residents of states newly admitted to the Union.

12. You can obtain census information from the National Archives, Washington, DC 20408. Be as specific as possible in your request.

13. Microfilm copies of the federal census, 1790-1910, can be found in National Archives branches and some public libraries. Many other public libraries have film covering their county, state, or region.

CHAPTER TEN

RESEARCHING THE RANK AND FILE

Military Records

164th Depot Brigade, Camp Funston, Kansas, 1918–19. National Archives

World War I troops relaxing in a club opened by a group of civilian women. Military records can sometimes help you fill gaps in your research for the period from 1775 to 1875. National Archives

ilitary records provide another resource to help us close the major "gap" in American genealogy — the century or so between the Colonial era, with its relatively abundant and well-preserved primary and secondary sources, and the time, about 1875, when the living memory of our families begins to fail. Like the census, military records are federal records and are therefore frequently more uniform and reliable than local records. Often more than one copy of a federal record was made, and many documents were deposited in Washington, D.C.

But federal records pose enormous problems of another kind for the researcher: they frequently lack adequate indexes and finding aids. Recognizing this problem, many genealogical scholars during the past twenty-five years have devoted much time to creating useful guides and indexes for federal data. Their efforts are detailed in the comprehensive *Guide to Genealogical Research in the National Archives.* Fortunately, some of the most genealogically valuable of the nation's military records are also now well indexed and can readily be examined. Such access may prove a boon to your research. Military records often supply the major information that identifies an elusive pioneer ancestor from the "gap" period of 1775 to 1875 — the "century of lost ancestors."

Created in large part by the wars and conflicts of the past three centuries — although peacetime records are included as well — the nation's military archives are massive. In addition to five Colonial wars, the American people have engaged in six international wars, several Indian wars, one civil war, and two "conflicts": the American Revolution, 1775-1783; War of 1812, 1812-1814; Indian Wars, 1817-1858; Mexican War, 1846-1848; Civil War, 1861-1865; Spanish American War, 1898; World War I, 1917-1918; World War II, 1941-1945; Korean Action, 1950-1953; and Vietnam Action, 1961-1975. We have gone to war almost as regularly as we have taken the census. While this frequently produced misery for our ancestors, it provides us with the means — muster rolls and pension records — to learn much more about them.

Military records, especially for the National period, divide into two basic types: those that provide evidence of military service and those that provide evidence of veterans' benefits. In the first category will be found a great diversity of documents, from muster rolls to correspondence to prisoner-of-war records.

As noted in *Guide to Genealogical Research in the National Archives*, "to use the service records, the researcher must know when and where in the armed forces his ancestor served and whether he was an officer or an enlisted man." There are no comprehensive name indexes. Unfortunately, this is asking most of us to put the cart before the horse. We are hoping that the military records will tell us when and where our ancestor served, not vice versa. One solution to this dilemma may be found in the pension and bounty land application files (see chapter 8), the second category of military records. The pension and bounty land files, which number in the millions, are arranged alphabetically by surname of veteran. Because a veteran or his wife or heirs must "prove" military service to be eligible for either pension or land, these files usually indicate when and where the veteran served. With this information from the pension files, you can then easily retrieve your ancestor's service records. Saving the best for last, we will focus first on service records and then examine the pension application files.

Service Records

Service records were generated in massive amounts throughout the nation's history. Military records from Colonial wars (including King Philip's War, 1675-1676; King William's War, 1689-1697; Queen Anne's War, 1702-1713; King George's War, 1744-1748; and the French and Indian War, 1754-1763) are found at the local and state level, not at the National Archives. Most are deposited in the various state archives of the original thirteen colonies. Look also for material among private papers. In Massachusetts, for example, many of the original muster rolls pertaining to King Philip's War are in the Hull Papers at the New England Historic Genealogical Society. Also note that many military records of the Colonial era are published. The muster rolls of King Philip's War appear in George M. Bodge's *Soldiers in King Philip's War*. Service records since 1775 are so massive and complex that you should consult the *Guide to Genealogical Research in the National Archives* (especially chapters 4-6) for a detailed description of each type of record and its availability.

We will focus on one collection that is indexed by veterans' surnames, the compiled military service records of the volunteer (nonregular) military units. Beginning with the Revolution, men were conscripted to serve in "volunteer" units when there were not enough enlistments in the regular army and militia. Such "volunteers" served in all the wars and disputes of the nineteenth century, as well as the Philippine Insurrection of 1898-1903.

Some years after the Civil War, the War Department began to compile information on each "volunteer" soldier from earlier wars, abstracting data from muster and payrolls, rank rolls, hospital records, prison records, and more. *Guide to Genealogical Research in the National Archives* states that the "card abstracts from each individual soldier were placed into a jacket-envelope bearing the soldier's name, rank, and military unit. The jacket-envelope, containing one or more abstracts and, in some instances, including one or more original documents relating specifically to one soldier, is called a compiled military service record."

Most important for the genealogist are consolidated indexes to the compiled military service records for each war and dispute except the Civil War. The War Department has prepared compiled service records and a consolidated index for Confederate officers, Confederate noncommissioned officers, and Confederate enlisted men, but there is no index to records for Union army volunteers. To locate the compiled service record of a Union army soldier, "the researcher must determine the name

Civil War troops. The National Archives maintains military records for every conflict from the American Revolution through the Vietnam War. National Archives

of the unit in which he served . . . . Separate indexes are available for each state and territory except South Carolina, which furnished no white troops to the Union Army." The compiled military service records and the consolidated indexes are available on microfilm at the National Archives and its regional branches.

There are no compiled service records or consolidated surname indexes for the regular army units and for other branches of the military, such as the navy and marine corps. Over the years, however, many specialized indexes have been prepared. They are described in *Guide to Genealogical Research in the National Archives*. Any military record created during the past seventy-five years is restricted by the Freedom of Information Act of 1967 (as amended in 1974) and the Privacy Act of 1974. The written consent of the veteran, or his next of kin if he is deceased, is necessary to obtain information of a "personal nature" from such a restricted record.

In 1973 a fire at the National Personnel Records Center in St. Louis destroyed most of the army records from 1912 to 1959 and more than half of the air force records from 1947 to 1963. This was the third major fire to affect the nation's military records. In 1800 and 1814 fires destroyed Revolutionary service records and numerous pension application files. Much work has been done to reconstruct information that was lost in these fires.

Muster Rolls

Of all service records, muster rolls often have the most value genea-logically. What is a muster roll? *Guide to Genealogical Research in the National Archives* calls it "a list of all troops actually present on parade or otherwise accounted for on the day of muster or review of troops under arms . . . . It was also the voucher from which the paymaster issued the pay. The several types include descriptive rolls, muster-in rolls, the regular pay rolls . . . ."

Muster rolls are genealogically valuable because of the personal information they often contain. It is not unusual to find a veteran's personal description, residence, and occupation in these records. Descriptive Rolls especially are likely to record such data. In *Massachusetts Soldiers and Sailors of the American Revolution* (vol. 8, pp. 45-50), for example, we find this entry for Francis Hale of Sandisfield, Massachusetts, abstracted from a descriptive roll dated August 20, 1781: "age, 24 years, stature, 5ft 8in; complexion, dark; hair, black; occupation, laborer; residence, Sandisfield."

Such detailed information allows us to pursue Francis Hale in other sources. A brief check of the *DAR Patriot Index*, vol. 1, reveals a Francis Hale "b. 3-4-1759 d. 1-28-1834 m. Olive Harrison Pvt MA." Now we know his wife's name. Next we look for a published genealogy of the Hale family in hopes that one will show a Francis Hale married to an Olive Harrison. Voila! In *Hale, House and Related Families* by Donald Lines Jacobus and Edgar Francis Waterman, the index lists an Olive Harrison on pages 145-147. Turning to these pages, we find a description of Francis Hale (born on March 4, 1757, *not* 1759) that includes many details about his parents, marriage, children, and occupation. The search will not always end as successfully. Rather than lead to a splendid gene-alogy such as *Hale-House* (one of the classics in the field), the hunt may take us to city directories, newspaper obituaries, or unpublished vital, court, or land records. Still, remember the fundamental point: a muster often includes enough data to start the search.

Pension Records

Like service records, pension and bounty land application files date from Colonial America, when governors and legislatures awarded pensions and offered land as an inducement to enlist. In the National period there have been three types of pensions: disability or invalid pensions (awarded for physical disabilities incurred in the line of duty), service pensions (awarded for serving specified periods of time), and widows' pensions, given to women and children whose husbands or fathers served or were killed in war.

Pensions were created by public and private acts of Congress. Several public acts passed between 1776 and 1853 created pensions for Revolutionary War veterans and their families. Private acts involved individuals who could not qualify for a pension under public law. Generally speaking, as time passed it became easier for veterans or their families to qualify. The first pension act in 1776 included only veterans who had been disabled. Later pensions were offered on the basis of specific periods of service. In 1832 Congress extended eligibility to Revolutionary War veterans (no matter how short their service) and their families. Subsequent legislation made it easier for widows to obtain pensions. Finally, in 1853, in its final legislation affecting Revolutionary War pensions, Congress declared that any woman who had been married to a Revolutionary War veteran was eligible for a pension, regardless of when the marriage occurred.

Why are pension application files so highly valued by genealogists? First, unlike service records, which focus largely on a veteran's life in the military, pension files often cover much of his later history. To obtain a pension, a veteran had to "prove" that he served in the military (and that he was impoverished, if his claim was based on need). Such proof often included evidence of name, rank, military unit, period of service, residence, birthplace, date of birth or age, postwar migration, and property owned (when the claim was based on need). Thus veterans' files will often have notarized statements from friends and neighbors, officials of the town, or members of their former military company, as well as deeds and other records — any kind of document the veteran thought would help his cause in Washington.

As time passed, pension applications became more interesting genealogically. By 1832, when Congress greatly liberalized the law governing pensions to veterans and their dependents, those veterans who were still alive (the great majority had died) had moved numerous times, and some had lost the vital documents that would prove their service in the Revolution. Many later files include wonderfully detailed accounts of what happened to veterans and their families after the war.

Widows' pension applications are frequently more useful genealogically than those of veterans. Besides including the data about her husband that you ordinarily find in a veteran's file, a widow's file contains her name, age, residence, maiden surname, marriage date and place, and her late husband's death date and place, as well as supporting documents such as Bible records and marriage certificates. Additionally, when children or heirs filed for their portion of a veteran's or widow's pension, they included documents that established the identities of both their father and mother, as well as the dates and places of their births, residences, and the date of their mother's death.

As was mentioned earlier, the pension application files are indexed and available on microfilm. *Index of Revolutionary War Pension Applications in the National Archives*, National Genealogical Society Special Publication 40, rev. ed., was a bicentennial publication of the National Genealogical Society. For each veteran included, it lists name, the state from which he served (except for service in the naval forces), the names of other persons filing for a pension under his name (a widow or children), and the pension application file numbers and bounty land warrant if appropriate. Symbols after the names indicate what kind of application was filed — S ("survivor was issued a pension"); W (widow's pension); BLWT (Bounty Land Warrant claim, see chapter 8); R (application rejected).

A final reminder: don't overlook rejected applications. Often these are the most useful genealogically because over the years the veteran or his widow or children continued to submit supporting documents in hopes that the government would act favorably. Also worth noting is the splendid series *Revolutionary War Period Bible, Family, and Marriage Records Gleaned from Pension Applications*, begun in 1980 by Helen M. Lu and Gwen B. Newmann of Dallas. They are proceeding through the alphabet slowly, for these pension-support documents are voluminous. When completed, this series will be a major addition to Revolutionary and pioneer genealogy.

A soldier's portrait, taken by the renowned photographer Mathew Brady. Yankee

Two Examples of Rejected Pension Applications

Let's examine two specific cases of pension applications. The first is taken from the Revolutionary War file (No. R2815) of John Dearborn of Scarborough, Maine. He petitioned for a pension in March 1818, but was rejected on the basis of desertion. The rejection is explained in a letter found in the file from the War Department to Stephen Longfellow of Portland, Maine, dated December 15, 1832. (It was not unusual for veterans to press their cases over many years, which could explain the fourteen-year gap between John Dearborn's original petition and the response quoted here.) The letter states that "on examination . . . it appears that John Dearborn, whose declaration was forwarded by you, enlisted, as he stated, into Captain Lane's Company; and deserted from the service. He is, therefore, not entitled to the provisions of the pension law, and his claim is rejected."

More than twenty years later, in 1853, Dearborn's heirs tried unsuccessfully to have the rejection overturned so that they could claim his pension. Moses Emery, a justice of the peace for York County, Maine, prepared the following affidavit listing the heirs:

Be it known that on this . . . day of November A.D. 1852, before me the undersigned, a justice of the Peace in and for the County and State aforesaid, personally appeared Dorcas Patterson, William H. Dearborn, Mary Jane Edgecomb, and Hannah L. Dearborn all residents of Saco in the said County, and Almira Lord a resident of Portland and Hannah Lunt a resident of Scarborough both in the County of Cumberland in said State, and made oath according to law that they are the legal heirs of the identical John Dearborn late of Scarborough in said state deceased, intestate, who was a soldier in the war of the Revolution, and who heretofore made application for the benefit of the Pension Act of the 18th of March 1818. That they are directly interested as claimants in said pension, and make this application affidavit to be filed with such additional evidence or arguments as own said agents or their substitutes may use in prosecuting said claim . . . .

A subsequent letter from S.V. Loring to the commissioner of pensions reveals the circumstances surrounding Dearborn's "desertion":

Saco, March 24, 1853.
To the Commissioner of Pensions:

Sir:

Having sometime since sent to the Pension office the required power of attorney, and affidavits of the children of John Dearborn, I now transmit to you a number of affidavits in support of his claim to a pension.

It will appear by the Rolls at Washington and by these affidavits that John Dearborn enlisted in the army of the Revolution April 1777, for three years, served out his time and was honorably discharged in April 1780, then enlisted for "during the war," got wounded, was assigned to the Invalid Regiment, and, there being little hope of his recovery in the camp, received a furlough to come home in September 1780 — that he did not get well enough to return to the army, but became a cripple for life — that he applied for a pension under the Act of 18th March 1818, and was informed that he deserted in December 1780.

John Dearborn was too poor and too much broken to make any attempt to have that entry corrected or counteracted, and his claim has lingered along without there being any one to prosecute it, till the present time, when his grand children have come forward to assist.

Besides the direct testimony in the affidavits, that Dearborn did not desert, you will find much indirect evidence. He could have no motive to desert at that time. He came home in company with a lieutenant in Carlton's regiment. His companions in the army from Scarborough all denied that he deserted. Dearborn practiced no concealment while at home, but wore his military dress and associated with those from the army on leave of absence.

Military gentlemen tell me, that if Dearborn did not return when his furlough expired, his officers would be likely to set him down as a deserter on the rolls, unless informed, that he was unable to return to action — but that they always correct such entry upon reason shown. The affidavit shows the reason. It will appear probable that Dearborn was told by his Captain not to return, till he got well enough to do duty, and that he had reason to believe that his officers had notice of state of his health by men going from Scarborough to the army and that they acquiesced in his continued absence.

The entry of December 1780 is attributed to a failure to receive notice of his inability to return, or else to a misapprehension on Dearborn's part or on the part of the officers as to which regiment he belonged, after he was wounded. That Dearborn supposed he had a right to do as he did, is believed to be perfectly certain.

Respectfully your
Obed. Serv't

S.V. Loring

Dearborn's file reveals both the historical and genealogical value of pension records. The letter by S.V. Loring tells us much about Dearborn's personal situation — that he was "too poor and too much broken" to have the desertion entry corrected. A check of Cumberland County land records — in which there is not a single entry for a John Dearborn — is further proof of his poverty. Loring's letter also refers to Dearborn's heirs (which, as you will recall, were listed by name in the document prepared by Moses Emery) as his "grand children." Together these documents provide essential facts about Dearborn himself and several members of his family. With this data in hand, we were able to find other records proving that Dorcas Patterson was actually Dearborn's daughter, while the others mentioned — William H. Dearborn, Mary Jane Edgecomb, Hannah L. Dearborn, Almira Lord, and Hannah Lunt — were indeed his grandchildren.

By the Civil War, military and pension records had become more complete, more voluminous, and more revealing. If you suspect that an ancestor served in the Civil War, first try to verify his service. In many cases, the gravestones of Civil War veterans indicate the company and regiment in which they served. A newspaper obituary notice or a "mug-book" sketch may give either vague or exact references to military service. Perhaps old letters, a diary, or a photograph of a soldier in uniform have survived in your family.

Our second example of a rejected pension involves Ezra Lyman Dearborn and Lucy Ann Bacon, both residents of Stanstead, Lower Canada (Quebec). They were married at Derby, Vermont, on September

14, 1841. To them were born three children: Frederick W., Susan Emeline (died young), and Ezra Lyman Jr. (or Lyman E). In the late 1840s the family moved to Rhode Island. By 1850 Ezra and Lucy had separated, for in the 1850 census we find Ezra boarding in a household in Scituate, Rhode Island, while Lucy and the two boys were living in Smithfield with Jonathan Buxton (Lucy is called Lucy Buxton). By 1855 Ezra was remarried, had another family, and was living in Springfield, Massachusetts, where he spent the remainder of his life. Although Lucy was later to claim in her application for a pension that she and Ezra had separated in 1858 or 1859, the above evidence shows that their parting occurred about ten years earlier. By the time of the Civil War, Lucy had moved to Barnston, Quebec, and was living with Guy Davis, ostensibly as his housekeeper.

Meanwhile, on October 29, 1861, in Ellsworth, Maine, young Lyman enlisted at the age of eighteen in Company C, 11th Regiment, Maine Volunteer Infantry. On December 26, 1861, he died of typhoid pneumonia in a Washington, D.C., military hospital. Upon receiving this news, his brother Frederick deserted from his own regiment (Company C, 2nd Regiment, New Hampshire Volunteer Infantry) and returned to Barnston, Quebec. In April 1862 Lucy applied for her deceased son's back pay and bounty under the name Lucy D. Buxton and again in January 1864 under the name Lucy B. Davis. In 1889 (File No. 410888) Lucy Dearborn petitioned for a pension as the dependent mother of her younger son, Lyman Dearborn. Her file not only reveals many of the above genealogical facts, but also tells a pathetic story. Because her account is self-

serving, full of half-truths and outright lies, we must weigh her statements against known facts. Lucy tried to prove that she had not remarried and that she was dependent on her late son Ezra at the time of his death, even though he had not lived with her for several years

Civil War soldiers. Pension records and applications — as well as actual service records — contribute to the body of military records. National Archives

prior to the Civil War. Federal officials interviewed Lucy and her son, Frederick, as well as numerous neighbors and acquaintances in Canada, Massachusetts, and at Dillon, Montana, where Lucy and Frederick later lived. Probably the most interesting of the depositions is one that Lucy Dearborn made before special examiner J.H. Anthony in 1901. Portions of the deposition follow.

Case of: Lucy Dearborn No. 410888

On this 26 day of July, 1901, at Dillon, County of Beaverhead, State of Montana, before me, J.H. Anthony a special examiner of the Bureau of Pensions, personally appeared Mrs. Lucy Dearborn who, being by me first duly sworn to answer truly all interrogations propounded to her during this special examination of aforesaid claim for pension, deposes and says:

I am 78 years of age; my post-office address is Dillon, Beaverhead Co., Mont. I was born in 1824. I am the applicant for pension as the mother of Lyman E. Dearborn who served in the 11th Regiment of Infantry and died while in the service at hospital at Washington D.C. I think it was Co. B he was in but I forget for certain. I think he was named Lyman Ezra Dearborn. His father's name was Ezra Dearborn, I was married to said Ezra Dearborn at Derby Line, Vt. I don't remember the date. I was 18 years old and I was born in 1824. I had three children by that marriage, Frederick, Lyman, and Susan Emeline. Lyman was born in the town of Stanstead, Canada. June the 5th I think. I dont remember the date. I think he was about 3 years younger than Frederick (Frederick present says he was born in 1842). Lyman lived at home with me until he was about 13 or 14 years old, and then he went off in the States somewhere and was there until he enlisted in the army.

Q. Did you see him or hear from him from the time he left home until you heard of his death in the army?

A. I don't think I did.

Q. Do you know where or with whom he had lived from the time he went away until he enlisted?

A. No — He went from place to place I suppose.

Q. Could he write?

A. Yes.

Q. He did not write to you?

A. No.

Q. Did he ever send you any money?

A. No.

Q. Then he had not contributed anything to your support after he was 13 or 14 years old?

A. No. But I had calculated that he would be my main support when he got back.

Q. At the time he went away where and how were you living?

A. I was living at Barnston, Canada. About 10 miles from Stanstead.

Q. Was his father Ezra Dearborn living with you when Lyman went away?

A. No.

Q. What had become of him?

A. I don't know.

● ● ●

Q. Who were you living with at the time Lyman left home?

A. I was keeping house.

Q. Who for?

A. I was keeping house for myself then. Just living alone.

Q. No one living with you at all?

A. No.

Q. What became of Ezra Dearborn?

A. Oh he went off and left me and died I heard by the boy.

Q. Where were you living when he left?

A. In the town of Barnston, Canada.

Q. How long had he been gone when Lyman went away?

A. Some time. I don't know how long, two or three years maybe.

Q. How old was Lyman when his father left?

A. I don't know.

Q. Was he 10 years old?

A. I guess so.

Q. Did Ezra Dearborn leave you or did you leave him or refuse to live with him?

A. Why he left me.

•••

Q. Had you lived in Canada all the time from the time you were married to him until he left?

A. Yes.

Q. When did you go to Rhode Island?

A. Oh. I don't remember. It has been a good many years ago.

Q. Where did you live in Rhode Island?

A. At Woonsocket Falls. Don't remember how long I was there.

Q. Five years?

A. Yes I guess so.

•••

Q. Now as a matter of fact were you not living there or Rhode Island when you separated from Mr. Dearborn?

A. No, it was after Mr. Dearborn left me that I went to Rhode Island. I had to go to work. I was in other places besides Woonsocket Falls. I worked in mills around there. At Blackstone one place and Slatersville I guess.

Q. Was it after Lyman left that you went to Rhode Island?

A. Yes.

Q. Then you had no family there at all?

A. No.

Q. Now as a matter of fact were you not divorced from Ezra Dearborn?

A. No.

Q. Are you sure of that?

A. Well long years after that I got a divorce.

Q. Where was it obtained?

A. In Rhode Island. I don't know what County. I think I was living at Slatersville. I don't know what year it was.

Q. Did you make the application for divorce or did he?

A. I did of course. He was gone long many years.

•••

Q. Now was that before or after Lyman's death in the army?

A. It was after — No I don't know. I guess it was before. I can't remember.

Q. Where did you first meet Jonathan Buxton?

A. In Rhode Island.

Q. When and where were you married to him?

A. I wasn't married. I kept house for him.

Q. You went with him from Rhode Island to Stanstead didn't you?

A. Yes.

Q. How long did you live with him?

A. I think I kept house for him six or seven years — five or six years.

Q. Did you have any children by him?

A. No.

Q. Now do you swear positively remembering that you are on oath that you were never married to Jonathan Buxton by any sort of ceremony or agreement?

A. I say positively that I was not.

•••

Q. Were you living with Buxton when you received news of Lyman's death?

A. No.

Q. Are you sure?

A. I know I wasn't.

Q. Did you not in April 1862 after you had heard of Lyman's death go over to Derby in Vermont and make an application for his bounty and back pay before Geo D. Wyman a Notary Public.

A. Yes. I think so.

Q. What name did you sign to it?

A. I can't remember.

Q. That application was signed Lucy Dearborn Buxton. Now were you not living with Buxton at that time?

A. I don't remember.

Q. Now in that application you stated that you had married Jonathan Buxton. That was sworn to. Now was that true?

A. No, I was never married to him. Folks called me Mrs. Buxton, but I was never married to him and I suppose I was kind of out of my mind a little and signed my name that way.

Q. On what terms did you keep house for him?

A. A dollar a week. I bought my own clothes.

Q. Did he actually pay you the wages or did you just live with him and was supported by him without any accounts being kept the same as a wife would be?

A. No he just paid me by the week a dollar a week.

Q. How were you living at the time of Lyman's death in Dec. 1861?

A. I was keeping house for Alpheus Kimpton at Stanstead. I don't know how long I kept house for him. It was on the same terms as before. A dollar a week. I think I was still keeping house for him when I made that application for bounty at Derby. I was never called Mrs. Kimpton. Never went by his name. His wife was dead. Had two boys who were away for themselves. I did not live with him in the relation of wife.

•••

Q. After you quit keeping house for Buxton was Mr. Kimpton the next one you kept house for?

A. I think so.

Q. And was Mr. Davis the next?

A. Yes. I can't see what is the need of all this.

Q. When and where were you married to Mr. Davis?

A. I never was married to him.

Q. Are you sure of that?

A. Yes I am sure of that.

Q. Were you not married to him, Guy Davis, by Proctor Moulton of the Free Will Baptist Church near Barnston and in the presence of Joseph Walker and a Mr. Thomas or either of them?

A. No.

• • •

Q. In your second application for bounty and back pay made in January 1864 you state in said sworn application that you had married since your former application and signed your name Lucy B. Davis. Why did you make that statement if it was not true?

A. Oh — I don't know. There were times when I was out of my mind and I hardly knew what I was saying.

Q. Who did you keep house for after Davis?

A. I don't know. Not anybody. Went to my brother's I guess.

Q. Have you kept house for anybody else since?

A. No.

• • •

Q. At the time of Lyman's death in December 1861 were you not being supported by Mr. Buxton or by Mr. Kimpton or by someone else in the same way that most men in their condition in life support their wives?

A. No — I wasn't. I was working at that time for Mr. Kimpton for one dollar a week, and he was not supporting me in any other way.

Q. Do you thoroughly understand and comprehend the questions asked you and have your answers been correctly recorded in this deposition?

A. I have tried to and it is all right — so far as I know.

(signed) Lucy Dearbon

The next day, special examiner Anthony filed his own report offering his opinion on the truthfulness of Lucy's statements.

Department of the Interior
Bureau of Pensions
Washington, D.C.
Butte, Mont
July 27, 1901
Hon. H. Clay Evans,
Commissioner of Pensions
Washington, DC

Sir:

I have the honor to return all papers, and to submit my report in the case Orig. No. 410888 of Lucy Dearborn, of Dillon, Beaverhead Co., Mont., who claims pension as the dependent mother of Lyman E. Dearborn, alias Durbin late of Co. C, 11 Me. Inf.

This case was referred for special examination to determine whether the claimant has legally remarried since the death of the soldier, identity of the soldier as claimant's son, celibacy, and dependence. The claimant's statement was taken subsequently by Special Examiner J. McD. Stewart. Witnesses testified that she had remarried two times at least, and the case was returned to this district for an additional statement from the claimant in the light of the new evidence procured.

I did not give the claimant any additional notice, but submit her deposition and that of her son, in which it will be seen that while she at first denied having obtained a divorce from the father of the soldier, she afterward admitted that she had done so, but she adheres to her statement that there was no marriage of any kind between herself and either of the persons mentioned or to any other person.

She also denies that she was being supported by a paramour at the date of the soldier's death, but brings in the name of another man for whom she says she was "keeping house" for one dollar per week.

The condition and surroundings of the claimant and her son, and the groans and grunting of the claimant are just as described by Special Examiner Randall but I should rate both as doubtful for truth, and that is their standing in the community. The people smile when asked as to their reputation for truth.

Besides, I do not think any dependence can be placed in anything they say in regard to where and how they have lived. I am inclined to believe, from the circumstances, and the application that was filed for the soldier's pay and bounty, that she was the mother of the soldier, but any statement that she was in any manner dependent on him for support is purely a fiction of law, if he had not yet reached his majority, for she says she had not seen nor heard from him from the time he was 13 or 14 years old, until she heard of his death. She will fix no time when she last saw him, and I believe if the facts were known he was with her but very little after she was divorced from his father, whenever that was.

The son, Frederick W. Dearborn, who seems to have been the one who informed the claimant of the service and death of this soldier, says he served in Co. C, 2N.H. Inf., and was given a "death furlough" at the time he heard of the serious illness of his brother Lyman, and went to see him, but found that Lyman was dead, and that he never returned to the company. Of course he deserted, but if a history of his service should be obtained it might be some corroboration of his statement if the record should show that he was granted a furlough, or deserted at about the time of the soldier's death.

Of course it may be possible that the claimant tells the truth when she says she was never married to either of these men. It would be not at all unlikely that they simply lived together, and from the character of the persons, I think it perhaps the more probable, and this seems to be a case of probabilities, and little of certainty.

I recommend further examination for testimony of Joseph Walker Boston, Mass., if he can be located, who is said by Mrs. Lydia Jane Davis (p. 13, Spl. Exr. Stewart's report) to be her brother, and to have said he had seen claimant married to Guy Davis, and who is said to have a store and summer house at Asbury Grove, about 30 miles from Boston.

The claimant professes to be unable to state where or when, even approximately, she was divorced from Ezra Dearborn, and denies positively that she married Jonathan Buxton, but admits that she went from Rhode Island back to Canada with him. Her brother, Orrin W. Bacon testified that she was divorced from Ezra Dearborn at Pawtucket, R.I., and that she was married to Buxton near there, or at Providence or Woonsocket, and the claimant also mentions Slatersville, and Blackstone as places in which she lived in Rhode Island, and I recommend further examination also for a search of the divorce and marriage records of the respective counties in which said places are situated to determine whether a record of such divorce or marriage can be found.

As claimant is shown to have been known as Mrs. Buxton at the time she filed the first application for pay and bounty in April 1862, the search need not be continued subsequent to that date.

Very respectfully,

These two documents in Lucy Dearborn's pension application file tell us much about her family and personal fortunes. As noted, the "facts" she relates are self-serving and confused. Nonetheless, her file contains a mass of personal data not available in any other source. She and her children come alive in these documents.

Bounty Land Applications

Federal land given to American soldiers as a reward for military service is discussed more fully in chapter 8 (on land records). We should note here, however, that pension files and bounty land applications are maintained together at the National Archives, for both the veteran or his widow and dependents submitted affidavits and documents to prove eligibility. Indexes for the two, also combined, are arranged alphabetically by veteran.

The examples presented in this chapter demonstrate the usefulness of military records in genealogical research. Many documents, especially in the pension files, amount to nineteenth-century oral interviews taken under oath. These oral histories can help us retrace the lives of our Revolutionary War and nineteenth-century ancestors.

❦ *Pointers and Pitfalls* ❦
Military Records

1. Military records provide another resource to help you close the "gap" in American genealogy — the century between the Revolution and the late nineteenth century.

2. As federal records, military records are frequently more uniform and reliable than local records.

3. Although finding aids for federal records are meager, some of the most genealogically valuable military records have been well indexed.

4. The *Guide to Genealogical Research in the National Archives* will introduce you to military records and their indexes.

5. There are two basic types of military records: those that provide evidence of military service (service records) and those that provide evidence of veterans' benefits (pension and bounty records).

6. To use service records, you must know when and where your ancestor served and whether as an enlisted man or an officer. There is no comprehensive index for service records.

7. The files for pension and bounty records are arranged alphabetically by surname of veteran. They often contain information you need to use service records.

8. Most Colonial service records are filed in the state archives of the original thirteen colonies. Some are found among papers in private institutions.

9. Consolidated indexes exist for military service records of army "volunteers" from each war and conflict except the Civil War.

10. Reminder: For regular army units and for other branches of the military (the navy and marine corps), there are no compiled service records or consolidated indexes.

11. Any service record created during the past seventy-five years is restricted. You will need written consent from the veteran or his or her next of kin to gain access.

12. Muster rolls are valuable because they often contain personal information such as soldiers' physical descriptions, residences, and occupations.

13. Pension application files are highly valued because they focus on a veteran's life after he left the service and may contain various materials intended to prove his service.

14. Widows' pension applications are sometimes even more valuable because they contain information about the veteran and his widow and/or children.

15. Pension files and indexes are combined with those for bounty applications.

16. More on bounty land applications can be found in chapter 8.

CHAPTER ELEVEN

OLD WORLD, NEW WORLD

Immigrant Ancestors and American Origins

A first generation Italian immigrant family, 1919. Fran Frasca

Japanese immigrants at California's Angel Island, a major receiving station for Asian immigrants. National Archives

Immigrant ancestors link us to another country and culture. The founders of our families in America, and in some cases the ancestors from whom we receive our surnames as well, are often our most elusive forebears. And we are very curious about them. We want to know who they were. When and where were they born? Where did they live in the "Old World"? When did they come to America? Whom did they marry? When and where did they die? In addition to this basic genealogical data, we are eager to discover the circumstances surrounding their immigration. Were they fleeing war or persecution? Were they running from starvation? Did they come as slaves or indentured servants? Were they attracted to the New World by a sense of adventure or the alluring promotions of railroad and land companies offering land and promising instant prosperity?

Whatever motivated them, Europeans, Asians, and Africans came to America in astonishing numbers, beginning with early seventeenth-century Spanish and English settlements in Florida and Virginia and culminating in the massive flood of people from eastern Europe in the decades around 1900. Altogether some fifty million people (not counting the American Indian) immigrated to America. The peak year, exactly three hundred years after the settlement at Jamestown, was 1907, when the nation accepted 1,285,349 new inhabitants. Our challenge is to identify among this great flood of people the handful (if recent) or several hundred (if seventeenth century) individuals and couples who began our own particular family lines.

The search for immigrant ancestors will employ many of the methods and sources that have proved helpful in tracing other generations. Like the native-born American, the immigrant leaves behind a trail of documents through which his personal history can be traced. Also, as is the case with American-born ancestors, parts or all of the trail have sometimes been destroyed. But what is distinctive about the immigrant is that his history begins outside the United States. To discover much about his early life, you may have to learn a foreign language and become familiar with local records in the country where your family originated.

In addition, our immigrant ancestors were often recorded while in transit from the Old World to the New. Information about them was sometimes noted by captains of ships on which they took passage to America and by customs officials as they entered the United States. We shall discover, too, that our immigrant forebears are noted in some rather unusual places, such as a published list of indentured servants or a missing persons column in a foreign-language newspaper.

Following the basic method of all genealogical inquiry, you should proceed in the search for your immigrant ancestors from the known to the unknown. First, be quite sure that your earliest known ancestor in any given line was indeed an immigrant — not the son, grandson, or great-grandson of an earlier settler. Second, exhaust all family and American sources before consulting foreign records. Unless you have an exact place of origin (town or parish, county or province, and country), using foreign records can be immensely frustrating.

Let's imagine, for example, that you descend from a Patrick Stewart who came to America from Scotland in the 1800s. You know only a name, a country, and a century. There may well have been hundreds of Patrick Stewarts living in Scotland in the nineteenth century; Stewart is a common Scottish surname, and middle names were not common at that time.

Scottish immigrant in native garb. Some families adopted "American" names after their arrival in this country, making it more difficult to trace their lineage. Clarissa Silitch

Tracking most of these names would take years of effort, and you still might not find or be able to identify *your* Patrick Stewart with certainty. Clearly you must be able to narrow the focus of your search — either to a specific locality and/or to a certain fairly narrow time period — to use foreign records successfully.

You may have better luck if your ancestor had an unusual name. Mark Wray of Brooklyn, New York, immigrated to New York City about 1850, where he thereafter practiced the trade of auctioneer. He died in Brooklyn on April 20, 1890, age seventy years, seven months, twenty-two days, which allows us to calculate a probable birthdate of August 29, 1819. Although it does give us his exact age, Mark's death certificate does not name his parents and states only that he was born in England. Research into published accounts of the surname of Wray in England show that the family is clustered mainly around Lincolnshire. An examination of the Mormon *IGI* (*International Genealogical Index*) for Lincolnshire reveals that a Mark Wray was baptized at Burton-upon-Stather on August 29, 1819, son of William and Hannah Wray. The marriage record of William and Hannah, in the same parish, shows that her maiden name was Pickersgill. It is no coincidence that Mark Wray named his first son Mark Pickersgill Wray.

The remainder of this chapter will list and discuss American sources likely to yield clues or specific information about immigrant ancestors, especially their exact addresses or birthplaces in the Old World. Research in Europe, the Old World home of most of our families, American Indian and black genealogy, and Colonial origin studies are all subjects requiring entire books, not single chapters. We shall attempt no general coverage of them here, but various pertinent sources and related topics are discussed in chapter 5 (on church records) and appendix B (on genealogical compendia). The archival depositories listed at the chapter's end can direct you to many other sources.

Starting with Family Memory

Several types of American sources, beginning with the family memory of your kinsmen, can help you trace immigrant ancestors. Just as genealogical investigations generally should begin with oral and written sources within your own family, so too should research on immigrant ancestors, especially if they came to this country after 1800. Someone in your family may have saved a diary or bundles of letters that document the move from the Old World to the New. When interviewing relatives, be sure to ask specific questions concerning the migration itself. What was the port of entry, the name of the ship, and the family's original surname if it was changed? Try especially to determine the town or province where the family resided in the Old World. Ask such questions of as many relatives as possible. Family memory often lasts much longer in some branches than in others, so although your close relatives may have forgotten the Old World origin of a great-great-grandfather, a third cousin may know it. Recovering surname changes is crucial, for only the original name will appear in foreign records.

The topic of surname changes requires further discussion. For many reasons, many family names were changed upon the family's arrival in America. African-Americans who came as slaves usually were given the names of their owners. Other surnames were affected by ship captains and customs officials who simplified spellings, recorded phonetically what they heard, or arbitrarily assigned an immigrant a new name. Many families retained their new name, believing it would simplify their lives in the New World. Some families deliberately Anglicized their names in order to appear less "foreign" in their new home. Thus "Le Blanc" became "White" and "Schmit" became "Smith." Frederick Debern, a native of Prussia who settled in Davis County, Iowa, in the 1840s, retained the original spelling of his name through his life (actually he was probably illiterate, for he signed his will with his "X" mark). Some of his

Hidalgo, Ana n.a.; New Orleans, La., 1778 *9436 p33*
Hidalgo, Bartolome Hernandez n.a.; New Orleans, La., 1778 *9436 p35*
   Wife: Isabel Hidalgo n.a.
Hidalgo, Francesca 9 *SEE* Hidalgo, Josef
Hidalgo, Gregoria n.a.; New Orleans, La., 1778 *9436 p15*
Hidalgo, Gregoro 10 *SEE* Hidalgo, Josef
Hidalgo, Isabel Hidalgo n.a. *SEE* Hidalgo, Bartolome Hernandez
Hidalgo, Isabel Sambrana n.a. *SEE* Hidalgo, Josef
Hidalgo, Josef n.a.; New Orleans, La., 1778 *9436 p13*
   Wife: Isabel Sambrana n.a.
   Son: Gregoro 10
   Daughter: Francesca 9
   Son: Juan 10 mos
Hidalgo, Juan 10 mos *SEE* Hidalgo, Josef
Hidde, Edward n.a.; Virginia, 1663–1679 *943 p157*
Hidde, Thomas n.a.; Virginia, 1663–1679 *943 p157*
Hiddeman, J W n.a.; Philadelphia, Pa., 1808 *9297 p203*
Hiddemen, William n.a.; Philadelphia, Pa., 1808 *9297 p203*
Hidden, E 32; New York, N.Y., 1823 *9268 p284*
Hide, . . . n.a.; n.d. *1222 p129*
Hide, Edward n.a.; Virginia, 1651 *2772 p159*
Hide, Elizabeth n.a.; America, 1773 *1222 p142*
Hide, Ffrancis n.a.; Barbados, 1663–1679 *943 p120*
Hide, James 22; St. Christopher, 1635 *3283 p81*
Hide, James 22; St. Christopher, 1635 *9151 p66*
Hide, Jane n.a.; America, 1698 *9151 p180*
Hide, John n.a.; America, 1775 *1222 p142*
Hide, John n.a.; New England, 1635 *702 p152*
Hide, John n.a.; New England, 1635 *1190 p769*
Hide, John n.a.; New England, 1635 *9151 p46*
Hide, John 18; Maryland, 1776 *1372 p265*
Hide, Joseph n.a.; Virginia, 1725 *1222 p142*
Hide, Joseph n.a.; Virginia, 1726 *1222 p142*
Hide, Richard 24; Virginia, 1635 *3283 p125*
Hide, Richard 24; Virginia, 1635 *9151 p105*
Hide, Samll n.a.; Virginia, 1643 *2772 p159*
Hide, Stephen n.a.; Jamaica, 1685 *943 p178*
Hide, William n.a.; Barbados, 1663–1679 *943 p139*
Hidebruner, Wolf n.a.; Philadelphia, Pa., 1754 *9041 p660*
Hidell, Antonio 27; New Orleans, La., 1823 *9268 p313*
Hidelston, John n.a.; New Castle, Del., 1784 *5243 p64*
Hidelston, John n.a.; No port mentioned 1784 *702 p18*
Hiden, Sarah n.a.; Boston, Mass., 1764 *9750 p30*
Hidenger, Peter n.a.; Philadelphia, Pa., 1841 *9297 p140*
Hider, George Abo 34; Texas, 1895 *528 p15*
Hider, I 28; Baltimore, Md., 1820 *9258 p162*
Hiderffer, Hans Georg n.a.; Philadelphia, Pa., 1772 *7820 p403*
Hiderhoff, Daniel n.a.; Philadelphia, Pa., 1867 *9297 p203*
Hiderick, Robert n.a.; Virginia, 1645 *2772 p159*
Hides, Samuell 29?; New England, 1639 *702 p180*

Hiebner, Christopher n.a.; Philadelphia, Pa., 1734 *9041 p138*
Hiebner, David n.a.; Philadelphia, Pa., 1734 *9041 p136*
Hiebner, Georg n.a.; Philadelphia, Pa., 1734 *9041 p136*
Hiebner, Georg Melchior n.a.; Philadelphia, Pa., 1753 *7820 p303*
Hiebner, Georg Milcher n.a.; Philadelphia, Pa., 1753 *9041 p525*
Hiebner, George Milcher n.a.; Philadelphia, Pa., 1753 *9041 p523*
Hiebner, Hans n.a.; Philadelphia, Pa., 1734 *9041 p139*
Hiebner, Johannes n.a.; Philadelphia, Pa., 1734 *9041 p137*
Hiebner, Maria n.a.; Philadelphia, Pa., 1734 *9041 p137*
Hiebner, Maria n.a.; Philadelphia, Pa., 1734 *9041 p139*
Hiebner, Melchior n.a.; Philadelphia, Pa., 1734 *9041 p136*
Hiebner, Melchior n.a.; Philadelphia, Pa., 1734 *9041 p139*
Hiedra, Domingo n.a.; New Orleans, La., 1778 *9436 p16*
Hiege, Christian n.a.; Philadelphia, Pa., 1846 *9297 p203*
Hiegel, Peter n.a.; Philadelphia, Pa., 1856 *9297 p203*
Hiegler, Rudolph n.a.; Philadelphia County, Pa., 1734 *7820 p475*
Hiel, Frederick n.a.; Philadelphia, Pa., 1878 *9297 p203*
Hielmdahl, C J 22; New York, N.Y., 1835 *6411 p16*
Hielmellar, Charles n.a.; Philadelphia, Pa., 1867 *9297 p203*
Hieman, Braun n.a.; Philadelphia, Pa., 1803 *9042 p135*
Hieman, Jacob n.a.; Philadelphia, Pa., 1749 *7820 p198*
Hieman, Jacob n.a.; Philadelphia, Pa., 1749 *9041 p399*
Hieman, Joh Hendk n.a.; Philadelphia, Pa., 1753 *9041 p564*
Hieman, Johannes n.a.; Philadelphia, Pa., 1754 *9041 p628*
Hiembuchner, Anna 8; New York (State), 1878 *6929 p48*
Hiembuchner, Anna 9; New York (State), 1878 *6929 p48*
Hiembuchner, Anna 37; New York (State), 1878 *6929 p48*
Hiembuchner, Catherina 7; New York (State), 1878 *6929 p48*
Hiembuchner, Conrad 18; New York (State), 1878 *6929 p48*
Hiembuchner, Conrad 41; New York (State), 1878 *6929 p48*
Hiembuchner, Georg 11 mos; New York (State), 1878 *6929 p48*
Hiembuchner, Johann 16; New York (State), 1878 *6929 p48*
Hiembuchner, Maria 11 mos; New York (State), 1878 *6929 p48*
Hiementz, Nicholas n.a.; Philadelphia, Pa., 1837 *9297 p203*

A page from Passenger and Immigration Lists Index, *mentioned on page 207. Passenger lists can help to confirm the arrival of an immigrant ancestor in America.*

sons, however, adopted the more common spelling of Dearborn. Frederick himself is enumerated as Dearborn at Davis County in the 1850 U.S. census.

Other immigrants chose English surnames that bore no relationship, linguistic or otherwise, to their Old World names. Because such changes often occurred informally, the only good source of information about them is the family itself.

Passenger Lists

Besides family documents and tradition, several types of public records — especially passenger arrival lists, naturalization papers, and census records — may help us identify our immigrant ancestors. Let's look first at passenger arrival lists. These can be divided into two categories — those created before and those generated after 1820, when the federal government began to record data on each passenger entering the country. Although a few early English and German lists are deposited in public archives and libraries, most pre-1820 passenger data is widely scattered. Undoubtedly, a large amount remains undiscovered, in private hands, but almost all early passenger lists found so far have been published. A master index to these printed lists, P. William Filby and Mary K. Meyer's *Passenger and Immigration Lists Index*, contains more than one million names and is constantly being expanded. This index lists the immigrant by name, age (when available), and place and year of arrival, and also gives the printed source from which the information is derived. Entries are drawn from a wide variety of sources, including customs lists; naturalization, court, and church records; newspapers; journals; and letters.

In 1820 the U.S. government began to record passenger arrivals in this country. Federal passenger arrival records consist of customs passenger lists, which date from 1820 to 1902, and immigration passenger lists which run generally from 1893 (although some in Philadelphia begin in 1883) through 1945. There is a fifty-year restriction on the latter lists.

Following a federal law passed in 1819, ship captains were required to file a list of passengers with the district collector of customs. These customs passenger lists state the names of the vessel and its master, the port of embarkation, and the date and port of arrival. For each passenger they include name, age, sex, occupation, and country of origin. The customs passenger lists have been microfilmed by the National Archives. In addition, the Works Progress Administration (WPA) compiled card indexes to the lists for Baltimore, 1820-1897; Boston, 1848-1891; New York, 1820-1846; and Philadelphia, 1800-1906. These indexes are also available as microfilm publications from the National Archives. A fifth such compilation, *A Supplemental Index to Passenger Lists of Vessels Arriving at Atlantic and Gulf Coast Ports (excluding New York), 1820-1847,* is incomplete, but may be helpful if an immigrant's port of arrival is unknown. A table showing available customs passenger lists and indexes appears in chapter 2 of *Guide to Genealogical Research in the National Archives.* Published lists to date largely cover Dutch, German, and "potato famine" Irish immigrants, as well as all arrivals in Baltimore, 1820-1834. For a bibliography and brief discussion of these works, see *Genealogical Journal*, vol. 12 (1983): pp. 112-117.

In 1882 the federal government itself began recording immigrants as they entered the United States. At first the form used was that employed by the State of Pennsylvania, but by 1893 the federal government had its own form which recorded the name of vessel, ports of arrival and embarkation, date of arrival, and the following information for each passenger: full name, age, sex, marital status, occupation, nationality, last residence, final destination, whether in the United States before, and if so when and where, and whether coming to join a relative, and if so the latter's relationship to the passenger. The format of the immigration passenger list was revised in 1903 to include race, in 1906 to include personal description and birthplace, and in 1907 to include the name and address of the nearest relative in the immigrant's home country.

Immigration passenger lists are arranged in the National Archives by port and thereunder chronologically. To find information about a particular individual in these voluminous records, you must know three facts: the port, ship, and exact date of arrival. If the port and an approximate arrival date are known, it may be possible to discover the exact date and ship from records of vessel entrances maintained at the ports. These records (also available on microfilm at the National Archives) list the name of each vessel, its captain, port of embarkation, and date of arrival. For some ports there are two series, one with entries arranged alphabetically by ship and the other with entries arranged chronologically. If, in addition to the port of entry and approximate day of arrival, you know the port of embarkation, the search can be narrowed further. If, for example, a passenger embarked from Stockholm for New York in a year when five hundred passenger ships arrived there, you need examine only the relatively few passenger lists for vessels sailing from Stockholm. The *Morton Allan Directory of European Passenger Steamship Arrivals* lists by exact date vessels arriving at the ports of New York, 1890-1930, and Baltimore, Boston, and Philadelphia, 1904-1926.

Italian immigrants. National Archives

Naturalization Records

Naturalization records also yield valuable information on immigrant ancestors. Beginning with the first naturalization act of 1790, aliens were required in most instances to establish residency and file for citizenship. Becoming "naturalized" usually required declaration of intention and, after meeting the residence requirement, a petition to become a citizen. An individual might also have to obtain depositions from friends and neighbors in support of his application. The petition, if successful, resulted in a certificate of naturalization.

Of the various kinds of naturalization records, declarations of intention and petitions for naturalization are the most helpful to genealogists. Before the immigration law of 1906, declarations of intention re-

Immigrants on the way to America. Photographer Lewis Hine captured the image of this impromptu band recital. Bettmann Archive

corded name, date, signature, and country of birth or allegiance. Some also stated the date and port of arrival in the United States. After 1906, the form was expanded to include each applicant's age, occupation, personal description, date and place of birth, citizenship, present and last foreign address, ports of embarkation and entry, name of passenger vessel traveled, and date of arrival in the United States. As is clear from this list, naturalization records are most useful for identifying our immigrant ancestors' places of origin. Remember, however, that many immigrants lived briefly in other countries (often Canada, the Caribbean basin, or South America) before finally coming to the United States. Thus last foreign address may reveal a migration pattern more complex than previously realized. Note too that the declaration of intention records the vessel and port of embarkation as well as the port and arrival date in the United States. With this information you can readily identify the immigration passenger list that records the arrival of your ancestor in America.

Locating an ancestor's naturalization record can prove frustrating.

Before 1906 an alien could go before any federal, state, or local court and petition to become a naturalized citizen. Records were maintained only by the court to which the petition was made. Checking each jurisdiction in which a forebear *might* have been naturalized for such data may require many hours. After 1906 all courts were required to forward copies of naturalization proceedings to the Immigration and Naturalization Service in Washington, D.C. A state-by-state description of naturalization records in federal district courts appears in chapter 3 of *Guide to Genealogical Research in the National Archives.*

A WPA project to abstract information from naturalization papers was, unfortunately, terminated after such work had been completed for the six New England states, New York City, and a few other areas. These extracts — two pages for each applicant — usually include place and date of birth, occupation, vessel, port of entry and date of arrival in the United States, place of residence at the time of application, and the name and address of a witness. An index of petitioners was compiled on three-by-five cards and is available at the Bayonne, New Jersey, (New York abstracts) and Waltham, Massachusetts, (New England abstracts) regional branches of the National Archives.

Thanks to this index, the naturalization papers of one genealogist's long-sought-for ancestor, William Banton, were located in the court of common pleas of Lincoln County, Maine (then Massachusetts), dated January 13, 1806. The papers proved to be exceptionally valuable because they provided a clue to Banton's place of origin. Such information is not usually found in documents of that early date:

⤳⦔

". . . William Banton now resident in Bristol in the County of Lincoln . . . an Alien, born in the Town of Manchester in the County of Lancashire within the Dominions of the King of Great Britain . . . ."

Census Records

Census records will prove immensely useful in tracing immigrant ancestors who arrived in this country after 1880. Beginning in that year census schedules asked (1) the birthplace of each parent (usually answered with a country or state, not a town, parish, or county), and (2) whether either was of foreign birth. The 1890 census, almost completely destroyed by fire, also asked (1) the number of years respondents had lived in the United States, and (2) whether they were naturalized or in the process of becoming so. A final additional column in the 1900 census asked mother tongue. Thus even if your ancestor immigrated to America much earlier, say 1840-1860, some information about his origins can be surmised from the 1880 and 1900 censuses — if he was still alive then. Often the 1900 census provides the only information you can find on a forebear's year of arrival. If from his residence you can reasonably guess the port of arrival, you can then search customs or immigration passenger lists with some hope of success. And if the census reveals he was naturalized before 1900, you can begin looking for naturalization papers as well.

Henry Dearborn, born in Canada in December 1810 of New Hampshire-born parents, was enumerated with his family at Georgetown Township, Ottawa County, Michigan, in the 1900 census, age eighty-nine. The census shows that he was a naturalized citizen and that the family immigrated to the United States in 1878. It is quite possible that his naturalization papers are filed in the Ottawa county courthouse. Among those enumerated in the household is a married daughter, Patience Crawford, and a grandson, James Crawford, who was born in South Dakota in December 1885. If this family group was a long-standing unit, then Henry's naturalization records could be in a South Dakota courthouse.

Danish mother and three children. Ben Watson

Passport and Homestead Applications

Until World War I, except for a brief period during the Civil War, U.S. citizens traveling to foreign countries were not obliged to obtain passports. As a precaution, however, many Americans did so. Passports generally recorded less information before the Civil War than after, but usually included the name, signature, residence, age, and personal description of the applicant. Also given were the names or number of family members intending to travel. Exact dates and places of birth of the applicant, his spouse, and any accompanying minor children were sometimes included. Most important for research on immigrant ancestors, if the traveler was a naturalized citizen, the passport would contain the date, vessel, and port of his arrival in the United States, as well as the date and court of naturalization. If you cannot find a forebear's court of naturalization, ask relatives if he ever revisited his native country. If so, look for a surviving passport. Even if your ancestor was not born abroad, you should still check the passport application because each document includes the applicant's birthplace and much descriptive data.

For example, in his application for a passport, dated at Boston, June 1, 1866, Joseph F. Dearborn stated that he was born at Hampton, New Hampshire, May 14, 1817, and described himself as age forty-nine; stature six feet; forehead middling high-retreating; eyes small gray; heavy eyebrows; nose long, nearly straight; mouth small; chin slightly projecting; hair very dark brown; beard black; complexion dark, florid; face long.

Passport applications received by the Department of State between 1791 and 1925 are deposited in the National Archives. Applications less than seventy-five years old may not be seen without permission. Finding aids for those filed from 1834 though 1923 are discussed in chapter 19 of *Guide to Genealogical Research in the National Archives*.

Because all homestead applicants had to prove that they were either U.S. citizens or candidates for that status, homestead application files often contain copies of naturalization papers. Like passport files, homestead files — further discussed in chapter 8 — sometimes identify an elusive court of naturalization. They, too, are found at the National Archives.

Newspapers

Foreign- and English-language newspapers can also be useful in tracing an immigrant's origin. If your ancestor was preceded here by relatives or friends, he may have tried to locate them by advertising in a newspaper that served his particular nationality or ethnic group. Such advertisements were quite specific, noting kinships between advertisers and the people they sought, and often citing town, parish, and/or county of origin in Europe. One major Irish newspaper, the *Boston Pilot*, ran a weekly missing persons column for almost a century. Here are three typical entries:

Of Nicholas Nautly, of Drumeagle, parish of Crossorlough, co. Cavan, who sailed from Dublin for N. York in the Chester St. John, in March 1849. He is 17 years of age, of good address — served 3 years in a grocery store in the City of Dublin. Any information respecting him will be thankfully received by his friend, Edward Smith, Taunton Ms.

Of Francis Moran, native of parish Allen, Kildare — served his time to Patrick Murphy, Baker, Francis Street, Dublin. Is now about 44 years of age — sailed for New York 16 years ago. Any communication respecting him will be thankfully received by his brother, Patrick Moran, care of Hugh Lacy, 178 Ann Street, Boston, Ms.

Of Thomas and Hugh Betton, natives of co. Longford, parish Bally-mahon. Thomas came to this country about 21 years ago and Hugh about 19 years ago. When last heard from were in Ulster County, N. York — they were married and had families — Thomas said he would go to Ohio to purchase land. Any information of them will be thankfully received by their brother, Ralph Betton, Coolide Point, Flushing, Long Island, N.Y.

Abstracts of all *Boston Pilot* missing persons columns from 1831 to 1916 are now being prepared for publication as a joint project of the New England Historic Genealogical Society and the Irish Studies Program at Northeastern University in Boston. Similar extracts from earlier German-language newspapers include "Notices by German and Swiss Settlers Seeking Information of Members of their Families, Kindred, and Friends Inserted between 1742-1761, in *Pennsylvania Berichte*, and 1762-1779 in *Pennsylvania Staatsbote*," by Anita L. Eyster, which appeared in *Pennsylvania German Folklore Society 3* (1938, pp. 32-41); and *Genealogical Data*

Immigrants — probably Irish — at Ellis Island. Sometimes you can locate information on an ancestor through "missing person" advertisements in back issues of ethnic newspapers. The Bettman Archive, Inc.

Relating to the German Settlers of Pennsylvania from Advertisements in German Newspapers Published in Philadelphia and Germantown, 1743-1800 by Edward Hocker.

In addition to missing persons columns, ethnic newspapers regularly published obituaries of near relatives of American immigrants who died in the homeland; bequests to local kinsmen would sometimes be mentioned as well. For further discussion of ethnic newspapers, see Lubomyr Wynar, *Encyclopedic Directory of Ethnic Newspapers and Periodicals in the United States.*

Ethnic Repositories

Many large public and university libraries are rapidly collecting ethnic materials. Specialized archives, institutes, and research centers are proliferating as well. A few are listed here:

National Immigration Archives, Balch Institute, Temple University, Philadelphia, PA. Its holdings include the originals of the customs passenger lists, 1820-1882, transferred from the National Archives (which retained copies on microfilm), plus microfilms of the later immigration passenger lists. The archives cosponsored publication with The Genealogical Publishing Company of Baltimore of the seven-volume *Famine Immigrants* series, listing all Irish immigrants to the port of New York between 1846 and 1851.

Center for Migration Studies, 209 Flagg Place, Staten Island, NY. Its holdings include records of American social welfare organizations and the private papers of many immigrants.

Indians, now referred to as the only "Native" Americans. National Archives

Edward E. Ayer Collection of Americana and American Indians, The Newberry Library, 60 West Walton Street, Chicago, IL. Its nineteen-volume *Dictionary Catalog,* published 1961 to 1970, lists one hundred thousand volumes covering North and South American Indians.

Schomberg Collection of Negro Literature and History, The New York Public Library, 102 West 135th Street, New York, NY. Its sixteen-volume *Dictionary Catalog,* published 1962 to 1974, lists more than sixty thousand titles. Annual supplements since 1975 have appeared as the *Bibliographical Guide to Black Studies.* Coverage is of all people of African descent, wherever they have lived in significant numbers.

Hispanic Society of America, Broadway (between 155th and 156th Street), New York, NY. Its fourteen-volume *Catalog of the Library,* published 1962 to 1970, lists more than one hundred thousand volumes covering the cultures of Spain, Portugal, and colonial Hispanic America.

The American Jewish Archives, 3101 Clifton Avenue, Cincinnati, OH and the *American Jewish Historical Society, 2 Thornton Road, Waltham, MA.* The major American institutions for Jewish genealogical research, they were cosponsors of Malcolm Stern's *First American Jewish Families.*

University of Minnesota Immigrant Archives, Minneapolis, MN. These archives house 23,000 printed works, 2,000 reels of microfilm, and 2,100,000 manuscripts (in 1974) related especially to immigrant groups from southern and eastern Europe. Especially noteworthy is its large collection of foreign-language newspapers published in this country.

More immigrants. National Archives

❧ *Pointers and Pitfalls* ❧
Immigrant Ancestors and American Origins

1. Our immigrant ancestors are among our most elusive forebears. One person's immigrant ancestors represent an infinitesimal portion of the fifty million immigrants to arrive in this country since the early 1600s.

2. In seeking immigrant ancestors, work from the known to the unknown.

3. Make sure that an ancestor you believe to be an immigrant is not, in fact, the child — or grandchild — of earlier settlers.

4. Begin your search by interviewing family members about the family's Old World origins.

5. Be aware of changes in family surnames. Often such changes were made informally, and only family members can provide accurate information about them.

6. Passenger lists contain valuable information such as name of vessel, port and date of arrival, and name, age, occupation, race, and country of origin of passenger. You can find these lists in the National Archives.

7. Naturalization records also contain valuable genealogical information, but can be hard to locate because they were maintained at the court to which the naturalization petition was made.

8. Other American sources of information on immigrant ancestors include census records, passport and homestead applications, and ethnic newspapers.

9. Many public and university libraries are collecting ethnic material. In addition, several specialized archives, institutes, and research centers can direct you to numerous other sources.

Chapter Twelve

COMPLETING YOUR WORK

Binding Past and Present

Alex Haley, author of Roots. *UPI/Bettman Newsphotos*

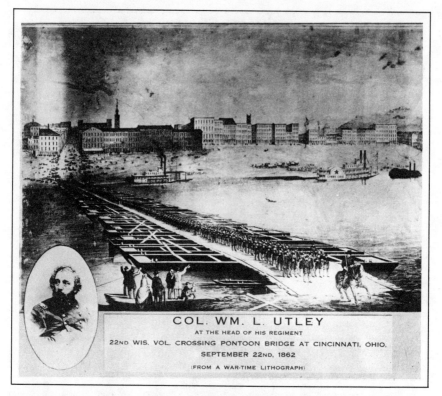

COL. WM. L. UTLEY

AT THE HEAD OF HIS REGIMENT

22ND WIS. VOL. CROSSING PONTOON BRIDGE AT CINCINNATI, OHIO.

SEPTEMBER 22ND, 1862

(FROM A WAR-TIME LITHOGRAPH)

Frontispiece from Ancestors of Col. William Lawrence Utley, *a genealogy in the* New England Historic Genealogical Society collection. *NEHGS*

---

our decision to research and write your family history undoubtedly reflects the fundamental interest we all have in knowing more about our ancestors. The motivation is always highly personal: through a study of our forebears, we hope to know ourselves better. But you should also be encouraged to share what you learn with others. At some point you must halt research and prepare for publication. Otherwise the ultimate fate of years of genealogical work may be forgotten storage in an attic or basement. Worse yet, your genealogical notes might simply be discarded by unsympathetic heirs. You must give careful thought to how to organize, compile, and publish your genealogy. You must have a method of organizing information as you collect it and, when you are ready to publish, a genealogical format that is easy to follow. Finally, you must make decisions about the best way to produce and/or publish your genealogy.

Organizing Family Data

As you gather information, you should record it on ancestral charts (referred to as four-generation charts in appendix E). Ancestral charts, showing all forebears for several generations, help you to visualize the various lines in your ancestry and allow you to record essential information on birth, marriage, death, and residence. Your first chart will begin with yourself and work back generation by generation through your great-grandparents. The last person on the chart, who would be your matrilineal great-grandmother, is listed as number 15. To trace her ancestry, you would begin another chart with her name, but continue to identify her as number 15. Following the same scheme, her father would be number 30, her mother number 31, and so on. (Although your other fourteen great-great-grandparents will not be shown on this chart, the numbers 16 through 29 must be left for them.) Each individual's number on your chart will be exactly half that of his or her father. Remember to number each chart as well, for family group sheets will be keyed to them.

The family group chart (also found in appendix E) is designed to help you organize and record data on individual "nuclear" units: husband, wife, and children. The form contains spaces for dates and places of birth, marriage, and death, as well as baptisms, residences, divorces, and remarriages. The form can also be used to note important biographical details such as military service, occupation, and religion.

Using the Computer.

Because the genealogist collects and organizes information in a systematic fashion, his research is particularly adaptable to computer management and manipulation. With a good database management program, you can enter directly into a computer information that you would ordinarily record laboriously on ancestral charts and family group sheets. Once you have stored it, you can search your genealogical material for information on a particular ancestor, and you can make corrections and add new material quickly and easily.

The options for someone seeking a computer program to aid genealogical research are enticing, but don't buy immediately. First become acquainted with the fast-growing and extensive literature devoted exclusively to genealogical computing. Start by reading Wade C. Starks' "The Computer and the Genealogist," in *The Source: A Guidebook of American Genealogy*, which offers an excellent introduction to the subject and lists various genealogical software programs currently available. See also *Computer Genealogy: A Guide to Research Through High Technology,* by Paul A. Andereck and Richard A. Pence, and *Genealogical Computing,* a bimonthly newsletter begun in 1981.

Citing Your Sources.

Whether you record information manually or by computer, it is vitally important to note the sources you consult. Such notes are not only necessary to verify information later, but they are essential if you decide to publish. There are different opinions of what you should include in a genealogical footnote, but one fundamental rule always applies: cite your sources so that another reader can easily locate the same information. When using a primary record, note the exact title of the document plus any further identification such as volume number, folio, docket number, name of the collection, and name and location of the repository. An example is as follows: "Will of Richard Smith," Docket Number 20747, Middlesex County Probate Records, Middlesex County Courthouse, Cambridge, Mass. The same basic principle applies to published sources. For example, if you take information from a published volume of vital records, note: "John Stockbridge married Mary Godfrey on 23 November 1681 in Haverhill, Massachusetts," *Vital Records of Haverhill Massachusetts to the End of the Year 1849* (Topsfield, 1910-1911).

For further discussion of genealogical citations, see Richard S. Lackey, *Citing Your Sources*: *A Manual for Documenting Family Histories and Genealogical Records,* and Donald R. Barnes and Richard S. Lackey, *Write it Right: A Manual for Writing Family Histories and Genealogies.*

Getting into Print

Because genealogy is such an absorbing activity, you will always want to continue your research. But at some point you should pause long enough to publish and distribute the best of what you have found to date so that others can enjoy and benefit from your investigations. Several options are available for presenting your work. Below are outlined some possibilities you might consider in terms of your budget and level of interest.

Photocopying.

The least complicated and inexpensive approach is to retype and arrange your ancestral charts and family group sheets, add whatever photographs and illustrations you think appropriate, photocopy this material, and insert it into three-ring binders to be presented to family members, friends, and libraries. You will be pleased by the warm and grateful reception this effort receives, and you may hear from relatives or other genealogists who have additions or corrections.

Genealogical Periodicals.

A second option is to publish your work in a genealogical periodical. Nearly five hundred genealogical serial publications range from newspaper columns to family association magazines, society newsletters, and major journals. The most notable genealogical journals include *The Genealogist, The American Genealogist, The National Genealogical Society Quarterly, Genealogical Journal, The New England Historical and Genealogical Register, The New York Genealogical and Biographical Record,* and *The Detroit Society for Genealogical Research Magazine.*

Before submitting an article to one of these publications, examine several issues carefully to determine the preferred type of article and format. *The New England Historical and Genealogical Register,* for example, tends to publish genealogical articles on Colonial New England families. Usually such articles begin with the immigrant ancestor and follow the male lines through several generations to the time of the American Revolution or the 1790 census. Likewise, *The New York Genealogical and Biographical Record* focuses on the early families of New York. *The American Genealogist,* on the other hand, likes to publish short articles resolving tricky problems or identifying immigrant origins and is less likely to accept long genealogies.

Most genealogical serials will publish primary materials — family Bible extracts, church records, cemetery inscriptions, etc. — and they usually welcome articles correcting genealogical errors in print, particularly if they affect probable ancestors of a large number of researchers. In short, while no genealogical periodical will publish your entire magnum opus from immigrant ancestor to the present, portions of such a work may well interest various editors and elicit considerable response from other genealogists. Indeed, in the long process of publishing a major family genealogy, you would be well advised to sharpen your analytical and writing skills with a few short articles. You might prepare a note that corrects a printed error or summarize your solution to a problem requiring little-used sources or unusual research techniques.

A good example of a correction was recently submitted to *The New England Historical and Genealogical Register* by Mrs. Frances E. Sage of Endicott, New York:

Printed below is material from the Boston Transcript *of 16 September 1925 concerning the ancestry of Stephen (1) Gates. Although it was published over sixty years ago and is absolutely correct, it is amazing how the error it mentions has persisted and been brought forth time after time . . . .*
[*Transcript* material follows]

GATES. There is a Gates genealogy, frequently quoted and apparently generally accepted, which gives Stephen Gates, the immigrant, as son of Thomas Gates of Norwich, Norfolk, England, and grandson of Peter and Mary (Josselyn) Gates of London. Mr. Charles Otis Gates in his book on the Gates family (*Stephen Gates of Hingham and Lancaster, Massachusetts, and his Descendants* (New York, 1898) gives this line and seems to be satisfied with the evidence, although he gives no proofs. Within the past month I have seen a Visitation of Suffolk made in 1612 and delivered in 1621 which includes further data, that shows that Stephen could not possibly have been a grandson of Peter and Mary Gates. Peter Gates was twenty-nine years old in 1612, and had one "son and heir, Josselyn, aged 3 and 2 daughters." Stephen's birth date is not known, but he was married and had five children, all born in England, when he came to America in 1634 or 1642. I have seen both dates given, but incline to the later one. Obviously Peter could not have had a son Thomas born after 1612, who would be a grandfather in 1642.

The Hon. Benjamin A.G. Fuller of Boston stated in the New England Genealogical and Historical Register (sic) in 1877: "From certain old manuscripts in my possession, it seems that Stephen Gates, second son of Thomas Gates of Norwich, Norfolk, came to this country and settled at Higham." There has never been any reason to question this statement, but the later claim that Thomas was the son of Peter seems now disproved.

Publishing Your Own Genealogy

As your interest in genealogy grows and your expertise increases, you will gain much satisfaction (and some scholarly reputation) by publishing in genealogical journals. But ultimately your goal may be to produce a book-length genealogy covering ten to fourteen generations of your own ancestors. This is a challenging assignment, so let's review the major steps involved in producing such a work.

First, you must convert the information on your ancestral charts to an acceptable genealogical format. When you prepare ancestral charts, you go from the known to the unknown, beginning with yourself (or someone else) and working back to parents, grandparents, etc. But when organizing a genealogy for publication, you must work in the *opposite* direction, beginning with the first known progenitor of the family (frequently the immigrant ancestor to this country) and tracing his descendants to the present. (This method is usually used in preparing genealogical articles for journals.)

In the mid-nineteenth century, when American genealogy was still in its infancy, published family histories followed a bewildering variety of formats. In 1870 Albert H. Hoyt, then editor of *The New England Historical and Genealogical Register,* lamented that "everyone who compiles a genealogy has his own plan for arranging his matter, hence there are as many plans as there are volumes." To reduce the confusion, Hoyt devised a system that subsequently became known as the Register Plan, or Register Form, and is now the standard format employed by professional genealogists and genealogical magazines in the United States. With the Register Plan, each family — head of household, his/her spouse(s), and their children — is treated as a discrete unit. Each generation of families is featured in a single chapter. To show how each head of household is descended from earlier generations and the immigrant progenitor, a special numbering system is used. The progenitor is assigned the number 1 as well as a superscript 1 (to indicate "first generation") after his first name. Any of his sons who marry and in turn leave sons of their own who marry are numbered consecutively 2, 3, 4, etc., in order of birth. They also receive superscript number 2 indicating membership in the family's second generation. Sons who die young, do not marry, die childless, leave only daughters, or leave sons who themselves do not marry, are not carried forward to the next generation; nor usually are daughters, although many genealogies use a modified Register Form that includes their progeny, or a section of it, for one or more generations.

To illustrate Register Form further, let's look carefully at the example given below, a small section of Edward W. Hanson's "The Hurds of Boston," *The New England Historical and Genealogical Register*'s lead article for April 1978.

1.   John[1] Hurd. (The coverage of John[1] Hurd includes six paragraphs that detail and document his arrival in Boston, various land transactions, a serious drinking problem, some confusion about the full list of his children, and the good works of his wife, Mary — .)

    i.   John[2], bp. 18 day 6 mo. 1639; d. young.

   ii.   Hannah, bp. 20 day 7 mo. 1640; m. John Cowell of Boston, and had issue. (See Edward S. Holden, "A Piece of Family Silver, and a Boston Silversmith of 1712," *Register*, 50 [1896]: 297-300.)

2.   iii.   John, bp. 17 day 5 mo. 1642.

3.   iv.   Joseph, b. 10th 7th mo. 1644.

   v.   Mary, bp. 8 day 9 mo. 1646; d. young.

   vi.   Benjamin, bp. 27 day 6 m. 1648; d. young.

  vii.   Mary, bp. 20 day 8 mo. 1650; not mentioned in father's will, 1687.

4.   viii.   Benjamin, b. 28th Nov. 1652.

5.   ix.   Jacob, b. 14 Mar. 1655 (Called Samuel on birth record).

   x.   Mehetable, b. 21st Dec. 1657; not mentioned in father's will, 1687.

The emigrant ancestor is John[1] Hurd, shown at the top of the list. His children are then listed in order of birth, but only those sons who married and left children are assigned Arabic numbers. Thus later in the article there would be full descriptions of 2 John[2] followed by 3 Joseph[2], 4 Benjamin[2], and 5 Jacob[2]. The given names in parentheses indicate the line of descent. Thus, for example, a later 9 Benjamin[3] (Jacob [2], John[1]) would be the son of 5 Jacob[2] and the grandson of 1 John[1].

A major variation on the Register Plan, used in many "multiancestor" genealogies that cover all known forebears of the compiler or sponsor, is to devote a separate chapter to each family in your ancestry, starting first with your own surname or patrilineal descent, and treating each family thereafter in either alphabetical or some logical genealogical order. Note that only the direct line or lineage from each immigrant forebear to the current compiler or sponsor is covered. Often preceding each chapter will be a generational chart showing how an "allied" family figures in the ancestry of the book's subject.

After settling on a format and numbering system, you must think about contents, title, index, and the best method of printing your manuscript. As for contents, you will readily note that a genealogy consists of a series of profiles or vignettes of family units that include father, mother, and children. What should you include in each of these family profiles? You must state the basic genealogical facts of birth, marriage, and death. Such information is essential for making generational connections. Beyond bare facts you should strive to make your genealogy readable. Biography is intrinsically interesting, and you should include what you have been able to discover about your ancestors' occupations, education, religious experiences, military service, and political offices, as well as any recorded contemporary assessment of personal characteristics, achievements, strengths, and weaknesses.

Don't exclude less pleasant facts if they are essential to the story. Objective reporting is fundamental to your role as family historian. John[1] Hurd had a drinking problem that eventually resulted in his being excommunicated from the First Church of Boston. On the other hand, his long-suffering wife, who bore him ten children, frequently nursed sickly neighbors, an activity reported by Judge Samuel Sewall of Boston in his famous diary (*The Diary of Samuel Sewall 1674-1729*). Personal details like this add flesh to your genealogy, enliven it for the reader, and in their own small way, contribute to our collective historical understanding of the American family.

You should give careful consideration to the selection of a title and the design of an index. Simply stated, the title of your genealogy should accurately reflect its contents. In "Creating a Worthwhile Family Genealogy," *National Genealogical Society Quarterly*, vol. 56 (1968): pp. 248-249, Meredith B. Colket recommends the following:

We think a family genealogy should have no more than one surname in the title and that it should also have the given name of a progenitor, usually that of the first American settler. Often there are several progenitors having a particular surname and it is unwise to imply by the title, as many have done, that a particular family genealogy relates to all families of that surname. A title should, we believe, show the place of residence of the progenitor and perhaps also the year of his settlement. Finally it should be made clear that it relates to the descendants of the progenitor.

Your index should also be kept simple and constructed according to a few basic criteria. It should be an "every name" index arranged in strict alphabetical order and keyed to *pages*, not genealogical numbers or generational superscripts. Usually a particular name (even if references to that name represent several different individuals in the genealogy) should appear only once in the index. Hence, "Morse, Daniel, 23, 45, 78, 96" might refer to the same person or to four people. This practice is acceptable because one of the main objectives of an index is to consolidate information. However, all variant spellings of a name should be listed, as well as the maiden and all married names of women. With variant surname spellings, entries should lead with the dominant spelling followed by variants in alphabetical order. Thus the Crandall surname might be listed as "Crandall, Crandale, Crandel, Crandell." Each variant, however, should be cross-indexed to the main entry — thus "Crandale, see Crandall," and so forth.

Pay particular attention to female entries to ensure that no marriage is omitted. Let's say, for example, that a woman with the maiden name of Elizabeth March married three times — to (1) John Hill, (2) William Creeden, and (3) Steven Grundy. Entries for her in the index would include:

Creeden, Elizabeth (March) (Hill)
Grundy, Elizabeth (March) (Hill) (Creeden)
Hill, Elizabeth (March)
March, Elizabeth

With this system, the index notes each marriage and all previous surnames by which the woman was known.

Finally, your manuscript must be printed. Just a few decades ago the only process for printing books was "letterpress," involving the formation of type from "hot lead." Letterpress is still an option for those bibliophiles who like the special feel and look of a fine edition. But a less expensive method is photographic offset printing, which requires that you first give the printer a clean, or "camera-ready," copy of your work. This means the manuscript has been carefully typed (often by a professional typist) and is free of creases, smudges, corrections, and all other unwanted marks. This camera-ready manuscript is then photographed, and the photo negatives are used to make printing plates. Binding is the last stage.

If you wish, you may have the printer typeset your manuscript as well as print and bind it. Professional typesetting affords you the flexibility of different typefaces and sizes. You can also correct mistakes in the text and reset whole lines and pages if necessary before the book goes to press. The difference between a manuscript that is typed and one that is typeset is the difference between the look of a term paper and that of a book. Although typesetting is expensive, personal computers and word processors now have many of the features and capabilities of typesetting machines, including italic, boldface, and "justification" (making type align at the right-hand margin as well as at the left). They can make corrections, add and delete text, and allow you to make changes up to the moment you hand camera-ready copy to the printer.

Other factors to consider in preparing your manuscript for publication include book design, paper quality, type of cover, front matter (prefaces, forewords, acknowledgments, title page), copyright, cost to include photographs or other artwork, and number of copies to print. Finally, you must consider ways to market your book at least to recover your costs. For those unfamiliar with book publishing, these are difficult and frustrating issues. Unwise decisions can result in a mediocre and unnecessarily expensive volume. One solution is to retain the services of a publishing or printing company that specializes in genealogy. Few, if any, commercial publishers will pay you for the right to publish your genealogy, but it is possible to pay some publishing companies to produce your book for you. Most genealogical publishers cannot review the accuracy or completeness of your work; they will print what you request. As professional publishers, however, they can prove immensely helpful with matters such as format, organization, typeface, paper, and filing for copyright. Probably the leading firm of this type today is Gateway Press, 1001 North Calvert Street, Baltimore, MD 21202.

You may, of course, decide to act as your own publisher and deal with printers directly. Specify that you want your volume to be of standard book size (usually six by nine inches), produced on good quality, nonacidic paper with a durable cover (but remember that a "hard" cover can add substantially to cost). Indicate the number and types of illustrations in your book and where they are to be located, whether you prefer letterpress printing or offset printing of typewritten or typeset copy, and the number of copies you desire. After establishing the criteria and determining the length of the manuscript, you should then ask the printer to prepare a quotation of the cost. Remember that typesetting and printing costs (as well as quality of the work) can vary greatly, so two or three quotations from different printers are advisable. Be sure also to ask for samples of their work.

Regardless of the quality of your research and the attractiveness of the finished book, sales and interest will be limited. Print runs of most genealogies are five hundred or less. Still, you should try to distribute your work as widely as possible, not only to recover out-of-pocket expenses, but more importantly to ensure that family members and many genealogical libraries know of it. Affordability is important, of course, but you should charge enough so that printing costs are offset by sales of one-half to two-thirds of the print run.

Begin marketing your book by preparing a prepublication flyer, which should be mailed once you have set the book's price. The flyer might offer a discount to all living individuals named in your work (your best market!) as well as to all genealogical societies and libraries. Once you have the book in hand, send copies to genealogical journals and newsletters to generate book reviews and listings in "recent book" sections. You can find pertinent addresses in Anita Cheek Milner's *Newspaper Genealogy Columns* and Mary K. Meyer's *Directory of Genealogical Societies in the U.S.A. and Canada*, 5th ed. You may wish, of course, to make gifts of your work to individuals and repositories that were especially helpful during the course of your research.

Seeing your own research in print is one of the greatest satisfactions genealogy can provide. The pleasure is multiplied many times over when the final product is an authoritative and attractive book. Such a work is a tribute to your ancestors and a contribution to American genealogical literature. Even more, among all your achievements, it is often the most compact and readily available, the longest remembered (because most often used), and the most enduring.

❧ *Pointers and Pitfalls* ❧

Binding Past and Present

1. It is important that you share your genealogical findings so that they are not forgotten or discarded.

2. Ancestral (or four-generation) charts and family group charts are the most helpful forms for organizing data as you collect it.

3. A computer can aid you in organizing information, but you should become acquainted with the literature on genealogical computing before purchasing software.

4. Always cite sources so that the reader can easily locate the same information.

5. Photocopying is the simplest and least expensive way to reproduce your findings.

6. Consider submitting some of your work to one of the many genealogical periodicals. Study a publication first to make sure your material is the type the editors choose for publication.

7. If you are planning a major family genealogy, writing short articles for a periodical is a good way to sharpen your analytical and writing skills.

8. When organizing a genealogy for publication, you must work from the past to the present, the opposite direction from that used in gathering information.

9. The Register Plan, or Register Form, is the standard format used in this country to organize genealogies.

10. Multiancestor works covering many families use a variation of the Register Form and often contain charts showing one person's descent from each family's immigrant ancestor.

11. All family profiles in your genealogy should include basic genealogical facts concerning birth, marriage, and death, as well as any information that makes the work more interesting and readable, including occupations, education, religious affiliation, and contemporary assessments of character.

12. Don't exclude unpleasant facts. As family historian, you must be as objective as possible.

13. The book's title should accurately reflect its contents.

14. Create an "every name" index, arranged alphabetically and keyed to page numbers.

15. A particular name should appear only once in the index, even if it refers to more than one person. All variant surname spellings, maiden names of married women, and surnames of women who married more than once should appear as well.

16. Letterpress printing is available for special quality editions, but photographic offset printing from camera-ready typed copy is much less expensive.

17. Other facts to consider in publishing your genealogy include book design, paper quality, cover, use of artwork, and number of copies to print.

18. A few companies specialize in publishing genealogies for a fee.

19. Interest in your book will be limited. Usually five hundred or fewer copies of a genealogy are printed. Attempt to recover your out-of-pocket expenses by promoting your book to family members, genealogical societies, and libraries.

APPENDIXES & INDEX

"Someone's ancestor," photographed in Chicago, 1882. Alison Scott

• APPENDIX A •

Reference Materials Recommended in this Book

This appendix provides a list of all the reference books and magazines recommended in *Shaking Your Family Tree*. Libraries with major genealogical collections will contain many — in some cases, most — of the items listed. Only a few of the items are likely to be found in a regular bookstore. You can order most items directly from the publishers, whose names and addresses are included.

The list is divided by chapter. A list of "general references" also appears at the beginning of the appendix.

The names of certain publishing companies have been abbreviated as follows: GPC for Genealogical Publishing Company, NEHGS for New England Historic Genealogical Society, and GSL for the Genealogical Society Library of the Church of Jesus Christ of Latter-day Saints (Mormons).

General References

The Source: A Guidebook of American Genealogy, Arlene Eakle and Johni Cerny, eds. Salt Lake City: Ancestry Publishing Company, 1984.

How to Find Your Family Roots, by Timothy Field Beard. New York: McGraw Hill, 1977. (See especially chapters 6, 7, 22, 30, 33-42.)

Beard, Timothy Field. Foreword to *Pedigrees of Some of the Emperor Charlemagne's Descendants*. A.L. Langston and J.O. Buck, eds. Vol. 2. Cottonport, LA: Polyanthos, 1974.

Library Services for Genealogists, by J. Carlyle Parker. (Gale Genealogy and Local History Series, no. 15), Detroit: Gale Research Company, 1981.

"Major Genealogical Publications of the Last Two Decades: A Selective List," by Gary Boyd Roberts. *Genealogical Journal*, Summer 1983, pp. 68-80; Summer 1984, pp. 65-70.

"The Most Needed Genealogical Reference Publications of 1960: An Update and General Review," by Gary Boyd Roberts. *Detroit Society for Genealogical Research Magazine*, Winter 1977, pp. 47-50; Spring 1978, pp. 93-97; Summer 1978, pp. 139-141; Summer 1979, p. 191.

Genealogy: A Selected Bibliography, by Milton Rubincam. 5th ed. Birmingham, AL: Banner Press, 1983.

Genealogical Research: Methods and Sources. 2nd ed. 2 vols. New Orleans, LA: Polyanthos, 1980-1983.

Genealogical Research in New England, Ralph J. Crandall, ed. Baltimore: GPC, 1984. See also Marcia Wiswall Lindberg, *A Genealogist's Handbook for New England Research*, 2nd ed. Boston: NEHGS, 1985.

Chapter Two: Joys in the Attic:
Discovering Clues Within the Family

The Tape-Recorded Interview: A Manual for Field Workers in Folklore and Oral History, by Edward D. Ives. Knoxville: Univ. of Tennessee Press, 1980.

Yankee Magazine. Dublin, NH: Yankee Publishing. Monthly magazine.

NEHGS Nexus Boston: NEHGS. Bimonthly newsletter.

The Connecticut Nutmegger. Glastonbury, CT: Connecticut Society of Genealogists. Quarterly.

National Genealogical Society Newsletter. Washington, D. C.: National Genealogical Society. Bimonthly.

The Genealogical Helper. Logan, UT: Everton Publishers. Bimonthly.

Chapter Three: Treasured Aisles:
Using Library Resources

American Library Directory. New York: Bowker. Biennial.

Directory of Historical Societies and Agencies in the United States and Canada, Madison, WI: American Association of State and Local History. Biennial.

Directory of Genealogical Societies in the U.S.A. and Canada. 5th ed., by Mary K. Meyer. Mt. Airy, Maryland, 1984.

History of the Military Company of the Massachusetts Now Called The Ancient and Honorable Artillery Company of Massachusetts, by Oliver Ayer Roberts. 4 vols. Boston: A. Mudge & Sons, 1895-1901.

American and British Genealogy and Heraldry: A Selected List of Books, by P. William Filby. 3rd ed. Boston: NEHGS, 1983.

Genealogies in the Library of Congress: A Bibliography, by Marion J. Kaminkow. 2 vols. Baltimore: Magna Carta Book Company, 1974.

Supplement to Genealogies in the Library of Congress, 1972-1976, by Marion J. Kaminkow. Baltimore: Magna Carta Publishing Company, 1977.

A Complement to Genealogies in the Library of Congress, by Marion J. Kaminkow. Baltimore: Magna Carta Publishing Company, 1981.

Family Histories and Genealogies, National Society, Daughters of the American Revolution Library Catalog, Vol.1, Washington, D. C.: National Society, DAR, 1982.

United States Local Histories in the Library of Congress, by Marion J. Kaminkow. 5 vols. Baltimore: Magna Carta Publishing Company, 1975-1976

A Bibliography of American County Histories, by P.W. Filby. Baltimore: GPC, 1985.

Index to American Genealogies. 5th ed. Joel Munsell & Sons, Publishers, 1900. (Reprinted Baltimore: GPC, 1967.)

The Genealogy Index of the Newberry Library, Chicago. 4 vols. Boston: G K Hall & Co., 1960.

The Greenlaw Index of the New England Historic Genealogical Society, by William Prescott Greenlaw. 2 vols. Boston: G K Hall & Co., 1976.

American Genealogical-Biographical Index. More than 135 vols. to date, 4 new vols. per year. Middletown, CT: Godfrey Memorial Library.

Index to Genealogical Periodicals Together With "My Own Index," by Donald Lines Jacobus. Baltimore: GPC, 1973.

Donald Lines Jacobus' Index to Genealogical Periodicals, by Carl Boyer III. rev. ed. Newhall, CA, 1983.

Genealogical Periodical Annual Index. 17 vols. Bowie, MD: Heritage Books.

A Survey of American Genealogical Periodicals and Periodical Indexes, by Kip Sperry. Gale Genealogy and Local History Series, no. 3. Detroit: Gale Research Company, 1978.

Index to Periodical Literature, 1960-1977, by Kip Sperry. Gale Genealogy and Local History Series, no. 9. Detroit: Gale Research Company, 1979.

The New York Genealogical and Bibliographical Record 113 Years Master Index, by Jean D. Worden. Franklin, Ohio, 1983.

Index to The Genealogical Magazine of New Jersey, by Kenn Stryker-Rodda. 4 vols. New Orleans, LA: Polyanthos (first 3 vols.); New Jersey: Hunterton Press (vol. 4), 1973-1982.

Index to The Virginia Genealogist, by John Frederick Dorman. Springfield, VA: Genealogical Books in Print, 1981.

Index to South Carolina Historical Magazine. 2 vols. Charleston, SC: The South Carolina Historical Society, 1961-1977.

Index to The New England Historical and Genealogical Register, by Jane Fletcher Fiske. Boston: NEHGS, forthcoming.

The Biography and Genealogy Dictionaries Master Index, Miranda C. Herbert and Barbara MacNeil, eds. 20 vols. Detroit: Gale Research Company, 1975-.

Passenger and Immigration Lists Index, by P. William Filby and Mary K. Meyer. 6 vols. Detroit: Gale Research Company, 1981.

International Genealogical Index. Salt Lake City: GSL, 1984.

Genealogists' Magazine. London: Society of Genealogists. Quarterly.

The New England Historical and Genealogical Register. Boston: NEHGS. Quarterly.

The New York Genealogical and Biographical Record. New York: New York Genealogical and Biographical Society. Quarterly.

The American Genealogist. Warwick, RI. Quarterly.

The National Genealogical Society Quarterly. Washington, DC.: National Genealogical Society. Quarterly.

The Genealogist. New York. Semiannual.

The Genealogical Magazine of New Jersey. Brunswick: Genealogical Society of New Jersey. Three times a year.

The Detroit Society for Genealogical Research Magazine. Detroit: Detroit Society for Genealogical Research. Quarterly.

Genealogical Journal. Salt Lake City. Quarterly.

The Genealogical Helper. See chapter 2.

The Kentucky Genealogist. Louisville, KY. Quarterly.

The Virginia Genealogist. Washington, DC. Quarterly.

The Maryland and Delaware Genealogist. Saint Michaels, MD. Quarterly.

The South Carolina Magazine of Ancestral Research. Columbia, SC. Quarterly.

Rhode Island Genealogical Register. Princeton, MA. Quarterly.

Chapter Four: Vital Signs:
Birth, Death, and Marriage Records

List of Vital Statistical Records. Washington, DC: U.S. Government/W.P.A.

Where to Write for Vital Records (U.S. Department of Health and Human Services Publication No. (PHS) 82-1184). Washington, DC: U.S. Government Printing Office. Updated frequently.

Chapter Five: Relative Revelations:
Church Records

First American Jewish Families: 600 Genealogies, 1654-1977, compiled by Rabbi Malcolm Stern. Cincinnati: American Jewish Archives/American Jewish Historical Society, Waltham, MA., 1978.

An Inventory of the Records of the Particular (Congregational) Churches of Massachusetts Gathered 1620-1805, by Harold Field Worthley. Cambridge, MA: Harvard University Press, 1970.

Encyclopedia of American Quaker Genealogy, by William W. Hinshaw, Thomas W. Marshall, and Willard Heiss. 7 vols. Reprinted Baltimore: GPC, 1969-1981. (vol. 7 Indiana Historical Society, 1962-1975).

Chapter Six: Unraveling the Plot: Cemetery Records

The Connecticut Nutmegger. See chapter 2.

Directory of Genealogical Societies in the U.S.A. and Canada. See chapter 2.

Markers. Dublin, NH: Association for Gravestone Studies. Irregularly.

Gravestone Inscriptions from Mount Auburn Catholic Cemetery, Watertown, Massachusetts, by Marie E. Daly. Cambridge, MA, 1983.

The various other periodicals mentioned in Chapter 6 are listed under chapter 3 in this appendix.

Chapter Seven: Probing Probate: Wills, Inventories, and Other Documents

Suffolk County Wills: Abstracts of the Earliest Wills Upon Record in the County of Suffolk, Massachusetts. Baltimore: GPC, 1984.

New Hampshire Provincial and State Papers. 40 vols. Concord, NH: State of New Hampshire, 1867-1943.

Archives of the State of New Jersey. 42 vols. Trenton, NJ: New Jersey State Library Archives and History Bureau, 1880-1949.

The Probate Records of Essex County, Massachusetts 1635-1861. 3 vols. Salem, MA: Essex Institute, 1916-1920.

The Probate Records of Middlesex County, Massachusetts, 1647-1664. Boston: NEHGS, forthcoming.

Plymouth Colony Probate Guide: Where to Find Wills and Related Data for 800 People of Plymouth Colony, 1620-1691, compiled by Ruth Wilder Sherman and Robert S. Wakefield. Warwick, RI, 1983.

Maine Wills 1640-1760. Baltimore: GPC, 1972.

The Probate Records of Lincoln County, Maine, 1760-1800. Portland, ME, 1895.

Chapter Eight: Reading Between the Borderlines: Land Records

Index of Revolutionary War Pension Applications in the National Archives (National Genealogical Society Publication No. 40). Washington, DC: National Genealogical Society, 1976.

American State Papers, Public Lands. Washington, DC, 1832-1861.

Grassroots of America, by Philip W. McMullin, ed. Salt Lake City, 1972.

Guide to Genealogical Research in the National Archives. Washington, DC: National Archives, 1982.

Federal Land Series, by Clifford Neal Smith. 3 vols. Chicago: American Library Association, 1972-1980.

Chapter Nine: Tallying to the Cause: Using Census Records

The Researcher's Guide to American Genealogy, by Val D. Greenwood. Baltimore: GPC, 1973.

Guide to Genealogical Research in the National Archives. See chapter 8.

"The Most Needed Genealogical Reference Publications of 1960: An Update and General Review." See General References.

A Census of Pensioners for Revolutionary or Military Services (1841). Baltimore: GPC, 1967.

State Censuses: An Annotated Bibliography of Censuses of Population Taken After the Year 1790 by States and Territories of the United States, by Henry J. Dubester, 1948. Reprinted New York: Burt Franklin, 1967.

Chapter Ten: Researching the Rank and File: Military Records

Guide to Genealogical Research in the National Archives. See chapter 8.

Soldiers in King Philip's War, by George M. Bodge. Reprinted Baltimore: GPC, 1976.

Massachusetts Soldiers and Sailors of the American Revolution. 17 vols. Boston: Secretary of the Commonwealth, State of Massachusetts, 1896-1908.

DAR Patriot Index. 2 vols. Washington, DC: National Society, Daughters of the American Revolution, 1967, 1980.

Index of Revolutionary War Pension Applications in the National Archives. See chapter 8.

Revolutionary War Period Bible, Family, and Marriage Records Gleaned from Pension Applications, by Helen M. Lu and Gwen B. Newmann. 6 vols. to date. 1980-

Chapter Eleven: Old World, New World: Immigrant Ancestors and American Origins

Passenger and Immigration Lists Index. See chapter 3.

Guide to Genealogical Research in the National Archives. See chapter 8.

Genealogical Journal. See chapter 3.

Morton Allan Directory of European Passenger Steamship Arrivals. Strasburg, VA, 1971.

"Notices by German and Swiss Settlers Seeking Information of Members of their Families, Kindred, and Friends Inserted between 1742-1761 in *Pennsylvania Berichte*, and 1762-1779 in *Pennsylvania Staatsbote*," by Anita L. Eyster. *Pennsylvania German Folklore Society* 3, 1938: pp. 32-41.

Genealogical Data Relating to the German Settlers of Pennsylvania from Advertisements in German Newspapers Published in Philadelphia and Germantown, 1743-1800, by Edward Hocker. Baltimore: GPC, 1981.

Encyclopedic Directory of Ethnic Newspapers and Periodicals in the United States, by Lubomyr Wynar. Littleton, CO, 1976.

Chapter Twelve: Completing Your Work: Binding Past and Present

The Source: A Guidebook of American Genealogy. See General References.

Computer Genealogy: A Guide to Research Through High Technology, by Paul A. Andereck and Richard A. Pence. Salt Lake City: Ancestry Publishing Company, 1985.

Genealogical Computing. Fairfax, VA: Data Transfer Associates, Inc. Bimonthly newsletter.

Citing Your Sources: A Manual for Documenting Family Histories and Genealogical Records, by Richard S. Lackey. New Orleans: Oracle Press Ltd., 1980.

Write it Right: A Manual for Writing Family Histories and Genealogies, by Richard S. Lackey and Donald R. Barnes. Ocala, FL: Lyon Press, 1983.

Newspaper Genealogy Columns, by Anita Cheek Milner. Bowie, MD: Heritage Books, 1984.

Directory of Genealogical Societies in the U.S.A. and Canada. See chapter 2.

The various periodicals mentioned in Chapter 12 are listed under chapter 3 in this appendix.

• APPENDIX B •

Major Genealogical Compendia

Genealogical compendia are large compilations of family pedigrees often organized by area or topic. You can find most in medium-size genealogical collections. You will probably consult them frequently. Major examples of genealogical compendia include the following:

1. The many Burke's and Debrett's volumes on the British peerage and landed gentry, plus the newer *Burke's Guide to the Royal Family, Burke's Royal Families of the World* (2 vols.), and the 1981 second edition of *Burke's Presidential Families of the United States of America.*

2. Multivolume sets covering most European princely, noble, or historically prominent families: Bartram on Wales; *The Scots Peerage* by Balfour; *The Peerage of Ireland* by Lodge; *The New Complete Peerage*; Anselme and de La Chesnaye des Bois on France; Prince von Isenburg, Baron Freytag von Loringhoven, Schwennicke, and Huberty on Germany; Bethencourt and Souza on Spain and Portugal; Litta on Italy; Wurzbach's *Biographisches Lexikon* on Austria; Dworzaczek on Poland; Elgenstjerna on Sweden; Ikonnikov on Russia; Prince Toumanoff on Armenia, Georgia, and Albania; Prince Sturdza on Greece; and Count Rudt-Collenburg on Crusader families. For full citations and descriptions of these works, see John Insley Coddington, "Royal and Noble Genealogy" in *Genealogical Research Methods and Sources* (1st ed., 1960; 2nd ed., 1980) and *Genealogical Journal*, vol. 12 (1983): pp. 68-70; and vol. 13 (1984): pp. 65-66. Also available are annual registers of noble or major bourgeois families, led by the *Almanach de Gotha* and its successor, *Genealogisches Handbuch des Adels.* These sets and registers are generally found only in the largest genealogical libraries.

3. Studies of all descendants for ten or more generations of various medieval or modern kings (Charlemagne, Gorm the Old, St. Louis, Edward III, Ferdinand and Isabella, James I of England, Louis XIV, and Peter the Great) or of all ancestors of the same (Edward III, Charles II of England, and the current Prince of Wales). For full citations, see the Coddington and *Genealogical Journal* items noted above.

4. Immigrant origins works: *Genealogical Gleanings in England* (2 vols.), *English Origins of New England Families*, (6 vols.), *Virginia Gleanings in England*, the first two volumes of *Eighteenth Century Emigrants from German-Speaking Lands to North America*, and various books by P.W. Coldham.

5. The periodical extract program of the Genealogical Publishing Company in Baltimore, which to date includes almost fifty volumes of compiled genealogical articles or source records on families in Massachusetts, Connecticut, Rhode Island, Pennsylvania, Maryland, Virginia, Kentucky, and Barbados. *South Carolina Genealogies*, five volumes of articles from the *South Carolina Historical (and Genealogical) Magazine*, has been published by Southern Reprint Company in Spartanburg.

6. The major New England genealogical dictionaries: John Farmer's *Genealogical Register of the First Settlers of New England* (1829, the first major American work of this kind); James Savage's *A Genealogical Dictionary of the First Settlers of New England* (4 vols., 1860-1864); Charles Henry Pope's *The Pioneers of Massachusetts* (1900) and *The Pioneers of Maine and New Hampshire* (1908); John Osborne Austin's *Genealogical Dictonary of Rhode Island* (1887); *The Genealogical Dictonary of Maine and New Hampshire* (1928-1939) by Sybil Noyes, Charles Thornton Libby, and Walter Goodwin Davis; and *New England Marriages Prior to 1700*, a listing by Clarence Almon Torrey of 37,000 married couples in seventeenth-century New England, together with all references to either partner in all pre-1960 works (microfilm version, seven reels, 1979; book version, without references, 1985).

7. Various Mid-Atlantic and southern works that are partial equivalents of New England's genealogical dictionaries. Examples are H.F. Seversmith's *Colonial Families of Long Island, New York and Connecticut*, J.E. Stillwell's *Historical and Genealogical Miscellany*, G.E. McCracken's *The Welcome Claimants; Proved, Disproved, and Doubtful*, C.P. Keith's *Provincial Councillors of Pennsylvania*, J.W. Jordan's *Colonial and Revolutionary Families of Pennsylvania*, G.A. Mackenzie's *Colonial Families of the United States of America* (especially useful for Maryland families), M.W. Hiden's *Adventurers of Purse and Person*, R.B. True's *Biographical Dictionary of Early Virginia* (on microfiche), H.E. Hayden's *Virginia Genealogies*, and *The Edward P. Valentine Papers*.

8. Nationality, ethnic group, or religious compilations such as Father Denissen's *Genealogies of the French Families of the Detroit River Valley*, Michel Call's Mormon Pioneer Genealogy Library, M.G. Turk's *The Quiet Adventurers in North America* (on Channel Island immigrants), Donald Whyte's and David Dobson's lists of Scottish immigrants, Malcolm Stern's *First American Jewish Families* (covering all pre-1840 immigrants, mostly Sephardic), and the seven-volume *Encyclopedia of American Quaker Genealogy*.

9. Lists of Colonial or Revolutionary soldiers. Note especially the recent Massachusetts volumes published by the New England Historic Genealogical Society and the Society of Colonial Wars; C.E. and S.G. Fisher's *Soldiers, Sailors, and Patriots of the Revolutionary War: Maine*; B.G. Moss's *Rosters of South Carolina Patriots in the American Revolution*; M.J. Clark's *Colonial Soldiers of the South* and *Loyalists in the Southern Campaign of the Revolutionary War*; and the three-volume *DAR Patriot Index* and *Index of Revolutionary War Pension Applications in the National Archives*. These last works are discussed further in chapter 10 on military records.

10. Although not genealogical compendia per se, biographical dictionaries generally, and those treating college graduates especially, can be helpful. Note especially the *Dictionary of National Biography* (British), the one-volume *Dictionary of Welsh Biography*, the ongoing *Dictionary of Canadian Biography* (French, German, and Italian sets are underway as well), the *Dictionary of American Biography* (with 7 supplements), the four volumes of *Notable American Women*, *The National Cyclopaedia of American Biography* (75 vols.), *Who Was Who in America* (8 vols., plus index), *Sibley's Harvard Graduates* (covering graduates through 1771), *Yale Biographies and Annals* (covering those through 1815), and the three recent volumes of *Princetonians* (through 1783).

Many more useful works are listed in P. William Filby's *American and British Genealogy and Heraldry*, 3rd ed. Boston: NEHGS, 1983.

• APPENDIX C •

Privately Published Federal Census Indexes (by State), 1800-1850

The information in this index is taken from "The Most Needed Genealogical Reference Publications of 1960: An Update and General Review," by Gary Boyd Roberts, published in *The Detroit Society for Genealogical Research Magazine*, vol. 41, (Winter 1977); pp. 48–50. Mr. Roberts has kindly updated this list to include works published through 1984. Note that exact titles have not been given, as they are almost always "Index to the _____ (year) Census of _____ (state)."

Alabama 1820 and **1830** Alabama Department of Archives and History, 1944 (reprinted by GPC, 1971).

Alabama 1830 — Pauline J. Gandrud, 1973.

Alabama 1840 — Betty D. Posey, 1973.

Arkansas 1840 — Mrs. Leister Presley, 1971.

Arkansas 1850 — Mrs. Leister Presley, 1974 (surname only).

Connecticut 1800 — Lowell M. Volkel, 1970.

Delaware 1790 — Leon de Valinger, Jr. (NGS Special Publication No. 10, 1962, reconstructed.)

Delaware 1800 — Gerald M. and D.O. Maddux, 1964 (GPC).

Delaware 1850 — Virginia L. Olmstead, 1977 (GPC).

Florida 1850 — Southern Genealogists Exchange Society, 1972.

Georgia 1790 — Delwyn Associates, 1975 (reconstructed).

Georgia 1820 — Mrs. Eugene A. Stanley, 1969.

Georgia 1830 — Alvaretta K. Register, 1974 (GPC).

Georgia 1840 — Eileen Sheffield and B. Woods, 1971.

Georgia 1850 — Rhea C. Otto, 1971.

Illinois 1820 — Lowell M. Volkel and J.V. Gill, 1966.

Illinois 1830 — James V. and M.R. Gill, 1968-1970.

Illinois 1840 — Maxine Wormer, 1973-1977.

Illinois 1850 — Chicago Genealogical Society, 1970.

Indiana 1820 — Willard Heiss, 1966.

Indiana 1840 — Genealogy Division, Indiana State Library, 1975.

Iowa 1840 — Bettylou Headlee, 1968.

Iowa 1850 — Iowa Genealogical Society, 1977.

Kentucky 1790 — Charles B. Heinemann, 1940 (reconstructed, reprinted by GPC, 1971).

Kentucky 1800 — Garrett G. Clift, 1954 (reconstructed, reprinted by GPC, 1970).

Kentucky 1810 — Ann T. Wagstaff, 1980 (GPC).

Kentucky 1820 — Jeanne R. Felldin and Gloria K.V. Inman, 1981 (GPC).

Kentucky 1830 — Dora W. Smith, 1973-1974.

Kentucky 1850 — Sam McDowell, 1974 (surname only).

Louisiana 1810, 1820 — Robert B.L. Ardouin, 1970-1972 (GPC).

Maryland 1800 — Lowell M. Volkel, 1967-1968.

Massachusetts 1800 — Elizabeth P. Bentley, 1978 (GPC).

Michigan 1840 — Estelle A. McGlynn, 1977.

Michigan 1850 — Michigan Genealogical Council, 1976.

Mississippi 1820 — Wilma B. McEllhiney and E.W. Thomas, 1964.

Mississippi 1830 — Norman E. Gillis, 1965.

Mississippi 1840 — Gwen Platt, A. Lanhert, and M. Peer, 1970-1972.

Mississippi 1850 — Norman E. and I.S. Gillis, 1973 (surname only).

Missouri 1830 — Mrs. Genevieve L. Carter, 1972.

Missouri 1840 — Frances R. Nelson and G. Boone, 1975.

New Hampshire 1800 — John B. Threlfall, 1974.

New Jersey 1793 — James S. Norton, 1973. (Reconstructed. Since New Jersey censuses before 1830 are lost, note also Kenn Stryker-Rodda's *Revolutionary Census of New Jersey. An Index, Based on Rateables of the Inhabitants of New Jersey During the Period of the American Revolution*, 1972.)

New Jersey 1850 — Margaruerite D. Owens and B.O. Tanco, 1973.

New York 1800 — Barbara K. Armstrong, 1984 (GPC).

North Carolina 1800 — Elizabeth P. Bentley, 1977 (GPC).

North Carolina 1810 — Elizabeth P. Bentley, 1978 (GPC).

North Carolina 1820 — Dorothy W. Potter, 1970-1974 (reprinted by GPC).

North Carolina 1840 — Gerald M. Petty, 1974.

Ohio 1820 — Ohio Library Foundation, 1964. (As the 1810 census of Ohio is missing, note also Esther W. Powell's *Early Ohio Tax Records*, 1971, and its *Surname Index*, 1974).

Ohio 1830 — Ohio Family Historians, 1964.

Ohio 1840 — Cleo G. Wilkens, 1969-1972.

Ohio 1850 — Lida F. Harshman, 1972.

Pennsylvania 1800 — Jeanne R. Felldin and Gloria K.V. Inman, 1984 (GPC).

Pennsylvania 1810 — Ohio Family Historians, 1966.

Rhode Island 1800 — Lowell M. Volkel, 1970.

South Carolina 1800 — Brent H. Holcomb, 1980 (GPC).

South Carolina 1820 — Gwen Platt, 1972.

South Carolina 1830 — J.P. and F.L. Hazelwood and T.L. Smith, 1973.

Tennessee 1820 — Elizabeth P. Bentley, 1981 (GPC).

Tennessee 1830 — Byron Sistler and Associates (East, Middle, West), 1969-1971.

Tennessee 1850 — Vera C. Carpenter, 1968, and Byron Sistler and Associates, 1974-1976.

Texas 1850 — Vera C. Carpenter, 1969.

Vermont 1800 — Vermont Historical Society, 1938 (reprinted in 1978).

Virginia 1810 — Elizabeth P. Bentley, 1980 (GPC), and Netti Schreiner-Yantis, *A Supplement to the 1810 Census of Virginia (reconstructed)*, 1971.

Virginia 1820 — Jeanne R. Felldin, 1976 (GPC).

• APPENDIX D •

Checklist of Published Special
and Reconstructed Censuses

Alabama — The extant part of the Alabama territorial census for 1820 was printed in the *Alabama Historical Quarterly*, vol. 6 (1944): pp. 333-515, and consolidated into *Alabama Census Returns, 1820 and Abstract of Federal Census of Alabama, 1830*, GPC, 1971.

Arizona — *Federal Census* — *Territory of New Mexico and Territory of Arizona* (89th Cong., 1st sess., S. Doc 13, serial 12668-1) includes the 1860 and 1864 territorial censuses and the 1870 Arizona census.

Delaware — The missing 1790 census has been reconstructed from local tax lists as *Reconstructed 1790 Census of Delaware*, National Genealogical Society Publication No. 10, Leon de Valinger, Jr., compiler, 1954, 2nd printing, 1962.

District of Columbia — Entries for the extant 1800 schedules appear in "U.S. Census of the District of Columbia in Maryland for the year 1800," *National Genealogical Society Quarterly*, vol. 38 (1950): pp. 105-110, vol. 39 (1951): 16-19, 56-59.

Georgia — Tax lists for a few counties were consolidated as *Some Early Tax Digests of Georgia*, Ruth Blair, ed. 2 vols. 1926. This publication is used as a substitute for missing 1790, 1800, 1810, and 1820 censuses. See also *Substitute for Georgia's Lost 1790 Census*, 1975, compiled from wills, court minutes, voter lists, and newspapers.

Illinois — For some 1810 schedules, the 1818 territorial census of Illinois, and the 1820 state schedules, see *Illinois Census Returns 1810, 1818 and Illinois Census Returns, 1820 (Collections of the Illinois State Historical Library)*, by Margaret Cross Norton, ed. vols. 24 and 26. 1934-1935. Both reprinted by GPC in 1969.

Iowa — See *Iowa 1836 Census*, by Ronald V. Jackson, ed., 1973 (part of the Accelerated Indexing Systems series mentioned in chapter 9).

Kentucky — Lost 1790 and 1800 censuses were reconstructed from local tax returns, as *"First Census" of Kentucky 1790*, Charles Brunk Heinemann and Gaius Marcus Brumbaugh, compilers, 1940, and *"Second Census" of Kentucky, 1800*, Garrett Glenn Clift, compiler, 1954. Both have been reprinted by GPC, in 1965 and 1968, respectively.

Minnesota — The 1849 census of the Territory of Minnesota was published as appendix D of the *Journal of the House of Representatives, First Session of the Legislative Assembly of the Territory of Minnesota, 1850*.

Mississippi — The 1816 territorial census was published in *Early Inhabitants of the Natchez District*, Norman E. Gillis, ed., 1963. Persons residing outside the Natchez district are listed in an appendix.

Nebraska — 1854, 1855, and 1856 territorial censuses were published as *1854-1856 Nebraska State Censuses*, Evelyn M. Cox, ed., 1973.

New Jersey — Substitutes for the missing 1790 census of New Jersey are: *New Jersey in 1793: An Abstract and Index to the 1793 Militia Census of the State of New Jersey*, James S. Norton, ed., 1973, and *Revolutionary Census of New Jersey, An Index, Based on Rateables of the Inhabitants of New Jersey During the Period of the American Revolution*, Kenn Stryker-Rodda, ed., 1972.

New Mexico — See *Spanish and Mexican Colonial Census of New Mexico, 1790, 1823, and 1845*, Virginia L. Olmstead, ed., 1975.

New York — For information about state schedules, 1825-1925, see *An Inventory of New York State and Federal Census Records*, Edna L. Jacobson, compiler. rev. ed. 1956. New York State censuses are among the best in the country — even better, at times, than their federal counterparts.

North Dakota — The 1885 census for North Dakota was published in *Collections of the State Historical Society of North Dakota*, vol. 4 (1913): pp. 338-448.

Tennessee — Some of the 1800 schedules have been reconstructed from local tax records. See *Early East Tennessee Tax Papers*, Pollyana Creekmore, compiler, 1980, a reprint of material originally published by the East Tennessee Historical Society.

Texas — See *The First Census of Texas, 1829-1836*, National Genealogical Society Special Publication No. 22, Marion Day Mullins, ed. 2nd printing. 1962.

Virginia — 1790 schedules have been reconstructed and published in two complementary volumes: *Heads of Families at the First Census of the United States Taken in the Year 1790: Records of the State Enumerations, 1782-1785*, Virginia, 1908 (part of the series published by the Census Bureau itself) and *Virginia Tax Papers, 1782-1787*, by Augusta B. Fothergill and John Marsh Nangle. Other than those published by the United States Census Bureau, 1940, reprinted by GPC in 1966, note also a *Supplement to the 1810 Census of Virginia: Tax Lists of the Counties for which the Census is Missing*, Netti Schreiner-Yantis, compiler, 1971.

• APPENDIX E •

Samples of Genealogical Information Forms

On the following pages are samples of several charts that you will find helpful in gathering and organizing genealogical information. Producing your own versions of these charts at standard 8½-by-11-inch size with holes punched for three-ring binders will greatly facilitate your research efforts. The charts shown include the following:

Four-Generation Chart — An explanation of the numbering system used with this chart appears in chapter 1. Always list yourself as number 1. Remember that an ancestor keeps his same number wherever his name appears on a chart. If your ancestor number 12 appears in the first position on chart 6, he remains number 12 and does *not* become number 1. Use the back of the form to list your sources.

Family Group Chart — This chart will contain information about a nuclear family and is one of the most important forms for genealogical data gathering. Use the back of the form to list information about divorces, additional marriages, residences, and data sources.

Birth, Death, Marriage, and Passenger Record Forms — These forms are self-explanatory and can be used to record vital data and immigration information. The chart below, when added to the bottom of any of these forms, enables you to record source information on the front of the form.

If not taken from original document, fill in below.

Microfilm No. _____ Roll No. _____

Microfiche No. _____ Card No. _____

Book Title _____

Author _____

Publisher _____

Publication Date _____

Volume & Page No. _____

Four-Generation Chart

Chart # _____

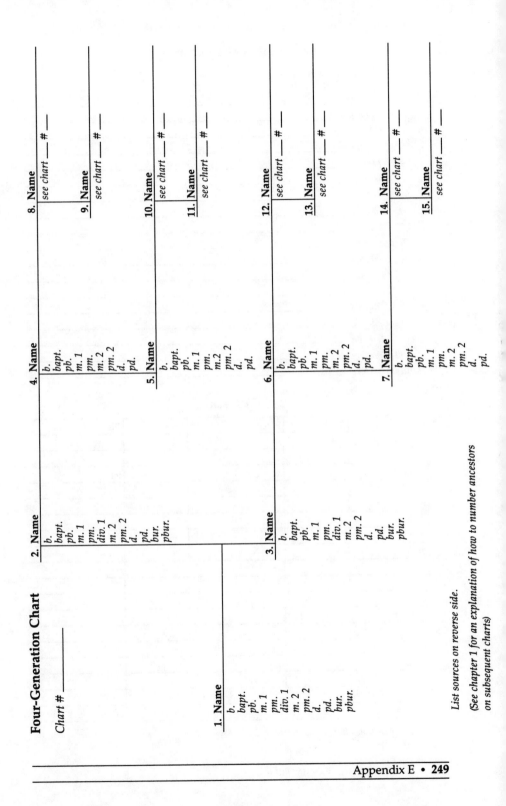

1. Name
b.
bapt.
pb.
m. 1
pm.
div. 1
m. 2
pm. 2
d.
pd.
bur.
pbur.

2. Name
b.
bapt.
pb.
m. 1
pm.
div. 1
m. 2
pm. 2
d.
pd.
bur.
pbur.

3. Name
b.
bapt.
pb.
m. 1
pm.
div. 1
m. 2
pm. 2
d.
pd.
bur.
pbur.

4. Name
b.
bapt.
pb.
m. 1
pm.
m. 2
pm. 2
d.
pd.

5. Name
b.
bapt.
pb.
m. 1
pm.
m.2
pm. 2
d.
pd.

6. Name
b.
bapt.
pb.
m. 1
pm.
m. 2
pm. 2
d.
pd.

7. Name
b.
bapt.
pb.
m. 1
pm.
m. 2
pm. 2
d.
pd.

8. Name
see chart ___ # ____

9. Name
see chart ___ # ____

10. Name
see chart ___ # ____

11. Name
see chart ___ # ____

12. Name
see chart ___ # ____

13. Name
see chart ___ # ____

14. Name
see chart ___ # ____

15. Name
see chart ___ # ____

List sources on reverse side.

(See chapter 1 for an explanation of how to number ancestors on subsequent charts)

Family Group Chart

	Husband	Wife
Name		
Born		
Place		
Father		
Mother		
Married 1		
Place		
Divorced		
Place		
Married 2		
Place		
Died		
Place		
Buried		
Place		
Religion		
Occupation		
Military Service		

Children

#	Name	B./Bapt.	Place	Died	Place
1.					
	m.				
	child of		at		on
2.					
	m.				
	child of		at		on
3.					
	m.				
	child of		at		on
4.					
	m.				
	child of		at		on
5.					
	m.				
	child of		at		on
6.					
	m.				
	child of		at		on

See Four-Generation Chart _____ number _____

Birth Record Form

Name _____

Born _____

Place _____

If Birth Not at Hospital, } State Address _____

Birth Certificate No. _____

Father _____

Father's Age _____

Father's Birthplace _____

Father's Occupation _____

Mother _____

Mother's Age _____

Mother's Birthplace _____

Mother's Occupation _____

Death Record Form

Name of Deceased _____

Died _____

Place _____

If Death Not at Hospital, } State Address _____

Cause of Death _____

Burial Date _____

Place _____

Death Certificate No. _____

Age/Birthdate _____

Birthplace _____

Father's Name _____

Father's Birthplace _____

Mother's Name _____

Mother's Birthplace _____

Marital Status _____

Spouse's Name _____

Deceased Residence at Time of Death _____

Occupation _____

Years Lived in U.S. _____

Citizenship _____

Informant _____

Relationship to Deceased _____

Marriage Record Form

Groom	_____
Groom's Age	_____
Groom's Birthplace	_____
Groom's Father	_____
Groom's Mother	_____
Date of Marriage	_____
Place	_____
Marriage Cert. No.	_____
Bride	_____
Bride's Age	_____
Bride's Birthplace	_____
Bride's Father	_____
Bride's Mother	_____

Passenger Arrival Form

Name of Passenger	_____
Date of Birth/Age	_____
Place of Birth	_____
Name of Ship or other mode of transport	_____
Date of Departure	_____
Port of Origin	_____
Date of Arrival	_____
Port of Entry	_____
Last Residence	_____
Citizenship	_____
Occupation	_____
Destination	_____

Family Members

Sex	Name	Age	Place of Birth
__	_____	__	_____
__	_____	__	_____
__	_____	__	_____
__	_____	__	_____
__	_____	__	_____
__	_____	__	_____
__	_____	__	_____
__	_____	__	_____

• INDEX •

American Revolution: "gap" in genealogy after, 25, 156, 158, 180, 181, 199
    Veterans. *See* Military records
Archives. *See also* Libraries; National Archives
    family, 13, 16, 22, 24, 29, 30, 31, 33, 34, 200
    immigrant, 216–217
    state, 182
Atlases, county: as source, 45

Bible, family: as source, 32, 33, 34
Bibliographies, genealogical: 52
Birth records. *See* Vital records
Boston Public Library: 176

Cemetery records: 98–112, 239
    caretaker's, 107, 108
    information from, 103–106
    locating, 99–100, 112
    recording inscriptions, 100–102, 112
    sources of transcribed inscriptions, 108–110, 112

Census records: 16, 158–178, 212, 239
    indexes of, 167, 171, 172, 173
    information contained, 168–171, 178, 212
    obtaining, 167, 175–176, 178
    organization, 167–173
    state, 174–175, 243–245, 246–247
    using, 176, 177–178
Church records: 65, 78–96, 237
    Baptist, 81, 92–93
    Catholic, 81, 83–85
    Congregational, 81, 88–89
    Episcopal, 65, 81, 85–87
    Jewish, 81, 93–94
    Lutheran, 87
    Methodist, 81, 92–93
    Mormon, 94–95
    Quaker, 90–91
City directories: as source, 47–48, 173, 178
Computer: use of in genealogy, 19, 22, 221–222, 231, 240
County histories: 18, 40–43

Dallas Public Library: 57
Daughters of the American Revolution (DAR): library of, 56, 59, 109
Death records. *See* Vital records
Deeds: as source, 144–153
    Colonial, 144–147, 152
    fractional, 149, 156
    locating, 152–153
    Multiple-grantor, 147–148, 152, 156
    quitclaim, 150–151, 156
Detroit Public Library: Burton Collection, 57

FINIS.